Students as Researchers

Falmer Press Teachers' Library

Series Editor: Professor Ivor F Goodson, Warner Graduate School, University of
                 Rochester, USA and Applied Research in Education, University of East
                 Anglia, Norwich, UK

Search and Research: What the Inquiring Teacher Needs to Know
Rita S Brause and John S Mayher

Doing Qualitative Research: Circles Within Circles
Margot Ely, Margaret Anzul, Teri Freidman, Diane Garner and Ann McCormack

Teachers as Researchers: Qualitative Inquiry as a Path to Empowerment
Joe L Kincheloe

Key Concepts for Understanding Curriculum
Colin J Marsh

Beginning Qualitative Research
P Maykut and R Morehouse

Becoming a Teacher
Gary Borich

Participatory Evaluation in Education
J Bradley Cousins and Lorna M Earl

Schooling for Change
Andy Hargreaves, Lorna M Earl and J Ryan

Studying School Subjects
Ivor F Goodson and Colin J Marsh

Perspectives: Key Concepts for Understanding Curriculum 1
Colin J Marsh

Planning, Management and Ideology: Key Concepts for Understanding Curriculum 2
Colin J Marsh

On Writing Qualitative Research: Living by Words
Margot Ely, Ruth Vinz, Maryann Downing and Margaret Anzul

Subject Knowledge: Readings for the Study of School Subjects
Ivor F Goodson with Christopher J Anstead and J Marshall Mangan

Fundamentals of Education Research (New Edition)
Gary Anderson

Students as Researchers: Creating Classrooms that Matter
Shirley R Steinberg and Joe L Kincheloe

The Falmer Press Teachers' Library Series: 15

Students as Researchers:
Creating Classrooms that Matter

Edited by
Shirley R. Steinberg
and
Joe L. Kincheloe

UK   Falmer Press, 1 Gunpowder Square, London, EC4A 3DE
USA   Falmer Press, Taylor & Francis Inc., 1900 Frost Road, Suite 101, Bristol,
            PA 19007

First published in 1998

A catalogue record for this book is available from the British Library

ISBN 0 7507 0630 9 cased
ISBN 0 7507 0631 7 paper

Library of Congress Cataloging-in-Publication Data are available on request

Jacket design by Caroline Archer

Typeset in 10/12pt Times by
Graphicraft Typesetters Ltd., Hong Kong

Printed in Great Britain by Biddles Ltd., Guildford and King's Lynn on paper which has a specified pH value on final paper manufacture of not less than 7.5 and is therefore 'acid free'.

Contents

Contents

To Ivor Goodson,
to whom it's all still rock 'n roll

Part One

Theoretically Grounding Student Research

Chapter 1

Students as Researchers: Critical Visions, Emancipatory Insights

Joe L. Kincheloe and Shirley R. Steinberg

We are passionate promoters of the idea that education should help one make sense of the world. At the same time it should help students make sense of themselves as 'players' in the world. This book explores this pedagogical assertion, arguing that a good education should prepare students as researchers who can 'read the world' in such a way so they not only can understand it but so they can change it. Students as researchers, as we envision them, possess a vision of 'what could be' and a set of skills to uncover 'what actually is'. Such students are empowered to delineate the social, political and pedagogical contradictions of schooling, in the process ascertaining the ways these contradictions have shaped their own and other students' consciousness. As our students as researchers progressively deepen their appreciation of the contradictory dynamics, they concurrently gain a power literacy — that is, the ability to recognize the ways power operates to create oppressive conditions for some groups and privilege for others. Thus, students as researchers gain new ways of knowing and producing knowledge that challenge the common sense views of reality with which most individuals have grown so comfortable.

Students as Researchers and the Critical Vision

No reason exists to preclude most elementary, secondary, and university students from becoming critical student researchers. A democratic and informal but intellectually disciplined classroom can become a venue in which teachers and students create and re-create knowledge. Myles Horton, the founder of Tennessee's Highlander Center, argued that students and teachers need to learn how to find answers to the problems that confront them. In his simple but not simplistic manner, Horton delineated the central theme of this book: students and teachers should be collaborators in inquiry into the obstacles that block the achievement of their goals and dreams. Teachers who facilitate the delicate task of engaging students as researchers must possess a well informed and sophisticated sense of how to involve students in an analysis and clarification of their goals and dreams. Horton argued that teachers needed to share their theory of where they were going with students, so students could decide how to respond to the purposes of the classroom. If students didn't agree with the direction the teacher and other members of the class were moving, then alternative paths could be devised. The important concepts at work in such a context involve both the teacher's effort to help students formulate a purpose for their research and education in general and the student's right to reject such a formulation (Long, 1995; Horton and Freire, 1990).

Recently, we talked with a group of teachers studying practitioner research and its various applications. As we listened to them it became increasingly apparent that while they understood a variety of action research techniques, they really had little sense of what larger purpose such research might serve. They were motivated to conduct teacher research but had no vision of what it could accomplish. The same is true of most new educational reforms: those who implement them often have no sense of the new ways of thinking they demand. Make no mistake about our purpose for students as researchers; as we engage students in such work, we want them to develop a higher level of understanding, a critical literacy. Such a literacy would allow them the ability to understand the social construction of the world around them and their relation to it. Student researchers in our vision learn to act in informed, socially just, and communitarian ways. We would not measure our success in terms of their ability to raise standardized test scores or gain admission into prestigious colleges. Our vision involves student inquirers as courageous citizens, not merely 'good students'.

In her essay in this book Kathy Berry writes of extending children's initial wonder about the world via student research. As student researchers analyze mainstream representations, they 'reclaim wonder' in a manner involving the illumination of the taken-for-granted. John Dewey focused our attention on such a process when he argued that individuals should operate on the basis of a reflective action that disembeds moral, ethical, and political issues from mundane thinking. As student researchers pursue such a reflective relationship to their everyday experiences, they gain the ability to explore the hidden forces that have shaped their lives. Just as Berry thinks of students reclaiming wonder, students as researchers relearn the ways they have come to view the world around them. Indeed, such students gain the ability to awaken themselves from a mainstream dream with its unexamined landscape of knowledge and consciousness construction. In their newly awakened state critical student researchers begin to see schools as human creation with meanings and possibilities lurking beneath surface appearances. Their ability to grasp these understandings moves them to a new level of consciousness — a cognitive domain where knowledge intersects with moral imperatives resulting in previously unimagined activities.

Students as researchers operating at a new cognitive domain go beyond so much: words on the page, dominant forms of ideology (constructs that maintain the status quo and its unequal power relations by producing particular meanings and interpretations of reality), and conventional purposes of education. This ability to go beyond is made possible by Paulo Freire's concept of 'problem posing'. Such a position, articulated in this book by Ellen Swartz, maintains that school curriculum should in part be shaped by problems that face teachers and students in their efforts to live just and ethical lives. Thus, in this context students as researchers become one feature in a problem-posed curriculum that seeks to foster critical reflection on the forces that shape the world. Such a critical reflection engenders a healthy and creative skepticism on the part of students. It moves them to be suspicious of neutrality claims in textbooks; it induces them to look askance at, say, Phillips Petroleum-legitimation commercials that position the oil company as the organization that has done more than any other to save our environment. Critically reflective students as researchers reject the traditional student request to the teacher: 'just give us the facts, the truth and we'll give it back to you.' Instead, critical student researchers ask: 'please support us in our explorations of the world'. Or as Penny Gilmer and Paulette Alli ask in their chapter on this book, please allow our science students the opportunity to conduct action experiments.

Both Primary and Secondary Research: Are We Being Rigorous Yet?

Instead of memorizing unexamined, teacher-delivered data, students as researchers reflect on the construction of their autobiographies, engage in the exploration of narratives (the grand stories) that shape their lives, devise (after rigorous study) revisionist interpretations of social and educational phenomena, and analyze canonized information within the frameworks of new contexts. Such activities all involve student production of alternate bodies of knowledge — a central theme throughout this work. In a critical pedagogy such production is an essential task, challenging, as it does, the unexamined Cartesian-Newtonian, scientific delineations of reality. Such articulations are typically connected with inequality and oppression around issues of race, class, and gender. Students as researchers operating in this critical mode understand the inseparability of their work from the exposure of knowledges produced by, and serving, the interests of power.

The research referenced in this critical context involves both primary and secondary forms of inquiry. Primary research involves conducting research directly in particular contexts whether they be ethnographic studies of events in their natural settings, semiotic studies of symbols, signs, and codes that inscribe meaning in everyday life, phenomenological studies of human consciousness and the meanings individuals give to certain phenomena, and historical studies of the unfiltered writings and other cultural productions of the past. Secondary research involves studying the ethnographies, semiotic analyses, phenomenological studies, and histories produced by researchers. Our contention is that students should be able to perform both types of research as early as possible. As far as secondary forms of research are concerned students should develop in depth library skills as soon as possible. In addition they should gain awareness of sources of information offered by the community — its institutions and particular members. A central aspect of secondary research involves the critical ability to evaluate the assumptions of researchers and to identify the vantage point from which they are observing a phenomenon.

An important aspect of this ability to locate and critique secondary research involves the skill to name what has been excluded. Students as researchers exploring secondary materials will find that school texts consistently leave out issues of social conflict, injustice, and institutional bias. In such secondary materials students will often discover what Henry Giroux (1997) calls a 'reified view of knowledge', meaning a form of knowledge that is beyond question, that erases the fact that it was produced by humans operating in a particular context with a specific set of values. Understanding these dynamics, student researchers gain an awareness of the subjective nature of all knowledge and of the need to interpret and deconstruct it in order to appreciate the tacit presuppositions about human beings and the world inscribed within it. In a time when traditional educators criticize progressives for a lack of intellectual 'rigor', we find such accusations odd in light of the type of scholastic abilities we want both teachers and students to possess. Democratic pedagogies are often connected by their opponents to low standards — the more authoritarian the pedagogy, the more conservative critics bestow the blessing of rigor.

In the eyes of the advocates of traditional education our efforts to democratize teaching and empower students are characterized as less-than-rigorous therapeutic sessions designed to help students get in touch with their feelings and to feel good about themselves — Bob Dole made this charge in his presidential campaign in 1996. While we have no problem with students who are happy and feel good about themselves, our purpose here is to produce emotionally and physically healthy students who possess numerous methods of gaining, interpreting, producing, and applying knowledge. There is nothing rigorous about pedagogies that require all students to concurrently 'master' decontextualized bits of information — a lockstep absurdity. In this context knowledge despite all of its complexity is reduced to a discreet entity that holds no past or no future.

Such data outside its context holds no significance. Students as researchers help explore and develop that context, as they search for the genesis of knowledge and analyze the reasons many have thought it was sufficiently important to place specific information in the official curriculum. Without such contextual understandings the memory-work pedagogies of traditionalists fail to achieve its most basic objective: the memorization of the validated knowledge of 'our cultural heritage'. Once the test is over most students no longer have any use for such information and quickly forget it. Students as researchers in our critical context not only delve deeper into topics and move to a deeper level of understanding, but they even remember data better than students in traditional pedagogies. Their contextualized understandings help them mentally file information in a manner that allows it to be easily recalled (Abercrombie, 1994; Capra, Steindl-Rast, and Matus, 1991; Fiske, 1994; Ayers, 1992; Fried, 1995).

As Melissa Butler argues in her chapter in this book, our conception of students as researchers involves developing their ability to read various texts through a liberatory/emancipatory lens. We are unembarrassed but cautious in our use of the term, emancipation. To move in an emancipatory direction involves the effort to achieve both self-direction and membership within a democratic community. It also implies a concern with the development of a consciousness that can see through surface appearances and the establishment of a just society. Emancipated students as researchers question their self-image, inherited dogmas, and comfortable ways of thinking. Many have critiqued the use of the term, emancipation, in the last few years. Such critics correctly point out that no-one is ever completed emancipated from the social context that has produced him or her. Also, many have questioned the arrogance that may accompany feelings of personal emancipation. These are important criticisms and must be carefully analyzed by those who operate in a critical manner. Taking these ideas into account, we retain the concept of emancipation with qualifications:

1   No one is ever emancipated — we only work toward emancipation;
2   We are humble in our quest for emancipation — while we search for those forces that tacitly shape who we are, we respect those who reach different conclusions in their personal journeys.

When students as researchers view classroom activity through an emancipatory lens, they view the curriculum not as an authoritative body of information but as inherently problematic. Textbooks become a specific effort by one scholar or a group of scholars to represent a body of knowledge. Students as researchers ask questions about textbook producers: Who are they? What are their goals? What market forces did they have to address? What are their assumptions? What have they left out of their text? How do other scholars from different perspectives view the topics addressed in this text? Students as researchers of textbooks understand that no-one can tell the whole truth about a topic. All we can ever get from a text is a partial story — obviously, this book included. Thus, textbooks in this critical emancipatory context become cultural artifacts to analyze in the same way an archaeologist examines pieces of ancient pottery.

As a young high school history teacher, I (Joe Kincheloe) attempted to engage my students as historiographical (pertaining to the study of the writing of history and the nature of historical research) researchers of our US history textbook. After reading the author's account of the US war with Mexico in the 1840s, students searched for a Mexican account of the war. What they found, of course, were two very different pictures of the conflict with vastly differing assumptions. This exercise helped my student researchers to realize that all texts have viewpoints, particular values, and unstated assumptions. Our purpose is not to find those texts which are unbiased — there are none. And, in addition, the biases of a text do not necessarily undermine its value, its social benefit. Kathy Berry makes this point well in her chapter when she argues that a 'text will generate different meanings dependant in many ways upon the challenge to the authority that the text represents.' Thus, not only do all texts have particular viewpoints, but all texts can be read in a variety of ways. Students as researchers operating in an emancipatory context learn to read in new ways, uncovering in the process challenging new meanings that take them to new pedagogical, political, and cognitive spaces.

Such students grow increasingly aware of the reality that no research finding is ever final. Student researchers learn to live with the ambiguity that comes with the critical terrain. We encourage such students to be self-critical of their own findings and humble in their presentations to fellow students, teachers, and members of the community. This ambiguity and humility we attach to our student research and our own inquiry is closely related to our work on post-formal thinking. We have written extensively about post-formalism in other venues (Kincheloe and Steinberg, 1993; Kincheloe, 1993; Kincheloe, Steinberg, and Hinchey, 1998), so we will not go into great detail here. It is important to note, however, that our understanding of student research cannot be separated from the basic assertions of post-formal thinking (Marker, 1993; Postman, 1995).

Post-formal Thinking, Ambiguity, and Students as Researchers

Post-formal thinking begins its challenge to mainstream educational psychology by questioning Jean Piaget's assertion that formal thinking is the highest order of human thought. Such thinking implies an acceptance of a Cartesian-Newtonian mechanistic world view that is caught in a cause–effect, hypothetical–deductive system of reasoning. Unconcerned with questions of power relations and the ways they structure our consciousness, formal operational thinkers accept an objectified, unpoliticized way of knowing that breaks an economic or educational system down into its basic parts in order to understand how it works. Emphasizing certainty (not ambiguity) and prediction, formal thinking organizes verified facts into a theory. The facts that do not fit into the theory are eliminated, and the theory developed is the one best suited to limit contradictions in knowledge. Thus, formal thought operates on the assumption that resolution must be found for all contractions. Schools and standardized test-makers, assuming that formal operational thought represents the highest level of human cognition, focus their efforts on its cultivation and measurement. Students and teachers who move beyond formality are often unrewarded and sometimes even punished in educational contexts.

As we describe post-formal thinking, one of our main concerns involves what types of cognition and action might occur when students move beyond the boundaries of Piagetian formalism. Of course, our conception of students as researchers fits well the criteria of post-formal cognition and action. Thus, students as researchers become part of a larger effort to construct a new vision of cognition, a new conception of what 'being smart' entails. As teachers and their student researchers move to post-formalism, they politicize cognition; here they attempt to de-socialize themselves from the conventions of school-based pronouncements of who's intelligent and who's not. Post-formal thinking is concerned with questions of meaning, self-awareness, the nature and function of the social context. Such concerns move post-formal thinkers beyond formalist concerns with proper scientific procedure and the *certainty* it must produce. This is where the post-formal thinkers' confrontation with ambiguity begins. When teachers and students gain a post-formal perspective, they grow more comfortable with complexity and the uncertainty and ambiguity that accompany it. This comfort with ambiguity is a central feature of post-formal thinking and the student research that we are promoting. Damian Kellogg's chapter on student inquiry into their dependence of technology is an excellent testimony to a post-formal researcher's engagement with ambiguity.

These post-formal teachers who promote student research expect more factual, analytic, and conceptual sophistication from student inquiry. Teachers comfortable with complexity and ambiguity are better equipped to establish a productive interaction between students and students and students and teachers. Such interaction heightens self-awareness, as student researchers are attuned to the power of their own words and those of others, and the nature of the contexts and codes and the ways they construct the meaning of communication. These higher-complexity teachers encourage the active interpretation and negotiation necessary to the critical process of cultural reconstruction. As they gain the power to reconstruct their own consciousness, they are able to help their student researchers re-interpret their traditions and re-invent their futures together in solidarity with other self-directed human agents. Teachers who are comfortable with ambiguity operate at a post-formal level that seems to be more tolerant, flexible, and adaptive and employ a wider repertoire of teaching models. They are better equipped to enter a post-conventional world where certainty is sacrificed in order to overcome bureaucratic definitions of the deskilled role teachers often play in school. This post-formal view of cognition helps us move beyond the negative consequences of the quest for certainty, as teachers and their students begin to imagine emancipatory educational futures. If the act of teaching followed the modernist pattern and was constant and predictable, teachers could act on empirical generalizations and teacher educators would know exactly what teachers needed to know to perform successfully. But teaching and learning are not constant and predictable — they always take place in the microcosm of uncertainty.

One of the main features of post-formal thinking is that in this microcosm of uncertainty it expands the boundaries of what can be labeled sophisticated thinking. When we begin to expand these boundaries, we find that those who were excluded from the community of the intelligent seem to cluster around exclusions based on race (the non-White), class (the poor), and gender (the feminine). The modernist conception of intelligence is an exclusionary system based on the premise that some people are intelligent and others aren't. Intelligence and creativity are thought of as fixed and innate, while at the same time mysterious qualities found only in the privileged few. The modernist definition of intelligence has stressed biological fixities that can be altered only by surgical means. Such an essentialism is a psychology of hopelessness that locks people into rigid categories that follow them throughout life (Bozik, 1987; Lawler, 1975; Maher and Rathbone, 1986).

Piaget's developmental description of thinking falls captive to the modernist tendency to separate the object of study from its environment — in this case one's intelligence is separated from the social context (their class, race , gender, ethnicity) that produced her or him. The theory walks into its own captivity because it views intelligence as a process that culminates in an individual's mastery of formal logical categories. The development of thinking seems to come from thinking itself, separate from the external environment. This reflects the innate fixity of earlier Cartesian-Newtonian views of intelligence as a spectre emerging from innate inner structures. The early Piaget, in particular, maintained that the desired pedagogical course was to move students' development away from the emotions so that rationality could dominate the progress of the mind. Stages were thus constructed around this logocentrism — stages that would become key supports in the common sense, unquestioned knowledge about intelligence (Piaget, 1969, 1970; Piaget and Inhelder, 1968).

Since one of the most important features of post-formal thinking involves the production of one's own knowledge, student and teacher research, it becomes important to note in any discussion of the characteristics of post-formality that few boundaries exist to limit what may be considered post-formal thinking. Post-formal thinking and post-formal teaching become whatever an individual, a student, or a teacher can produce in the realm of new understandings and knowledge within the confines of a democratic pedagogy, social and economic justice, and a critical communitarianism. Much of what cognitive science, and in turn the schools, have measured as intelligence consists of an external body of information. The frontier where the information of the disciplines intersects with the understandings and experience that individuals carry with them to school is the point where knowledge is created (constructed). The post-formal teacher facilitates this interaction, helping student researchers to re-interpret their own lives and uncover new talents as a result of their encounter with school knowledge.

Viewing cognition as a process of knowledge production presages profound changes in education. Teachers who frame cognition in this way see their role as creators of situations where student experiences could intersect with information gleaned from various bodies of information. In contrast, if knowledge is viewed as simply an external body of information independent of human beings, then the role of the teacher is to take this knowledge and insert it into the minds of students. Evaluation procedures that emphasize retention of isolated bits and pieces of data are intimately tied to this view of knowledge. Conceptual thinking is discouraged, as schooling trivializes learning. Students are evaluated on the lowest level of human thinking — the ability to memorize, the ability to follow directions. Thus, unless students are moved to become knowledge producers who connect such information with their own lives, schooling will remain merely an unengaging rite of passage into adulthood.

The point is clear; the way we define thinking exerts a profound impact on the nature of our schools, the characteristics of education, and the everyday life of students. Notice in the brief delineation of the characteristics of post-formal thinking that follows, each feature contains profound implications for the future of schooling. Self-reflection would become a priority with students and teachers, as post-formal researchers attend to the impact of school and work on the shaping of the self. In such a context, teaching and learning would be considered acts of meaning-making that subvert the technicist view that thinking involves the mastering of a set of techniques. Education could no longer separate technique from purpose, reducing teaching and learning to deskilled acts of rule-following and concern with methodological format. Schools guided by empowered post-formal teacher and student researchers would no longer privilege white male experience as the standard by which all other experiences are measured. Such realizations would point out a guiding concern with social justice and the way unequal power relations in school and in everyday life destroy the promise of self-determination. Post-formal teachers would no longer passively accept the pronouncements of standardized-test and curriculum makers without researching the social contexts in which their students live and the ways those contexts help shape student performance. Lessons would be reconceptualized in light of a critical notion of student understanding. Post-formal educators would ask if their classroom experiences promote, as Howard Gardner (1991) puts it, the highest level of understanding that is possible.

A Brief Description of Post-formal Thinking

Critical teachers and students as researchers expand 'what counts' as intelligence by using these four basic features of post-formal thinking.

1 Etymology

   Etymology (the origin of validated knowledge) — the exploration of the forces that produce what the culture validates as knowledge. Individuals who think etymologically inquires into the sources of their intuitions and 'gut feelings'. Rarely do we come up with such feelings independently, for most thoughts and feelings are collective in origin (Bohm and Edwards, 1991; Senge, 1990). Consider, for example, language — it is entirely collective. We may think that our assumptions are self-generated, but typically we get them from the core of culturally approved assumptions. The concept of 'thinking for oneself' must be reconsidered in light of these concerns; indeed, without an awareness and understanding of etymology, women and men are incapable of understanding why they hold particular opinions or specific values. Without such appreciations, the ability for reflection and analysis is seriously undermined. It is not an exaggeration to maintain that the capacity for critical thought is grounded upon the post-formal concern with etymology.

2 Pattern

   Pattern — the understanding of the connecting patterns and relationships that undergird the lived world. Having in 1992 spent a harrowing night in a small bathroom with three of our children and three dogs seeking shelter from Hurricane Andrew, we are aware of the power of the cyclonic weather pattern that creates unfathomable power. High and low pressure centers developing in differing locations are part of the hurricane system, as they interact with prevailing wind patterns to direct the path of the storm. Each component of the pattern influences the others in a way that is typically hidden from view. One can only comprehend the system of a hurricane by thinking of it as a totality, not as independent, discrete parts. Knowledge of various types is also constructed by invisible patterns characterized by interlocking activities. From our vantage point in the middle of these patterns, they are extremely difficult to identify. Modernist science and education have typically focused on separate pieces of the patterns, many times missing the system itself. As a result, serious problems go unsolved as mainstream 'experts' focus on specific events. 'American worker productivity falls again', Tom Brokaw tells his nightly news audience, fragmenting our understanding of long-term deskilling patterns in the workplace and causing us to fight the wrong battles in the effort to increase productivity. Indeed, no matter how educated individuals become, if they cannot escape the confinements of formal thinking they will be held hostage by unseen patterns. A critical dimension of student research involves learning to discern patterns in the data collected. Post-formal teachers must be able to model this ability in their efforts to sophisticate their students' research abilities.

3   Process

Process — the cultivation of new ways of reading and researching the world that attempt to make sense of both ourselves and contemporary society. The way modernist civilization has developed with its Cartesian-Newtonian logic and scientific reductionism has taken its toll on human creativity. All human beings naturally hold the potential for creative thinking processes, but through their acculturation and especially their education, many men and women have lost such a capacity. Many analysts argue that prehistoric peoples lived a more creative existence than we do now — a shock to our modernocentric systems. They devised not only tools and useful objects but creative ornamental and spiritual articles as well. Unlike many workers and students today, they did not follow a mechanical routine. For prehistoric humans everyday was different, new, and possibly quite interesting and exciting. The post-formal notion of process attempts to recapture that excitement and interest, by devising new of perceiving the world, new methods of researching. The post-formal process attempts to break the mold, to rethink thinking in a way that repositions men and women as active producers, not passive receivers of knowledge.

4   Contextualization

Contextualization — the appreciation that knowledge can never stand alone or be complete in and of itself. When one abstracts, one takes something away from its context. Of course, this is necessary in everyday life because there is too much information out there to be understood in detail by the mind. If an object of thinking cannot be abstracted, it will be lost in a larger pattern. The post-formal thinker is certainly capable of abstraction, but at the same time such a thinker refuses to lose sight of the conceptual field, the context that provides separate entities meaning (Raizen and Colvin, 1991). For example, modernist schooling typically has concentrated on teaching students the 'what' of school subjects. Life and job experience has traditionally taught us 'how' and 'why'. If deeper levels of understanding are desired, tasks must be learned in the context in which they fit. In light of such a pronouncement we can begin to see that novice workers are people who possess no specific knowledge of a particular work setting even though they may come to the situation with everyday knowledge and academic information. Such greenhorns become seasoned veterans only after they gain familiarity with specific social, symbolic, encoded, technical, and other types of workplace resources — i.e., the context of the workplace (Raizen, 1989). Thus, student researchers become researchers of contexts. As post-formal researchers operate, their ability to focus their attention to the contexts in which a piece of data is found becomes second nature. Meaning making is possible only when information is contextualized.

Thus, our conception of students as researchers is a post-formal practice that promotes an ethical awareness and a higher-order of thinking. No fixed definition of a post-formal practice is necessary outside of the general principles delineated here. The definition is always contingent on post-formalism's interactions with its ever-changing experiences, the new contexts in which it finds itself. John Dewey, as usual, anticipated our conception of post-formal students as researchers decades ago. Describing what he called reflective thought, Dewey maintained that individuals should inquire carefully and persistently into any form of knowledge in the context of the arguments that support it and the conclusions it is taken to imply. Teachers, he continued, should be ever mindful to the cultivation and monitoring of students' doubt and perplexity and the facilitation of research into the reasons for their cognitive dissonance (Dewey, 1933). In addition to Dewey's reflective thinking, we find Freire's problem posing, Henry Giroux's teachers as intellectuals, and many other educators calling for pedagogical practices very similar to our students as researchers — indeed, our notion is less-than-new. Nevertheless, the notion of student research promoted here is still a challenge to the mainstream everyday theory and practice of many educational leaders and practitioners concerning the nature of knowledge and the role of research.

The Role of Student Research in Mainstream Schooling

There is no doubt that the easiest way to teach is for teachers to give students answers to questions contrived by experts far away from the classroom. Still, at the turn of the twenty-first century this easy form of teaching still dominates schools — public and private. Such teaching fits seamlessly into the dominant epistemology of western science that has fragmented the world to the point that many people are blinded to particular forms of human experience. This fragmentation is the antithesis of our critical notion of student research, as it weakens our ability to see the relationships between our actions and the world. Contemporary schools still emphasize quantities, distance, and locations, not qualities, relationships, or context. These epistemologically guided assumptions about the fragmented nature of knowledge are deeply embedded in various aspects of school life. The exams typically given in North American schools, for example, prepare students to think in terms of linear causality and quantification — the foundation of a scientific modernist epistemology. Such ways of thinking squash efforts to develop a research-oriented curriculum, hidden assumptions in school conventions and everyday life. Though it takes place in the name of scientific neutrality, such teaching promotes a specific ideology, a specific way of looking at knowledge and the world.

The epistemology, the way of knowing that underlies mainstream practice is an arrogant point of view. Condescending toward other ways of knowing, mainstream educational apologists contend that students come to school to learn the true nature of reality, a body of knowledge that has been neutrally gathered by objective scientists. Such a perspective is antithetical to our notion of students as researchers, as mainstream apologists maintain that questions concerning where the truth came from or how it was produced are irrelevant. Indeed, the message from many mainstream schools is clear: they do not want students to be researchers. In my (Joe) own school experiences in elementary, secondary, and undergraduate education, I was consistently punished for seeking knowledge beyond classroom lectures and assigned textbooks. In a series of political science classes in my undergraduate curriculum I was motivated by my passionate interest in politics to read and research a variety of viewpoints on particular political questions referenced in class. My meta-analytical delineation of various schools of political thought about particular issues limited me to a grade of 'C' or 'C-' in these classes. My less motivated classmates studied key phrases used by the professor and easily obtained their 'A's'. Our children learned quickly not to ask me for help in school, for to act on my suggestions was to guarantee themselves a low grade. In this context we worked out an agreement stipulating that I would suggest readings about particular assigned topics, they would read and analyze them and then turn in to their teachers a brief summary about the topic from an encyclopedia in order to obtain a good grade.

In schools like the ones our children attended and many of those in which we have conducted research, students are taught to surrender themselves to the system and become passive recipients of official truths. The idea of students as researchers who explore their own lives and connect academic information with their own lived experience is alien to many schools. When the term, research, is used, students (like our children) are required to go to official sources (like the *World Book Encyclopedia*) in order to obtain the 'correct' answers to specific questions. Such official sources, including, of course, classroom textbooks, present knowledge as if it was a product to be leased to students until after a 'factual test' when it is no longer useful. The leased product has to be returned in the same form it was when leased. No discussion of the knowledge's complexity and ambiguity is needed, as its veracity is not in question. In this context students engage in a form of pseudo-research that like so-called 'lab experiments' in biology classes have predetermined outcomes and prearranged steps to follow.

In this traditional context schooling's focus on individual, isolated activities involving the manipulations of linguistic and mathematical symbols removed from the experience of the world makes post-formal research activities very difficult to inject into classrooms. Teachers and educational leaders dedicated to promoting student research must thoroughly understand the context of such scientific schooling, its epistemological assumptions and its discomfort with students exploring the world around them. Through such understandings they will be able to address the mind-set that privileges pedagogies grounded upon the sequential learning of skill hierarchies and developmentally appropriate basic skills that remove students from contact with the world. No wonder when the teaching of reading is approached in this skills-hierarchy manner, many students while learning to decode words off the pages don't really learn how to read for meaning. They don't understand that reading is best conceived as a form of research, an act of finding out something about oneself and the world. We often find students who don't learn to read in this conceptual way until they are in graduate school.

Operating in this context students are cognitively numbed by a form of teaching that rarely induces them to think about the purpose of education or the development of their own thinking. In such an educational context students are prohibited from taking part in real research where one's findings are not preordained. Such forms of teaching place limits on student curiosity in the process killing the passion for learning that first brought the teacher to the profession. In this context the ability to ask questions — a basic skill of critical teaching — is lost. Until teachers learn (or regain the ability) to ask questions, there is little possibility of students becoming researchers. But questions are dangerous, often perceived as an attack on authority — nothing got us in more trouble in school than asking questions. Paulo Freire and Antonio Faundez (1989) in their book about questioning maintain that schools either reject questions or they formalize the process of questioning. We don't merely ask questions of students between 10:15 am and 11:00 am on Thursdays, they argue. Instead, we view questions as a basic act of human existence. As an act of human existence, questions don't contain within them their answers — these are bureaucratized questions. Teachers who cultivate students as researchers study questioning as an art that pushes us beyond the boundaries of what we thought was possible (Sholle and Denski, 1994; Postman, 1995; Raizen, 1989; Marker, 1993).

Democratizing Access to Research Skills: Motivating Students to Become Researchers

Research in a critical education is no longer only the province of the expert. Students can become sophisticated researchers who produce their own knowledge and when facilitated by an adept teacher construct their own curriculum. With the teacher as co-researcher students can achieve as many unprecedented goals as creative learners can imagine. A few years ago I (Joe) was asked to teach a course entitled 'Anthropology and Contemporary American Culture' for a local high school. In order to understand the foundations of the critical insights I was presenting, I introduced the class to the evolving critical theoretical tradition. Many people argued that high school students could not learn such difficult theoretical material. Almost without exception students not only understood this admittedly difficult material, but were able to apply it to the formulation of their research projects concerning the community surrounding the school. Examples such as this one abound; indeed, as Nina Zaragosa relates in this book, student research can be encouraged among even younger students than mine.

The question for teachers in this context is not whether students can become researchers; the answer to that one is simple — they can. We believe the relevant question is: how do we induce students to become researchers? This question is especially important to teachers cultivating student research because by the time we get them students have often been educated to be passive recipients of data. Most of our students are bored by school and the uncreative, stifling routines it imposes on them. Teachers must become researchers of this boredom, its sources and consequences. In many pre-industrial societies, for example, young people went around with their parents participating in the affairs of the day. During this time they were learning as participants, gaining first-hand knowledge of the ways of the world. At the end of the twentieth century young people are isolated from everyday affairs, unconnected with the adult world. One aspect of our promotion of students as researchers is designed to address this isolation, to provide the young with new paths of access to the adult world. Such a connection, We believe, will help ease the boredom of contemporary youth (King, 1990; Long, 1995; Bohm and Edwards, 1991).

In this context the teacher becomes a researcher of students, their concerns, their self-perceptions, their relationship with reality. Understanding these particular aspects of their students enables teachers to design research strategies that have meaning for particular students. Connecting these individualized needs and interests with larger concerns, teachers can begin to overcome the disincentives for scholarly activity school often generates among young people. The larger concerns about which we are thinking involve important reasons teachers can provide students for engaging in research. In our teaching we seek to engage students as researchers on the basis of the emancipatory action necessitated by a critical system of meaning. Such a system of meaning returns us to our notion of emancipation, as it helps students gain a consciousness that is aware of the ways power shape our identities. Understanding this emancipatory system of meaning, students begin to seek out the forces that shape us. In addition, they appreciate the need to rethink who they want to be, as they struggle to understand how they have come to see themselves and the world.

Critical teachers help student researchers engage with a system of meaning by using Michel Foucault's (1980) concept of geneology to trace the formation of the identities. Student researchers begin to see themselves at various points within the web of reality, ever-confined by their placement, but emancipated by their appreciation of their predicament. Thus, in the spirit of research within a critical system of meaning, students begin to understand and disengage themselves from the meta-narratives that have laid the basis for dominant ways of seeing. Engaged in the ability to see from a variety of perspectives, students as researchers set the stage for a long running, meta-dialogue with themselves. This inner conversation leads to a perpetual redefinition of their images of both self and world. Teachers operating on the basis of this critical system of meaning respect students enough to give them real work to do, research that matters. It is amazing what students are capable of when they engage in activities they feel are important. Research as real work involves teaching students to do work that historians, anthropologists, or physical scientists perform. Operating with the benefit of social theory — a critical system of meaning — our student researchers can perform research even better than the experts.

In the chapter on my (Joe Kincheloe) student researchers in my elementary social studies methods class and their analysis of the water problem in Shreveport, Louisiana, I point out the expertise that these inexperienced students brought to this issue. In many ways their final report was more sophisticated than the one the city later commissioned for several hundred thousands of dollars because of their social theory-informed perspectives. My students produced social and political insights that were unaddressed by the expensive experts. Picking up on Ellen Swartz's concern in her chapter with student researchers learning from the methods of various expert researchers, we maintain that part of the education of a student research would involve inquiry into the culture and practice of communities of expert researchers (Lave and Wenger, 1991). In this manner student researchers could learn both ways of emulating the experts as well as understanding and transcending the limitations such professionals face. Such activities would not only make schools challenging in ways previously not considered, but they would make schools far more interesting.

Wanted: Teachers with Skills to Promote Student Research

We can talk at length about the many teacher skills needed to facilitate student research, but our discussion must begin with teachers' ability to conduct primary and secondary research. In the same manner that we don't want to take flying lessons from an instructor who can't fly an airplane, students can only learn to become researchers from teachers who are capable of doing research. Teachers must model research and share their own research with their students. In the context of teacher education this means that one aspect of the curriculum should be devoted to teaching prospective teachers how to conduct their own research and how to encourage it among their students (Slaton, 1993). This means — as Nancy Dana maintains in her chapter in this book — that teachers come to see themselves as Freirean co-investigators with their students.

Our debt to Paulo Freire (1972) is immense in our conceptualization of students as researchers. Freire engaged his students as partners in his research activities, immersing himself in their perceptions of themselves and the world around them and at the same time encouraging them to think about their own thinking. Everyone joined in the investigation, learning to criticize, to see more clearly, to think at a higher level, to recognize the way their consciousness is socially constructed. When teachers put Freire's methods to work in their own classrooms, they teach students the research techniques that they have learned. Students are taught such fieldwork skills as observing, interviewing, picture taking, videoing, tape-recording, note taking and life-history recording. Such activities provide an opportune context for teachers to engage students in meta-analytical epistemological analysis — the heart and soul of the movement to post-formalism. Freire's lessons in research were subversive; his invitation to students to take part in the conceptualization, criticism, and reconceptualization of research can be correctly construed as a direct challenge to the modernist cult of the expert. At the same time, his insights provided critical teachers employing research with a sense of direction, a consciousness that transforms the notion of research from simply a data-gathering strategy into a post-formal, consciousness-raising, transformative pedagogical technique.

Freire, especially in the last years of his life, was very concerned with the role and authority of the teachers in a critical, problem-posing, research-oriented classroom. Teachers cannot deny their position of authority in such a classroom. It is the teacher, not the students who evaluate student work, who are responsible for the health, safety, and learning of students. To deny the role of authority a teacher occupies is insincere at best, dishonest at worst. Critical teachers, therefore, must admit that they are in a position of authority and then demonstrate that authority in their actions in support of students. One of these actions involves the ability to conduct research/produce knowledge. In our view the authority of the critical teacher is dialectical; as teachers relinquish the authority of truth providers, they assume the mature authority of facilitators of student inquiry. In relation to such teacher authority students gain their freedom — they acquire the ability to become self-directed human agents.

These aspects of democratic teaching are often misunderstood. Facilitating student research does not mean abandoning the authority of the social role of teacher, nor does it mean never providing students with content knowledge. No teacher who teaches students research skills can maintain a passive, out-of-the-way status. Developing students as researchers is a pedagogical process where students and teachers work together in the activity known as learning. Make no mistake, teachers need to know subject matter content, the history of that content, and ways of teaching it. What is at issue here is how we put forward ideas or teach the content we know. To be a teacher is to assert ideas; we can assert them in an authoritarian or a democratic manner. Democratic teachers working to cultivate student researchers need to provide ideas to their students without disaffirming the right of students in a democratic classroom to interpret and react to such ideas in their own manner. Thus, to use Freire's metaphor, teachers don't simply 'deposit' information in students' minds, but use their content knowledge to guide them in particular interaction with students: to help students formulate problems, to challenge student certainty, to develop generative themes, to help them correct student misunderstandings, etc. . . . (Horton and Freire, 1990; Bartolome, 1994; Macedo, 1994; Freire and Faundez, 1989; King, 1990).

Critical teachers with subject matter knowledge use their authority to provide a context where knowledge can be produced. Such a research-oriented context induces students to reflect on the knowledge presented, to learn from other perspectives on this knowledge, and to use the knowledge to rethink accepted social practices. When teachers induce students to refuse to see themselves in classrooms as consumers of knowledge, the foundation is laid for students to discover personal meaning in the knowledge circulating in the classroom. Students in authoritarian traditional classrooms consume data; students as researchers examine data in relation to their own lived experience. Pat Hinchey writes of this dynamic in her chapter in this book, as she shares with readers the way she builds her classes around particular questions. One of her most important goals involves using her knowledge of content to engage students' disposition to question. Hinchey understands that critical teaching and knowledge production begin with good questions. She shows teacher who want to cultivate students as researchers how to ask good questions, so they can subsequently model such behaviors for their students (Giroux, 1992; Hauser, 1991).

The authors of the chapters in this book understand the difficulty of teaching students to be critical researchers. A critical teacher has to create a learning environment that is safe and intellectually supportive of students' initial, fledging efforts to get beyond the passivity with which they have grown accustomed. One of the first understandings such teachers have to get across to their students is that the traditional ways teaching and learning take place in contemporary society are not natural and divinely provided. Like other socio-cultural dynamics they are socially constructed and, as such, they can be reconstructed by deliberate human action. In this context the teacher promoting critical student research illustrates different assumptions about epistemology and knowledge production, the nature of authority, the purposes of education, and the nature of power and its role in the construction of self and society that a critical pedagogy entails. To engage student research as called for here is to rethink numerous assumptions about the pedagogical act.

In some academic circles observers have recently argued that with the advent of the internet and other forms of information access, student researchers can teach themselves with no need for teachers (Postman, 1995). In this construction teachers become the roadkill along the information superhighway, as students sitting in front of their computers garner all the data that they will need to make their way in the world. Such a perspective reflects not a unique vision for an educational future but a tired and regressive view of knowledge and learning. Epistemologically, such a position assumes that knowledge needs no interpretation, that no form of analysis or contextualization is necessary because the data speaks for itself. It forgets that the gathering of data is merely a first step in the research process. Anyone who surfs the net knows that information in cyberspace is produced by a wide variety of groups and individuals with an extensive range of assumptions and agendas. To argue that students need no help sifting through this rugged terrain is both pedagogically and social irresponsible. In this cyber-context we can clearly see one of the roles for teachers who are committed to the production of critical student researchers; indeed, such an interpretive, analytic role is important in any textual context, whether it be the internet, approved textbooks, libraries, TV and popular culture, etc. . . . .

Involved in these types of interpretative and analytical activities, teachers as facilitators of student research expand the envelope of student activity. Often teachers have told us at this point in our discussion of students as researchers that they understand the value of such a pedagogy, but they are not sure of how they can demonstrate its worth in a manner that convinces their administrators of its importance. In this context we advise them to become PR (public relations) experts for the promotion of a critical pedagogy of teacher research. In this role teachers can arrange with other teachers for student researchers to present their findings to their classes (Fried, 1995). Thus, students not only learn research skills but pedagogical skills involving the determination of how to arrange their research findings for presentation, what to leave out and what's essential, how to contextualize their findings in a way that makes them meaningful for other students and teachers. In addition researchers can prepare booklets for the school library, contact community organizations about the possibility of presenting their research findings at a public meeting. Most administrators will be impressed with the positive public exposure their school will receive from students uncovering, analyzing, and presenting such impressive research. Indeed, administrators will more than likely bask in the positive light on their schools provided by such students and their teachers.

When the work and understandings of teachers as researchers are followed by a concern with students as researchers, pedagogical possibilities abound. The authors of this volume address the relationship between teacher and student research, in the process defining inquiry in a variety of creative ways from a plethora of diverse pedagogical perspectives. Teachers and teacher education students will find a gold mine of instructional ideas in these chapters that will not only challenge and expand their storehouse of pedagogical methods but will induce them to rethink their purposes as educators. We have become very interested in recent years in the problems of scholarship in the area of teaching methodology (teaching teachers to teach) — especially its tendency to separate educational purpose, social context, and ethical concerns from the process of teaching. Our attempt here is to bring these dynamics together, to convince teachers and teacher educators of the deskilling that occurs when these issues are not viewed in relation to one another. We hope that a pedagogy of critical student research helps accomplish these goals and at the same time sophisticates the conversation about and the practice of contemporary education.

References — see p. 245.

Chapter 2

Reclaiming Wonder:
Young Students as Researchers

Kathleen S. Berry

Introduction

Access to cultural/critical literacy for young children provides an arena of study into which teachers seem to either willingly enter or politically avoid. Reaction to the introduction of critical literacy, with other names such as cultural studies or cultural criticism influencing the field, seems to range from hesitant curiosity to redundant fears. With whichever theoretical mood teachers approach literacy, none can reject or circumvent the increasing need to include critical literacy as a daily ingredient in classroom practices beginning with the early years of a child's education. In fact, many would claim that critical literacy begins at home.

To simplify classroom practice for a complex field such as literacy has, intermittently over decades of debates, caused pedagogical arrests. On the other hand, literacy discussions have created dynamic, intellectual energy in a curriculum field that is constantly susceptible to backlash and cries of 'back to the basics'. Cultural/critical literacy is not intended as a response to the debates and discussions nor as a panacea that excludes other theories and practices of literacy. In fact, without the inclusion of other approaches to literacy, critical literacy does not fill its mandate as a theory of inclusiveness and resistance.

What is Cultural/Critical Literacy?

The introduction of cultural/critical literacy in the classroom requires clarification of certain semantic points. One of the first is the various titles under which cultural/critical literacy falls. Terms such as cultural criticism, cultural studies, post-modernism, post-structuralism, post-colonialism, and de-constructionism can, in essence, convolute the theoretical clarity of a teacher's thinking and prevent the evolution of practices. To define the terms might confuse the issue even further. However, for the purposes of 'getting on with it', I will attempt some brief, simple definitions and background to the field.

Since critical literacy arises out of a socio-cultural context, it goes without saying, that any text in which there are representations and relationships is a source for critical literacy. Young children, even at birth, are already immersed in social, cultural contexts in which meanings, symbols, behaviors, knowledge, values, history, and truths are generated and consumed by the young child. Immersed in literacy environments, the task of critical literacy is to shape a child's oppositional readings of the world.

The major task is one of reading the text, whether oral, printed, visual, media, or a host of other available symbolic texts. It is not simply a matter of reading the text for meaning but of reading against the grain; i.e. to question or challenge the representations and relationships of the text in order to deconstruct what are mainstream, taken for granted worlds. Cultural criticism or critical literacy demands a type of questioning that dismantles exclusions and misrepresentations within the text based on cultural constructions such as gender, race, class, age, mental and physical qualities, history, and institutional structures such as family, marriage, church, schools and a host of other cultural artifacts.

With this in mind, the type of questioning that becomes, from birth, crucial to critical literacy is very specific and different to the usual mainstream questions of young children. Questions of wonder which predominate in a young child's life range from 'where're my toys?' and 'what's for supper?', to the big questions such as 'why is the sky blue?' and 'who is God?', and finally to silent questions such as 'do you love me?' and 'who is going to take care of me?'

However, the engagement of children in critical literacy extends their initial questions of wonder about the world to those types of questions that reclaim wonder by addressing and challenging mainstream representations and cultural exclusions. In other words, children are researchers; they search for answers to their questions. Students, equally so, are returned to their initial insertion into a world of knowledge already constructed for them but not necessarily by them.

Cultural/criticism literacy inserts additional ways of thinking and wondering about the world. Some authorities claim that literacy begins at birth. The argument here supports this claim and furthermore, adds that critical literacy also begins at birth. There is little doubt that young children hear from adults a world of questions that are already in play to shape cultural constructions that misrepresent or do not include others or their own.

To further clarify critical literacy, I will place it on a continuum in comparison to traditional and current approaches to literacy, such as basal programs and whole language. Each approach develops a different kind of reader orientation. In the traditional approach, the representations and relationships create a preferred reading, e.g. the construction of the modern, nuclear family consists of a mother, father, and children. This is the accepted, traditional reading of family in modern times. Prior to this time, of course, the preferred reading of family was the extended family in which parents, grandparents, and other relatives lived under the same roof, and everyone was responsible for the raising of the children, especially the grandparents.

In the current dominant structure of family, there is a negotiated reading, e.g. a single parent family in which children are raised by one parent who is both the breadwinner and the domestic caregiver. Negotiation exists in the fact that there is still a parent — most likely the mother. Fathers, grandparents, and other relatives have very limited to nil responsibility in the household and child care. Thus, there is still the presence of the parent as in the preferred reading of the family as nuclear. However, a negotiated reading of family permits a slight variation and compromise to the traditional, nuclear family for a variety of reasons (women at work, education, mobility).

In critical literacy, a reading of family would oppose or resist the traditional, dominant, or negotiated reading of family. For example, in the former readings of family, representations and constructions of family would exclude homosexual relationships or parents since traditional and negotiated readings are still based on heterosexual constructions of family. A homosexual reader exposed to a symbolic text (e.g. oral, printed, visual, media) in which the representations and relationships are preferred or negotiated would have to oppose or resist those representations based on the fact that it is not true to, or inclusive of, homosexual families. Since critical literacy is directed at challenging the authority of the text, the development of oppositional and resistant readings is a prime expectation for teachers of young children.

In addition to the recognition of exclusions and misrepresentations, critical literacy includes theoretical information from contemporary fields such as post-modernism, post-structuralism, post-colonialism, and de-constructionism. In an attempt to expand the reader's notions of critical literacy, I will attempt to provide some background on the influence of these contemporary theories.

One of the easiest ways to understand post-modernism is to ask what is modernism, and how is it problematic to the theories and practices of literacy? Modernism has no clear beginnings or ends, but there seem to be some common denominators that frame modern life. It seems that modern consciousness has constructed or shaped our world in particular ways over the past five to seven centuries with the most obvious start being the rise and value placed upon science and technology. Cartesianism, that is the split in the pre-modern consciousness, constructs the world as subjective and objective. In other words, the world can be constructed and studied as separate from a human consciousness if indeed it is studied as an objective realm. In this way, technology or techniques (and education is filled with techniques of 'how to' on teaching, learning, behavior management) become the major way in which the world is constructed. Problematic to our interest here is that the world can be constructed in such a way that human values, histories, truths, knowledges, gender, class, and so forth, are excluded or dominated by one particular cultural construct such as male over female, European white race over other, races, or ruling classes over working classes. Consequently, modern constructs that are dominant, privileged, powerful, and mainstream can rule out any cultural, social constructs that do not fit within the frameworks or borders of these dominant groups.

While challenges to the constructs of modern life come from the theories and practices of fields such as post-modernism, post-structuralism obviously acts as a challenge to the world of modern formalism and structuralism. Structures in modern society, although they are said to be natural, are in fact, exclusive or oppressive. The task of post-structuralism becomes one of dismantling modern day structures, demolishing historical and taken for granted structures, and reconstructing theories and practices that no longer exclude, misrepresent, or oppress. For example, in modern life, the major construct of family has evolved as mother, father, and children. However, this structure is challenged on many fronts and is changing our concept of what a family structure is. Institutions are entrenched with modern structures such as family, school, church, business, government and so forth, that even presently are being restructured by contemporary, cultural, social differences, and impact upon the way we act, learn, survive, think, and live.

Post-colonialism is related to the modern life surge of early and late colonialism by European and American powers respectively. The influence of colonialism on other cultures leads to the assimilation and contamination of the differences created by the inclusion of various cultures. The elimination of cultural differences by colonialism provides a world in which the dominance of western, Euro/American structures and power (education, law, medicine, social services) are prevalent to date. These colonial structures appear to be challenged currently by the rise of economic and political power of Asian, African, and South American cultures. Although these powers are constructed along national and geographical lines, the borders of culture are gradually crossed, especially by the power of media and information technology which crosses borders without necessarily recognizing cultural differences.

The discourses and practices of post-colonialism are beginning to change and challenge dominant cultural texts that range from print to politics, from economics to media. For example, school curriculum is incorporating, we hope, literature written by colonized populations from the position of the colonized and not the colonizer. Representations of Afro-Americans reposition them as active political agents through the rewriting and restructuring of traditional canons of literature. A shift, for example, relates the history of the United States of America from the experiences, knowledge, truths, and so forth of the Afro-American and not from the position of a white, middle class American male. The slave is represented as an agent of change, not as a powerless, inactive, apolitical being. Literature that traditionally positions the colonized as dependant upon dominant white, European power and privilege is rewritten to represent the slave as an intelligent, political agent. In other words, Afro-Americans are writing culture and history. Another example of post-colonial theory in action are the challenges against the arrogance of *Lawrence of Arabia*, in which, the author, T.E. Lawrence (1935) writes as though the Arabs were rescued by the British, and without them, would not have survived.

Finally, critical literacy is being informed by the theories and practices of de-constructionism in which there is no-one fixed meaning in a text. De-constructionism claims that each reading of a text will generate different meanings dependant in many ways upon the challenge to the authority that the text represents. Although some people claim similarities between critical analysis, and de-constructionism, the two are quite different in both theory and practice. De-constructionism works out of the notion that a text is embedded with more than literary or strategical devices that the reader of the text can analyze for the purposes of evaluating the text as good or bad. On the other hand, de-constructionism has very specific strategies and purposes for taking a text apart.

Considerations of when the text was written, by whom it was written, and who the reader is are important to de-constructionism. A reader positioned by gender, race, class, age, and other cultural constructions would be able to abduct different readings from the text than a differently positioned reader. If I read a text from my position as a white, middle class, Maritime Canadian woman, the text carries different meanings or untruths than for an Asian upper class male. This leads us into multiple meanings and thus, multiple and infinite readings; a possibility that could shake up the standardized, fixed readings currently in place in literacy curriculum.

Together, these contemporary theories place an enormous responsibility upon parents and teachers to introduce critical literacy into the lives of young children.

Why and When Does It Start?

As previously mentioned, literacy begins at birth, and critical literacy is not any different. Parents and teachers may not have the specific terminology and discourse available to them. However, they have a responsibility to immerse children in environments that encourage and evoke critical literacy. From day one, an informed parent and teacher can immerse the child in activities and thinking that engage the child in critical literacy.

Since talk is the first and foremost literacy of a child's life, in which the child learns the parent tongue, it is imperative that the literacy environment engages critical literacy. On the surface, parents can ensure that toys are gender neutral or gender specific. Girls can play with trucks and boys can play with dolls. The modeling that a parent provides is the key to a child grasping the concepts and language of critical literacy. One mother, for example, talks out loud in the presence of her child about how many of the advertisements on TV are directed at women having a very specific body type. 'It's too bad that they can only sell cars if there is a blond, skinny, big breasted woman draped near the car', claims one mother in front of her 3-year-old daughter. Another parent who reads to her two daughters every night makes them aware of the dominant gender and racial values and privileges represented in fairy tales. Even on a trip to a local fall exhibition, Barb Fullerton (1994) listens to her 3-year-old daughter make statements about how the cows must all be female because they have bangs. Aware of her daughter's gender constructions, she reminds her daughter that men have bangs also.

Just as children 'have to be carefully taught' to love and to hate, they are also, at a very early age, becoming literate about their world, both immediately and through literature books and media technologies. If parents fail to practice critical literacy and point out the exclusions and misrepresentations of texts, young children's literacy is only partially begun. To be fully literate, and to nurture a critical consciousness, is very dependant on the early contacts a child has with the language and constructions of culture.

In addition to the coaching statements made by parents in the presence of their children, other caregivers also have a responsibility to engage in critical literacy. Grandparents, aunts and uncles, neighbors, community, media, and other significant aspects of a child's life have to lose both the history of past discourses and the thoughts that are means of oppressive actions and thoughts. To release past and present stereotypes and cultural biases may seem impossible or unimportant to do. However, since these people and environments are the initial sources of a child's literacy, it seems the key to the future literacy of the child lies with these people. Everyone is responsible for educating the child into the realm of critical literacy.

Continuing at School

If indeed, critical literacy begins at home, the task for school is to continue the initial work that parents and others have begun. Of course, this implies that critical literacy has been started and addressed before a child enters school. This assumption, in turn, must be addressed by teachers. Contact and involvement with parents and community is necessary to both continue and connect critical literacy to the home and school environments. Teachers, in cooperation with school administrators and school districts (from the local to the national levels) need to introduce policies which ensure that critical literacy begins at home and continues at school. However, it is only recently that literacy curriculums are including notions of critical literacy in their curriculums and emphasizing home–school literacies.

Needless to say, there is an increased amount of backlash when attempting to introduce critical literacy in the classroom. Teachers and parents have an adversity to change and to political confrontations in an area as pronounced as literacy. Back to the basics in critical literacy includes an assumption that what is basic are human rights and dignity. Backlash should be to the lack of critical literacy in the classroom instead of a lack of phonics, grammar, and meaningless exercises that have proven to retard language acquisition and development instead of advance a more expanded notion of what it means to be literate. On the one hand, awareness and political action that supports the introduction of critical literacy in the classroom needs to be strongly supported by policies that legitimize the introduction of critical literacy. On the other hand, without the awareness and connection with parents and educational administrators, critical literacy in the classroom will suffer.

Teacher's Role

In addition to connections with home and educational administrators, the teacher in the early years of a student's life is as responsible for the introduction of critical literacy into the curriculum as parents are. Initially, teachers need to be informed about the theory and complementary practices before they introduce critical literacy into the curriculum. The foundation lies in how aware the teacher is of cultural constructions in the texts (whether printed, visual, or oral), that need to be challenged based on the exclusions, misrepresentations, and stereotypes of gender, race, class, age, sexuality, and other cultural constructions.

Fast Starts and Slow Results

While a teacher may wish to jump into the bath without the bathwater, as so often happens when new curriculum becomes politically enticing or exciting, immediate results are slow to come — and well this should be. Any attempts to see results in a short period of time may result in political upheavals or pedagogical damage. There is as much unlearning to occur in critical literacy, as there is learning. Influences from a student's environment and background have probably, even at a very early age, shaped their knowledge and perceptions of gender, race, class, age, sexuality, and so forth. From several indications, such as research and personal experience, young children are very entrenched in mainstream cultural knowledge, values, truths, representations, and so forth.

Scrunity preceeds implementation. An investigation of the materials in the classroom serves as a cautionary start for teachers. Materials such as books, posters, and magazines could be surveyed for balanced representations of different gender, race, class, sexuality, and so forth. A balanced environment would also be included in the investigation. Seating arrangements, task assignments, illustrations in books and worksheets, entrances and dismissals in the classroom, responses to students, questions answered and acknowledged are only a few of the symbolic environments that need to be scrutinized for dominant, privileged, marginalized, and oppressive constructions.

These initial investigations of the classroom environment provide the teacher with an opportunity to organize and plan the classroom curriculum prior to the arrival of the students. Whatever the grade level, especially in the early years where environmental literacy plays such an important part, teachers can hasten the implementation of critical literacy without the danger of having too fast of a start that might interrupt or upset parents and school administrators, which in turn might slow down the implementation process. In fact, critical literacy demands an inclusion of other literacies which indeed demand that the symbolic environment is filled with a plurality of cultural representations and structures. If not, challenge the conditions in which students are emergent researchers.

In addition, interaction between the students and teacher in the multiple settings of a school, such as hallways, recess, gymnasiums, lunchrooms, washrooms, and playgrounds is perhaps one of the major arenas in which critical literacy can be slowly, but profoundly, introduced. One teacher on playground duty who had a group of grade 2 children around her, wondered out loud why it was that only boys were playing soccer and baseball, and how was it that only girls were playing hopscotch and skipping? Another teacher in passing the washrooms asked her grade four students why one washroom was labeled 'men' and the other was labeled 'girls'? The students pondered for a moment, and seemed to have no problem with the labels until the teacher mentioned that the girls' washroom should be labeled 'women', thus elevating the girls to a more mature position as had the discourse over the men's washroom. In another school, all the murals and posters are visual images of men (boys) playing sports or working with computers. The images of women (girls) are invisible and absent. These spontaneous interventions in a child's thinking about gender (and of course, other cultural constructions) is probably one of the best ways to contextualize critical literacy and thus, move the theory into the concete world of the children.

Redundant Fears

No other area of education seems to evoke as much backlash and fear as does the debates over what theories and practices should be part of a literacy curriculum. Cries of 'back to the basics', 'children are not literate if they don't know their phonics', 'teachers already have too much curriculum to cover without introducing something else like critical literacy', 'the parents don't want to have their children exposed to topics about other races, feminism, sexuality, and the values and knowledges of other groups', 'if we teach our children this stuff, they could end up thinking that their whole world is wrong' are only a few of the overheard conversations that instill fear about introducing the sensitive topics and issues that follow from introduction of critical literacy. However, these fears are redundant. They have been heard since the times when education was dominated in the past by the Church; presently by government; and surely, if history does repeat itself, in the future the cries will continue from big business. In fact, today, churches and schools still carry the remnants of the fear of inclusions based on homosexuality — the last respectable prejudice of the twentieth century.

Daily and Long Term Practices

As mentioned before, intervention by the teacher on a daily basis happens spontaneously and unpredictably. The same would hold true for teachers' intervention in other activities of the child's daily life in the classroom. Questions introduced while children are reading or writing are an excellent opportunity for the slow, but sure, method of awakening the oppositional or resistant reader and writer. While the teacher models a critical consciousness through questioning, the cultural texts which are placed before the student offer a host of cultural constructions that are open to challenge from the teacher and the students. Ms Saunders, while reading a folktale to her grade 2 students pauses during the reading to wonder why Chinese rulers are always males. Her wondering is infectious. When Aylissa read a folktale during USSR (uninterrupted, sustained, silent reading) following Ms Saunders' reading, she yelled out to the rest of the class, 'why are all the heroes men?' It was obvious that the teacher had influenced the student's thinking and moved her into the realm of critical literacy.

Nuturing Resistant Imaginations

Once the process of critical literacy begins at home and continues at school, everyone becomes involved in nurturing the imagination of resistance. Every text of a child's world is challenged by questions and informed imaginations. Children soon learn to research their world through their questions, and by reading/writing against the grain of mainstream, status quo, and dominant texts, they constitute a world of inclusion. In other words, they begin to challenge the cultural constructions in any text including environmental, print, oral, visual, media, and others. The emergent imagination of resistance is received as is the first utterance of recognition of the other in their lives. As parents rejoice at a child's babbling of 'mama, dada', so too do teachers celebrate a child's emerging, critical literacy.

Celebration of the emergent critical literacy of young children is orally recognized by the teacher as 'great question, shows you have a good eye/ear for noticing how some people or groups are more powerful than others', or 'that's true (name of child), that most of our stories are about boys. How can we change that?' Could somebody in the class rewrite stories so that they include, are about, or make a certain gender, race, or class important? (be careful to avoid stereotypes and tokenism and remind the children that they should write from their cultural positions. The rejoicing of children's emergent critical literacy is endless. Indeed, like all aspects of literacy, it is a lifelong process.

Examples of Critical Literacy Lessons

Given that teachers are aware of the theoretical background to critical literacy, everyday lessons using oral and printed text seem to follow more easily and frequently. Printed materials are readily at hand, whether basal readers, or literature books that are outdated or updated in terms of cultural/critical literacy. Students are introduced to a text in various ways, and in so doing, the teacher is aware that the approach to talking about, and activities centerd on, the book are based on the theories and practices of critical literacy. As a teacher reads to the children, or the children read to each other, or read silently to themselves, momentary stops are made in which the reader challenges or opposes the cultural constructions in the text. Especially with young children, the teacher should introduce the text in such a way that the children are focused on one cultural construction such as gender. Comments made before, during, and after the reading could be centred around cultural constructions related to gender. 'What gender gets to be the heroes? What gender is the most important in the story? What gender is always doing the action or rescuing or in power? What gender is always waiting to be rescued or depends on the opposite gender for strength or their power? Are there characters who seem to have more power than others? Are there characters who are left out or do not have any voice/say in the story? What particular qualities do boys/men have in the story compared to those of girls/women? Whose activities are important, and whose are of less value? Are there characters who seem to have more power than others based on their gender (age, race, class, religion, education, physical appearance, mental abilities, and so forth)?' The list is endless. However it is important for the teacher of young children to keep them focused on one cultural construction at a time. Not only do these comments and questions focus the reader, they also influence their consciousness as they read/write in a manner that evokes critical reading against the grain.

Once the text has been introduced, it is important in critical literacy as it is in traditional (basal reading) and current approaches (whole language and literature based programs) to have the students talk about the text in particular ways. In the traditional, basal approach, students are required to answer questions formulated from a literary analysis perspective. The type of reading here is that of a preferred reading of cultural constructions. The discussion that follows a traditional, basal introduction to the text includes questions about characters, setting, plot, main idea, factual information, inference questions, judgmental and evaluation questions, and synthesis and analytical questions. The first four set of questions arise from literary analysis, and the latter questions are derived from Bloom's taxonomy.

In the whole language approach the questions are derived from a reader response and personal connections response to the text. This assumes there is a negotiated reading between the text and the reader. Both generate meaning and, in the interaction between the reader and the text, there is a response that is both personal and connected to the real world outside the text. The text talk in whole language derives from questions such as: 'What is your favorite part? What part puzzled you the most? What do you think of the main character? What is your opinion of the main character's thoughts and actions?' And in the personal connection mode, whole language questions are formulated as follows: 'Is there someone in this story who is like somebody you know? Has anything ever happened to you or someone you know like what happened to any of the characters of the story?' Each question is related to negotiating meaning and evoking a personal response from the reader.

In critical literacy, young children discuss the cultural constructions in the text and are asked to challenge or oppose the representations and relationships based on race, age, gender, class, physical and mental differences, knowledge, truths, histories, and so forth. Teachers frequently mention how this is the most difficult, most sensitive, and potentially volatile area of literacy. As mentioned before, the redundancy of their fears is real, however, their reluctance is unnecessary. Policies are in place both at the governmental/state level and in curriculum documents that support teachers' entrance into critical literacy. My experience has been that teachers will risk discussions based in the critical literacy field but will only stay within particular cultural boundaries such as gender, race, and age. The most neglected or avoided aspect of critical literacy still continues to be homosexuality. Avoidance ranges from 'the parents would never let us do it', to 'there's no way I'm gonna do that in school because the children are too young' to the ultimate statement 'it's just plain wrong' (these are actual statements made by classroom teachers/administrators at a workshop on critical literacy).

Restoring Agency to Young Children

Lindfors (1980), a teacher educator at an American university, had her students collect samples of children's questions from age 2 to 7. What they found was that before children were of school age, they were generating their own questions that were very philosophical and scientific. However, when children entered school environments, they reduced the amount of questions to only 15 percent, and in addition, the questions were usually procedural ('Where do I put the date?') or asking for permission ('Can I please sharpen my pencil?'). Although this was only the findings of a mini-research project, the implications speak of the role of critical literacy in the lives of young children.

Once people stop asking questions, they are no longer agents of their own learning or action. Thus, by implication from Lindfors' students and from my own personal experience, I find that each year a child is in school, it seems to remove both their initiative in asking questions, and also demand a conformity of thought. Teachers, even in the early years, seem to give limited time and credibility to students' questions. In fact, research seems to indicate that classroom questions are asked mainly by the teacher (85 percent of the questions are asked by teachers) and as stated before, the only questions students seem to ask are procedural or for permission. Over the years, needless to say, children are gradually displaced as agents in their own learning. What happens is teachers control the child's literacy and hinders any active responsibility on the part of the child to oppose, resist, or challenge constructions in texts.

With this in mind, teachers as well as modeling and introducing critical thinking, and thus, critical literacy into the child's curriculum must also withdraw from controlling the questioning opportunities of young children. If teachers consistently model critical literacy both spontaneously and planned, and in collaboration with parents and others, then young children begin to reclaim their initial wondering about the world. What has been added is a consciousness that is shaped and directed toward critical literacy.

Counter-hegemonic Literacy

One of the major concepts in critical theory is hegemony. Basically, it is a theory of consent (please note that it does not mean consensus). This theory looks at how it is that people come to accept cultural constructions that are dominant, privileged or oppressive and do not challenge or oppose the text that govern and rule their lives. In fact, hegemony is a history and system of consent that allows the rulers to produce, circulate, and maintain cultural constructions that oppress the ruled. The theory of hegemony attempts to explain the workings of consent through education, manipulation, and subtlety without using coercion or force. With this in mind, a major direction for critical literacy is to develop counter-hegemonic practices for young children.

When Carolyn's father asked his 4-year-old daughter to do something in the house, she asked why, and he answered, 'because I'm the boss.' Carolyn, versed in counter-hegemonic thinking, said 'no, I don't have to. I'm the boss of myself.' Granted, Carolyn lives in a household that encourages and accepts challenges to authority in young children. Carolyn's father, although he does not call it counter-hegemony, hopes that this early exposure will prepare her for future challenges to authority.

Teachers, like Carolyn's father, are responsible for providing opportunities and environments in which counter-hegemonic practices are modeled, expected, and allowed without rudeness or danger to the young child's emergent critical literacy. It seems that teachers, in many cases, take counter-hegemonic statements from young children as disrespectful, disruptive, and misbehavior. Instead of hearing a child's opposition or resistance to constructs that are not compatible, teachers tend to assume that the young child is misbehaving or rude. A grade 1 teacher, Ms Laws, takes children's consent as dangerously passive and producing 'gutless thinkers'. She lyrically takes their challenges, oppositions, and resistances to dominance and mainstream thinking as authentic learning situations. When most teachers comebacks to children's challenges or resistances are stated as 'don't you speak to me like that', 'you have no right to talk like that', 'I'll have to punish you for acting like that (disrespectful)', or 'that's not the right answer (when they are reading or doing other activities)', they are shutting down a child's opportunity to produce counter-hegemonic or non-consent practices. We seem to have many statements and practices in place that create consent, however, there is limited to nil modeling or permission for opposition or resistance through counter-hegemonic practices. Critical literacy demands that young children, as argued before, starting at birth, question, challenge, oppose, and resist mainstream, dominant, privileged, preferred, or negotiated readings of the world.

Socialized Subjects

Young children are constantly surrounded by symbolic representations and relationships that are influencing and shaping their consciousness. Whether watching television (now a major text in the lives of late, modern children), hearing stories read to them, reading their own stories, shopping in a mall or a host of other activities which engage children with culturally constructed texts, they are being constructed as subjects.

Subjectivity does not exist in isolation. Each of us are who we are from multiple socio-cultural influences. Throughout my 53 years, I have been shaped as a working class child, middle class, white, heterosexual, Canadian, academic woman by family, church, school, community, media, and a host of other institutions and technologies. This is my subjectivity. I do not exist as an individual, but as a subject construction. I have been socialized more so than individualized. Most of these influences come from a taken-for-granted world.

Teachers (and others) cannot afford to allow young students to take the world for granted. They are of it but can also change it. This means reclaiming wonder by researching that world; in turn, reclaiming their voice and becoming political agents. They are constructing and being constructed; subjected to the images, representations, and relationships of dominant texts. If indeed, their history, knowledge, values, structures, gender, race, experience, literacy and so forth, are excluded or mis-presented, they become marginalized, oppressed, silenced, or invisible through the hegemonic practices of schooling — a responsibility that is in the hands of the adults in their environment.

Post-modern Babies

Lise Nicholson, a personal friend, is a French Canadian married to an English Canadian. When she carried her first child in her arms, she asked, in tears, an important post-modern question — was Michael (and later his siblings, David and Lyette) to be raised French or English? The two cultures are in conflict in Canada and her choice could determine the future inclusion or exclusion of her baby. Born into a modern world, children like Michael are inserted into particular dominant, cultural constructs that, in many cases, determine his future if they are not challenged or opposed. Distinct society is what some French Canadians, in a national cultural dominant by English Canadians, want and the politics demand separation and political borders more so than plurality of distinctions and no borders. Lise's question was a political question. What power does Michael have if he is French in a country that is constructed along British lines?

The same question is asked for all babies at the end of the modern era — what kind of world are we born into and if I don't fit, how do I change it? Obviously, the cultural critic answers — research it, ask the *big* questions like Lise did, challenge, oppose, resist, be a politically active agent in thought, word, and actions by researching your *big* questions.

References

FULLERTON, B. (1994) Young girls constructions of gender: A mother's search, University of New Brunswick: Unpublished Master's Thesis.
LAWRENCE, T.E. (1935) *Seven Pillars of Wisdom: A Triumph*, London: Penguin.
LINDFORS, J. (1980) *Children's Language and Learning*, NJ: Prentice-Hall.

Chapter 3

Nurturing Critical Dispositions in the Classroom

Patricia H. Hinchey

As I sat down to write this chapter, the back page commentary of the current *Education Week* was headlined 'How Teachers Would Change Teacher Education'. In it, the author summarized (and obviously agreed with) the results of a survey calling for specific reforms in teacher education. Perhaps not surprising, but nonetheless alarming, is the article's criticism that 'emphasis on theory over practice is not only inappropriate, it is damaging and has resulted in ineffective preparation for the classroom', and its insistence that 'schools of education must shift the balance from theory to practice and emphasize school-based experiences' (Ridgen, 1996). Speaking for the Council for Basic Education, the author argued for less *thinking* and more *doing* in teacher education programs.

This is not surprising to me because of my own experiences any time the words 'philosophy' or 'theory' come up. Colleagues in philosophy courses I took hated them, judging them a waste of time because they offered no advice on what to *do* in a classroom. Students in courses I've taught, both undergraduate and graduate, have stoutly resisted reading or thinking about theory for the same reason. Goodlad's extensive study of teacher education (1990) indicates that my experience is typical, that there is widespread resistance to any theoretical coursework. What many are demanding of teacher educators is more and more emphasis on what critical theorists would call 'instrumental rationality', a line of thinking that assumes the goals of teaching are self-evident and that practitioners need only advice on *how* to get there. In short, a common mindset in relation to teacher education is 'Yeah, yeah — we all know *what* to do. Just tell us *how* to do it, and save those philosophical discussions for the college cocktail parties'.

Traditional Coursework

As educators everywhere try harder and harder to placate an increasingly hostile public, none of this criticism bodes well for the study of theory and philosophy. What will happen as critics push for more and more practical courses and experiences, crammed into the shortest feasible amount of time because of students' increasing financial problems? Like introductory composition courses in the English department, introductory teacher education courses have already been diminished by senior professors who scorn anything considered 'introductory' for undergraduates and have largely pushed its teaching off on to adjunct faculty. Far too often, this has meant that the first teacher education course that undergraduates encounter has been taught by the local retired principal or superintendent who may have had 30 or 40 years 'practical' experience — and who well may not have read a professional publication or attended a serious academic conference for the last quarter century or so. In courses taught by well-meaning and experienced but inexpert instructors, the pedagogy often equates to a 'read this chapter, then take this multiple choice test' approach that quickly convinces students that everything they've heard about education courses being 'Mickey Mouse' fluff is true. After all, how much specificity and passion can a sort of hobbyist infuse into courses which are roughly the equivalent of the history department's 'History 101: From the Big Bang to the Big Band Era'?

The professoriate has, then, exacerbated scorn of 'non-practical' introductory coursework by treating such courses as unimportant and by affording them only cursory care and token status in teacher education programs. In my college, for example, few of the curriculum faculty have the foggiest notion of what is taught in our introductory theory and policy courses and why it might matter. But to admit that such courses are routinely undervalued and badly taught is not so say they should be eliminated. To do away with early, theoretical study in response to criticisms of 'too much theory!' (as many urge) would be a mistake for several reasons.

First, while it's certainly true that teachers need to know *how* to teach a class, any *how* without a *why* is sterile and self-defeating. Teaching has a good deal in common with writing, and it may be useful to consider an analogy here. Writers cannot *effectively* compose a piece without having some goal in mind. If I were writing to inform an interested audience about which specific words frequently offend feminists, I'd write one way; but if I were writing to persuade *dis*interested or hostile readers to think about avoiding sexist language, I'd write very differently. While there would probably be some overlap in content, the strategy, tone, and emphasis would be very different. Similarly, teachers cannot design an *effective* class without clear and explicit goals. Introductory coursework in theory and policy, where subject matter routinely includes discussion of various purposes for schooling and of various curricula designed in response to those purposes, offers a time and place for students to begin thinking about goals and about how different choices lead to different kinds of classroom experiences and learning.

Moreover, research on teacher thinking indicates that introducing new methodology (the *practical* aspect of teacher education) is pointless until certain groundwork has been laid. Specifically, the research finds that students are unable to seriously consider and implement classroom alternatives until they have recognized and questioned the unconscious ideas they bring to the teacher education classroom (Kennedy, 1991). Methods like collaborative problem solving and portfolio assessment will seem impractical and/or irrelevant to them until they have acknowledged and critically examined reified ideas like 'a good classroom is a quiet classroom; teacher talk is more important than student talk; textbook curriculum is not only appropriate, but appropriate for all students; those handy tests provided by publishers will tell us all we need to know about student "learning"'. Before students can even *think* about the practical, about the new goals and new pedagogies many reformers urge, they have to become aware of such deeply held, unconscious beliefs because those beliefs often constitute barriers to new practice. For example, the teacher who values a quiet classroom will not be quick to adopt group work. Until students can grasp the initial idea that common practice is not necessarily the best and only possible practice, they can make little progress toward becoming the flexible, creative and effective practitioners we so badly need.

Many of us want teachers who realize that schooling might be very different than it now is. We want teachers who actively analyze what is happening around them and who can imagine a more desirable scenario. We want teachers who will not only be able to envision change, but who will think of themselves as change agents and take action to improve things. All of this is to say — whether reformers are aware of it or not — that we want *critical* educators for tomorrow's classrooms. Shaped by a critical perspective, introductory coursework offers opportunities to seed and nurture dispositions that are prerequisites for critical practice.

If those of us working with undergraduates rethink our own goals, and then rethink what strategies might suit those goals — if we undertake just the kind of reconceptualizing we ask of our students — we can create a different kind of introductory academic experience, one that helps our students develop a mindset necessary to become the skilled practitioners that the public demands — and one that also helps them to begin assuming the role of autonomous agent, an essential goal of critical teacher educators. In this process, the critical educator will quickly find familiar ground. Creating conditions that encourage others to question their own assumptions is, after all, the heart of critical theory, which seeks to empower people to change whatever they determine needs changing. This seems a natural and valuable center for our classroom efforts with students just beginning their professional preparation.

A Critical Classroom

General Goals

Moving people to challenge their unconscious assumptions is no mean feat. Not only are many people unaware of the specific assumptions they make about schooling, but they tend to hold those assumptions as self-evident truths about the way things are and must be, rather than ideas that have alternatives. For example, many teachers cannot imagine school without imagining that homework will be part of it, even though the practice could be eliminated by a simple decision to eliminate it (Hinchey, 1992). Even when teachers complain that students never do homework, they assign it anyway because they can't imagine *not* assigning it. For any teacher education interested in reform, then, the instructor's questions become: How do I move students to become aware of their assumptions? How do I help them begin to distinguish between alternative ideas and immutable facts? And, once they can imagine change, how do I encourage them to believe they can — and must — act to realize it? If these are my goals, what classroom strategies might be appropriate? For the critical teacher educator, other questions are also important: Whom does this situation benefit? Whom does it disadvantage? Is it just? Should I act to pursue change?

Narrowing Goals

The goals laid out above — to raise awareness of assumptions, of their malleability, and of the possibility and responsibility for change — are the umbrella goals we can all work toward. How each of us approaches them, however, will depend in large measure on who our students are and on what knowledge, skills and dispositions they bring to our classrooms. My own students are, like the national profile, overwhelmingly Caucasian and middle-class. While I teach at an excellent institution, most students do not come because of our excellence, but because of our comparatively low tuition as a state-related university. Many are drawn to my campus, too, because we're close to their homes, where they want or need to live while attending college. Like the communities they come from, my students are also notably racist, sexist, homophobic and Eurocentric. Most have traveled little, and few have seen evidence of the vast wealth reflected in Palm Beach mansions and Neiman Marcus price tags. For the most part, they imagine teaching students just like themselves, preferably in the very schools they themselves attended. And, for the most part, they are entirely devoid of intellectual curiosity, having suffered 12 years of passive, authoritative schooling.

Where to begin? For me, the starting place in planning has been to articulate the specific questions I hope the course will move students to ask: 'Where did I get *this* idea [about education or other people]? Is it accurate? . . . Why didn't anyone ever tell me *this* before? . . . Why didn't I ever want to do *this*? . . . Why did I think I couldn't do this? . . . If I don't like *this*, what exactly can I do to change it?'

Given the conservative and prejudiced ideas I know my students often bring to the classroom, I find no shortage of topics that might push against students' mental boundaries. In fact, to encourage an inquiring disposition, I usually center courses around a series of explicit questions I tell students we'll explore; often, my syllabi open with a quote from William Ayers: 'Questioning everything in the environment, from the bottom up, is an important task for teachers' (1993). While I know I won't succeed with every student, I trust that in the process of exploring these questions, many students will become aware that they routinely base firm opinions on limited information; that those opinions are usually transferred to them from others; and that they are perfectly capable of deciding what to think for themselves if they are given — or go out and pursue — substantive information. Specific questions I often pose include these:

1 What kind of education have non-white, non-middle-class, non-male students had in American classrooms? What do those experiences suggest

about the credibility of the ideas that public schools provide equal opportunity for everyone, and that anyone who works hard in school can and will be successful?

Students read historical and imaginative texts (detailed below) that offer information about the experience of Native American, Mexican American and African American students; females; poor students; and Puerto Ricans. We talk about the concept of Manifest Destiny and we read the history of Native Americans and educational policies relating to them. Subsequently, students learn that a book exists titled *Lies My Teacher Told Me: Everything Your American History Textbook Got Wrong* (Loewen, 1995). We see a documentary comparing the experience of a black student in a ghetto school and of a white student in a nearby, affluent enclave and talk about the work of Jonathan Kozol. We read results of the AAUW (American Association of University Women) survey on gender bias in math and science instruction. Students learn that the Harvey Milk School in New York City was created for homosexual students, and that New York City's Rainbow Curriculum was outlawed by citizens who objected to its two paragraphs suggesting that books about families with gay parents be available to students. We discuss tracking and second generation segregation.

In this way, sheltered students can be introduced to the idea that 'American' students do not all look, sound, and live like they do; that their school experience is far removed from the school experience of many others; that historical events and conditions are reflected in current conditions; and that the history they learned in high school selectively omits a vast quantity of important information. Typically, at least some students begin to question why they've generally assumed that poor children are stupid and come from stupid families (or else they wouldn't be poor); that minority students are frequently hostile toward the white, middle-class population and its institutions for no good reason; and that poor schools are full of delinquents who don't want, deserve, or already have any good teachers.

2   What do unions have to do with teaching children?
We examine a teaching contract from early in the century and ask what assumptions about the relative status of women and men might have led to the title of 'Miss' being preprinted on contracts, and to such restrictions as teachers being forbidden to leave town without administrative permission or to ride in a vehicle with any man except a father or brother. We examine statistics on how many women and how many men teach in elementary schools; how many of each are in administrative positions; how many on school boards; we count how many women and how many men are in our class. Then we ask how gender statistics might influence teaching salaries and conditions. We talk about whether any of the students were told by someone that they're 'too smart' to be a teacher, and we talk about the unions' struggle for respect and professional level salaries. We look at local newspaper articles about teacher strikes, looking for media bias. When we

find it (as we routinely do), we ask why teachers are so frequently blamed for being greedy and insensitive to the needs of children. We talk about the effect of such criticisms as 'unions protect incompetents' and 'unions make unreasonable demands' when those charges are true.

Because many of my students have experienced teacher strikes first-hand, they frequently enter my course thinking *their* teachers had been selfish and greedy during the strikes that inconvenienced seniors and foot-ball players. This material offers information suggesting that greed and selfishness are not the *only* way to explain teacher strikes. It also prompts the question of who *is* responsible if incompetents remain on a faculty and of what responsibility good teachers might have to help ensure the professionalism of the school community as a whole. We discuss a hypothetical situation poses the problem of what a new teacher should do when it becomes clear the veteran teacher in the classroom next door has a serious drinking problem that is affecting his classroom performance.

3 What purposes do public schools serve? Who has what kind of power? Who should control what happens in schools?
Here, we ask why exactly public schools were founded at public expense, and what practical purposes they serve public institutions. We read about the difference between public and private goals, and about social, economic and political purposes of schooling. We examine current rhetoric about schools, asking which purposes are being promoted by whom, and why. We look at legislation being proposed and consider the different impact of block grants and categorical aid, and why Republicans routinely support one and Democrats the other. We read about and explore ties between the Republican party, conservative Christian groups, what their stances are on such issues as vouchers, and why. We think about how different kinds of curricula support different kinds of goals, and how different interests are served by different curricula. Students ask their parents and grandparents if they remember whom they voted for in the last school board election (many don't), and if they do, why they voted for those particular candidates (sometimes because the candidate was Irish or Polish or Italian, sometimes because he's a good butcher). Students read, and then re-read in disbelief, the portion of a text that tells them the Supreme Court has found corporal punishment constitutional; they do the same with a copy of an *Education Week* article from a year or so ago that includes one state's regulations about the legal size, shape and material for classroom paddles. They read court decisions both affirming and limiting students' and teachers' constitutional rights in the classroom.

Much of this information strikes students as startling. When they begin to see that classroom routines like pledging allegiance and coloring silhouettes for classroom displays on Presidents' Day were originally implemented by someone to shape their thinking in some specific way, they feel duped (as they do when they learn about omissions in their knowledge of American history). Having been chagrined earlier by the information that the government removed Indian children from their homes in an attempt to 'Americanize' them, students become uneasy when they realize that they, too, have been 'Americanized' by their schools. (This is not to suggest that schools should not be concerned with patriotism, or should undermine patriotism. The emphasis here is prompting students to realize to what extent they have unconsciously adopted attitudes and ideas that someone else has worked *consciously* to instill in them.) When they learn that parents do not have a constitutional right to protect their children from corporal punishment in school, they are outraged and start thinking a great deal about what exactly a constitutional right is and how state governments can help shape local policy in ways its public considers desirable.

4 How could a dull, dry textbook possibly play a political role in schools? Here students learn a lesson in the economics of textbook publishing. They learn that some states adopt one set of texts for every school district, a policy that encourages publishers to produce books that will be particularly appealing to those states. We talk about publishers frequently eliminating topics (like information on AIDS and euthanasia) because they want to please heavily religious and conservative states like Texas. We talk about Harold Rugg's social studies texts having been burned by school boards earlier this century on the grounds they were 'anti-American' because they suggested one could not believe every claim in every ad. Students hear my story of recently looking something up in a grammar text I used in a high school in the early 1970s and being stunned to find the text full of exercises based on very nasty, anti-Communist prose — which I never noticed when I used the book with students. The American climate was so rabidly anti-Communist at the time that the text was just a part of the way things were; nothing out of the ordinary at all. We talk about *People for the American Way*, which tries to keep religious bias out of textbooks. While we're on the subject of books in the classroom, we talk about censorship, and efforts to ban the lyrical children's book *I Love You Forever* (a story which ends with an adult son cradling his aged and infirm mother in a rocking chair) on the grounds that it promotes incest, and to ban *Snow White and the Seven Dwarves* on the grounds that it promotes homosexuality (if Snow White slept in a dwarf's bed, then that displaced dwarf must have slept with one of his comrades).(!)

Traditional vs. Critical Approaches to Information

Of course the above outline cannot summarize every discussion topic that might be useful in encouraging students to develop the habit of interrogating their own assumptions. But information on any of these topics is easy to come by — even standard — in a variety of texts. Like every instructor, I supplement standard information with personal experience and outside sources like newspapers, research reports, videos, and so on. But as a writer may take the same information and shape it differently for different audiences and goals, I believe that a critical focus and critical goals imprint a very distinct shape on what is fairly generic information.

The crucial difference in a critical approach is that all of this information is provided to students in the format of food for thought rather than as content that has some intrinsic importance which makes it worth memorizing and regurgitating on standard exams. Consistently students are asked to articulate how the information presented affects their answers to such questions as 'Does this information confirm or contradict the idea that American schools offer equal educational opportunity? That women's struggle for equality is over? That if you are not gay, you don't need to think about gay issues in your classroom? That government is a sort of lumbering irrelevancy that has little to do with daily life? That teachers need be concerned only with events within their own classroom?' And so on and so on and so on. Always, the central theme is 'You spent 12 years in schools — did you learn *this* there? Why or why not? Does this information change your thinking in any way? Where did you get the ideas you held on this topic before? Whom does it benefit if a lot of people think that way?'

Of course, the difference in a critical approach must go beyond the shape of information offered. If student habits and dispositions are to change, if students are to be nudged out of their roles of passive recipients and into new ones of active questioners, then classroom routines must change as well. We need to think beyond providing information, inquiring into what sorts of activities will help genuinely empower our students.

Affective Goals and Classroom Strategies

Before detailing some specific strategies from my own classroom, I want to make two disclaimers. The first is that I choose here *not* to discuss certain strategies I use because they are widely discussed in texts on reflective practice: journals, for example, or autobiographical writing. That literature has *much* to offer the critical theorist in the way of methodology that can be adapted to critical ends, and I would prefer that readers explore that field on their own instead of receiving a secondhand account of it from me (see especially Clift, Houston and Pugach, 1990; Russell and Munby, 1992; and Osterman and Kottkamp, 1993). The second is that I would remind readers that the very tenets of critical theory deny that there can be *one* correct version of anything. As I continue describing my own practice in some detail, I remind readers that I offer this information as food for thought for them as they chart their own classroom journeys.

Cultivating Climate and Voice

My students have difficulty looking each other in the eye on the first day of class, offering a cheerful hello and saying 'Hi. I'm John. Who are you?' Males sit in the back, females mostly in front. My courses have a reputation for being difficult, and students stare at me fearfully, lambs in the lion's den. They want me to like them, and they want their colleagues to like them. They don't want to be laughed at for being wrong, and they won't take risks if they're fearful of being 'wrong'. They don't want to end up with a poor grade because they held views their instructor didn't like.

But students who are frightened or intimidated cannot learn, nor can they voice an honest opinion even if they do happen to have one. Discussion cannot happen in a classroom characterized by fear and conformity. And so, the first task is to build a climate that makes it safe and comfortable for students to voice opinions. First, we — the students and I all together — learn names, though there might be over 30 students in the class. If we have two Christines, we develop tricks to keep them straight. We learn which nicknames everyone prefers, and what mis-pronunciations of their names make people crazy. We divide and subdivide in small groups and switch parts of groups around until we work our way up into a large circle where we practice saying everyone's name together. I make mistakes, and laugh at myself, indicating that perfection is not required in my world. I ask students for help when I can't name someone, and I encourage them to help each other out when they're stuck: we all want to 'get it', but it's ok if the process takes longer for some of us than for others, and it's not only ok but actually a good idea to help each other out. I encourage them to practice their naming by calling across the cafeteria or campus, 'Hey! Aren't you Sean from my education class?' *Every* individual student is given every indication that he or she matters as a distinct individual.

No doubt spending so much time learning names will seem frivolous to some, but I believe — and students routinely agree in course evaluations — that learning each other's names is an important element of classroom life. Nearly everywhere else, students are an undifferentiated mass and treated as one. In my university, for example, exams can be taken by filling in circles on computer forms, which are subsequently scored by computers, generating grades that are often e-mailed to students. In this process, there is virtually no human reaction to individual work and results. Students who do not feel like individual human beings will have a difficult time imagining themselves able to make any difference in the larger world. So much of university life sends students the signal that they are very small indeed, and quite undistinguished and insignificant — especially when they enter a large research institution as freshmen. Signals to the contrary must be loud, clear and frequent in the critical classroom in order to counter institutional climate.

Moreover, risk-taking requires a sense of safety that is difficult to develop in an anonymous crowd. It's one thing to be afraid that 'everyone' will think an idea is stupid, and quite another to anticipate that Joe and Sue will probably disagree with you, but Rachel at least might agree with you. Faculty who complain about the lack of classroom discussion usually have done little to cultivate the climate that makes it possible.

Other strategies to develop confidence and voice include giving students time to jot down responses to a question before beginning a discussion, which allows the instructor to invite quiet students into a conversation by asking them to read what they've written. If we know that everyone has written *something*, then we don't need to worry about embarrassing someone by calling on them and finding them struck dumb by the attention. And small group work, of course, allows students to try ideas out in a small, and therefore fairly safe, forum, allowing less confident students to bring their ideas to a full class discussion more confidently because they've already been found worthy by some of the class.

Developing Skills

If students are to be empowered to analyze information on their own, then they must have practice in reading and analysis. Unfortunately, textbooks routinely require a kind of 'reading' that is antithetical to intellectual inquiry. What most texts require, even when they have pretty sections of questions labeled 'critical thinking' at the chapter's end, is for students to simply shuffle the exact words of the text. Dexterity, not understanding, is required. Starting very early in grade schools, students learn that the best words to explain something are the words of the text or the words of the teacher. If a text asks 'What are the five parts of a gagizmo?' then students must begin their answer with the words 'The five parts of a gagizmo are . . .' and fill in the blanks with the exact words of the textbook. They might as well be rearranging silverware as 'reading'. The same is true of copying the teacher's exact words into their notebooks: they might as well be coloring in the lines, using a key that tells them which color they must use where.

My students are both stunned and resentful that I will *not* accept the exact words of the textbook in answer to my questions about information they've read. I explain that being able to *say* something doesn't indicate that you know what it means, and they can only convince me that they understand something by rendering it in their own words. Of course, much language research indicates that capturing an idea in our own words is an essential tool for developing genuine understanding, so my students actually develop their understanding of course material by rephrasing ideas in their texts. And, while I will clarify difficult passages, I will *not* lecture on the textbook. In fact, I discourage my colleagues from such lecturing every chance I get, being sorely tempted to scream every time someone implies that the logical response to a lack of reading ability among students is to ask them to do *less* reading. Students can only become more skilled and more active readers by practicing active reading. When a faculty member makes it unnecessary for students to grapple with texts, they are actually eliminating practice essential for student growth — not to mention for informed participation in a democracy. Our job is to nurture students' growth, not to collaborate in their permanent dependency.

Developing a Sense of Agency

In line with the comments on reading above, I routinely insist that students can do more than they think they can — more reading, more independent analysis, more research. We've known for a very long time that student performance improves or worsens in relation to expectations their teachers have of them; why do we continue to behave as if there's nothing in our teaching that might encourage poor performance rather than excellence?

When students need information they can't find in the library, I point them to a telephone book and a telephone: yes, they can call someone they don't know and ask for information. When we wonder if history textbooks have become more inclusive because of recent criticism, I put them in small groups with new texts I've not looked at and ask them to decide what they think, and then to share their findings and the evidence they're based on: yes, they are entitled to formulate their own judgments based on the data at hand, and it is not a teacher's job to always and everywhere provide answers. When we're going to talk about various responses to an assignment, I put one or a few of them in charge of the class discussion: yes, they can have an intelligent discussion without a teacher and it's an important skill for them to practice. I may intervene as coach, but to help them improve their performance rather than to chastise them for not yet being perfectly skilled. Yes, they can analyze media stories and decide whether or not to accept the perspective in the article; no, 'news' is not routinely objective, given that some events are covered and others aren't, that some facts are included and others aren't, that one word has one connotation and an alternative word would have had different implications all together.

My husband and I often wonder why people who don't seem to like small children ever have them, and it's a parallel wonder to me why teachers who can't tolerate imperfection in students ever go into education. If students had already polished all their skills, if they already knew or could find everything they needed to know, what would they need us for? In general, I think university instruction would improve enormously if faculty stopped complaining about what their students don't know and can't do and instead set about *teaching* them those things. If they need to be able to read and write and think, and if they do all of those things poorly, then let's give them plenty of practice and constructive feedback.

Representative Assignments

I learned long ago that the best assignments address multiple goals at once, and that's a criteria I apply to specific assignments. Believing that both of the following meet that standard, I offer them as samples of the kinds of assignments a critical education instructor might make.

Attending and Analyzing a School Board Meeting

I often require my students to attend a school board meeting before we arrive at that topic in class — usually that means they have maybe six weeks or so to get themselves to a meeting. When the class is going to take up the topic, they read a selection in their texts explaining different kinds of power configurations that are possible among board members themselves as well as among the board and/or the superintendent and/or the community. When they come to class, they must be prepared to describe the meeting they attended and to explain which of those power arrangements they believe they saw in action. When we have this discussion, I don't worry about whether the labels students choose are the 'right' ones; I merely monitor whether the evidence they offer seems to support the conclusions they draw.

This assignment creates panic in students but it also produces lively class discussions and greatly heightens sensitivity to politics in the local community. The first problem that unnerves students is that I don't hand them a list of school board meetings and times to choose from. Why would I do that, I ask, when they are perfectly capable of reading a newspaper or picking up a telephone and calling a school to inquire about its board meeting schedule? On the heels of their complaining about their logistical confusion, they ask incredulously 'Well, would we be *allowed* to attend?' I point out that the assignment involves a public meeting of public school officials who are responsible to the taxpayers who elected them; why wouldn't they be 'allowed'? Invariably, a productive discussion of the responsibilities of elected officials to the public and of the right of the public to be informed about what they're doing follows.

Students return from the meetings with a variety of reactions, depending on their experience. Some are dismayed at the rudeness of board members toward each other and the public; at their refusal to provide information that was requested; at the number of decisions that are made without discussion — which even my inexperienced students can tell signals that issues were discussed and settled previously, out of public hearing, probably at the town pub. Others come to class energized by the warm reception they received, the amount of information they were provided, and the professionalism of everyone at the meeting. Once, a student even became addicted to attending school board meetings because he found the board members such buffoons that their antics provided a never-ending source of entertainment for him. Almost without exception, students return from the meetings feeling more *real* because they had been part of an audience at an official event. Once in a while, they say something like '*I* could have discussed the issues more intelligently than any of them did', and I say 'Well, why don't you run for school board?' I consider that a valuable seed planted.

Discussion (tied to their interviews with parents and grandparents about whom they voted for and why) also explores the question of how buffoons could win — again and again — seats on the board. I always ask if *they* voted, and if so on what grounds. And, I point out to them that if they did not vote *against* the buffoons or help campaign for a more worthy candidate, then in fact they provided support to whoever won. When some vague 'elected officials' acquire specific faces and names, and when students observe them in action, making decisions that affect the experiences of students in the schools they attended, the political process becomes much more *real* to them than it had been. We consider, too, if any teachers attended the meeting, and whether teachers *should* have been there or not.

I like this assignment because it makes students rely on their own resources to get information they need; it puts them in touch with ideas from the course in a forum far outside the classroom; they learn about their right to monitor the actions of public officials; they consider whether and how far teachers' responsibilities might extend into the political realm; they consider whether voting matters, and what grounds people might choose to base their votes on; they learn that the same structure can operate very differently in two different places, demonstrating that the way things are is not the way they *have* to be; they must be active rather than passive; and, they (not I) bring the 'answers' about power structure to class. On the whole, I believe that it provides practice in 'reading the world' in the way Freire suggests.

Writing a Persuasive Letter

This assignment works less well than the school board meeting, but I am reluctant to abandon it because every student can complete it with at least some success, and it offers students who become genuinely engaged in it the opportunity to experience a sense of power and agency. This assignment, which usually serves as a culminating activity, asks students to identify an educational issue they care deeply about; to determine a specific, productive action that someone with power might take; and to write a letter to that person persuading him or her to take that specific action. I explain the general structure of a piece of persuasive writing (establish common ground; demonstrate that a significant problem exists; suggest a remedy and explain why it's the most desirable one; answer potential counterarguments; and provide the specific information necessary for action). While students are at first pleased because the letter may not be longer than two pages, as they begin to work on the assignment they soon learn why it's especially challenging.

First, many of them have trouble settling on a topic. While this doesn't bode well for the assignment, I won't tell students what to write about when they come to me complaining that they can't find a topic. Instead, we have a conversation about what it means to be truly invested in work we undertake, either in the classroom as students or in the world as professionals. Is it possible to not care deeply about what you're doing and still become expert at it? If none of the issues we've discussed interested and engaged them, what might that suggest about their declared desire to teach? If they are interested in a topic but think doing a good job on it would be too hard, what does that suggest about the kind of professional they might become? Then, I turn them around and send them out of the office to find an idea; I promise to offer practical help if they come back with at least a starting place. But I cannot tell them who they are and what they should care about. I know who I am as a professional; they need to explore their own concerns and identity.

Doing the research for the kinds of projects students develop is often an adventure. Of course, many of them do fairly straightforward library research to get facts and figures straight, but many have to strike out in very different directions. One student, who wanted a stop sign installed near a school bus shelter, stood out in the cold and counted the number of cars that whizzed by children waiting for the bus on a typical morning. Another who wanted traffic patterns changed at an elementary school measured the width of a typical mid-size car and of a school bus, then calculated how much room there would be left for a child if cars were parked on both sides of the street and a school bus were squeezing through the opening. Others have interviewed school board members, principals, teachers, students and superintendents, or conducted written surveys with such groups. This semester, one student began the assignment intending to write to the governor either applauding or criticizing his stance on pending legislation to change teacher certification requirements. The first step, of course, was to find out what his stance actually was. She wrote; she phoned; she faxed; she suffered countless transfers of her phone calls, only to be told repeatedly that the *next* office worker would be able to give her the information she wanted. She visited her state legislators' offices, but they couldn't help, either. Finally, with my grinning blessing, she wrote a strong letter to the governor reminding him that education is a serious state responsibility; that teachers need to have informed opinions and share them with their representatives; and that elected officials are obliged to share their thinking and plans with the folks who elected them. She urged him both to clean up his communications act *and* to see that she was informed about his stance on alternate routes to certification.

I mail these letters, moving the assignment beyond role-playing and into the real world. Many students tell me that for that reason, they take it much more seriously and complete the assignment feeling somehow less like 'students' and more like 'real people'. The feeling that they matter and have a voice is strongly affirmed when they receive responses to their letters, as many report they do. The student who wrote about the stop sign picked up his phone one day and found himself invited to oversee the exact placement of the stop sign he requested when it was installed. A mother who wrote to complain about inconsistencies in spelling instruction in her daughter's elementary school was invited to attend a meeting between administrators and teachers, many of whom shared her concerns. Several students have framed letters from the White House.

Generally, the experience is as productive as individual students make it. For some, it is powerful and clearly constitutes the first step on their journey toward becoming active professionals. For others, it is an opportunity lost through inertia and lack of ambition. But having thought hard about it, I refuse to withhold the opportunity for a significant experience from some students simply because not all students will take advantage of it.

Helpful Materials

One text I like is Joel Spring's (1996a) *American Education*, though it contains much the same information as many other texts. Spring is himself a critical educator, however, so I find the emphasis in his work useful. A text which would *not* be easily duplicated is his *Deculturalization and the Struggle for Equality*, a brief work which provides a wealth of information about minority education and its relation to politics and economics. Other pieces I find useful include Studs Terkel's (1974) *C.P. Ellis*, the first person narrative of a Klansman turned educational activist; Tony Cade Bambara's (1972) short story 'The Lesson', in which an edu-cated black woman takes a group of Harlem children to the exclusive FAO Schwarz toy store in New York City; and a first person account of Lame Deer's childhood on a reservation and his experiences with forced attendance at a boarding school.

Of course, this list is meant to be suggestive rather than comprehensive. There are any number of literary pieces which can inform students' understanding of the effect of events on individual human beings with faces and names; multicultural readers and readers for composition courses (almost sure to be found in abundance in the office of any faculty member in English) are wonderful sources for such materials. Videotapes exploring relevant topics are also readily available and useful in helping students to connect personally with historical or theoretical material. Cases for teacher education, hypothetical situations that ask readers to make deci-sions about practical dilemmas, help students understand what it means to take a stance on issues after thinking options through carefully — including the option of doing nothing (which amounts to supporting something by default).

Final Words

When a course ends, I remind students that it was intended as a vehicle to explore who they were when they came into my classroom and who they might become as a professional after they leave it. Similarly, I remind readers that this piece is intended as a vehicle to help them explore which goals they've pursued and what strategies activities they've incorporated into their own classrooms, as well as which goals and strategies they might choose for the future. Students learn what we teach them, and foundations courses are what we make them. I, for one, hope we work to make theoretical and philosophical questioning an integral part of tomor-row's very best teacher education programs.

References

AYERS, W. (1993) *To teach*, New York: Teachers College Press.

BAMBARA, T.C. (1972) 'The lesson', in HUNT, D. (ed.) *The Riverside Anthology of Litera-ture*, 1988, Boston: Houghton Mifflin.

CLIFT, R., HOUSTON, W. and PUGACH, M. (1990) *Encouraging Reflective Practice in Educa-tion: An Analysis of Issues and Programs*, New York: Teachers College Press.

GOODLAD, J. (1990) *Teachers for Our Nation's Schools*, San Francisco: Jossey-Bass.

HINCHEY, P. (1992) 'Using the practical problems novice teachers articulate as routes to the theoretical thinking they dread', Unpublished doctoral dissertation, Teachers College, Columbia University.

KENNEDY, M. (1991) *An Agenda for Research on Teacher Learning*, East Lansing: Mich-igan State University, National Center for Research on Teacher Education.

LAME DEER and ERDOES, R. (1993) 'From Lame Deer: Seeker of visions', in RILEY, P. (ed.) *Growing up Native American: An Anthology*, New York: William Morrow.

Listening to America with Bill Moyers: Unequal education (1992) Videotape, Alexandria, VA: PBS Video.

LOEWEN, J. (1995) *Lies My Teacher Told Me: Everything Your American History Textbook Got Wrong*, New York: The New Press.

OSTERMAN, K. and KOTTKAMP, R. (1993) *Reflective Practice for Educators: Improving Schooling Through Professional Development*, Newbury Park, CA: Corwin Press.

RIDGEN, D. (1996, December 11) 'How teachers would change teacher education', *Education Week*, pp. 64, 48.

RUSSELL, T. and MUNBY, H. (1992) *Teachers and Teaching: From Classroom to Reflection*, New York: Falmer Press.

SPRING, J. (1996a) *American Education*, Seventh edition, New York: McGraw-Hill.

SPRING, J. (1996b) *Deculturalization and the Struggle for Equality*, Second edition, New York: McGraw-Hill.

TERKEL, ST. (1974) *C.P. Ellis, Working*, New York: Avon.

Chapter 4

Interpretive Inquiry as Student Research

Julia Ellis

In a number of graduate courses I have asked participants to undertake interpretive inquiry projects as their major assignment. To provide us with a shared language for talking about the process, we worked with Packer and Addison's (1989) text, *Entering the Circle: Hermeneutic Investigations in Psychology*, and David Smith's chapter, 'Hermeneutic inquiry: The hermeneutic imagination and the pedagogic text'. In this chapter I wish to present the kind of discussion I offer in an introductory lecture which draws from these writings and previous students' work. While Gadamer and other writers in hermeneutics have made it abundantly clear that the processes or dynamics of interpretation constitute our very mode of being in the world, rather than a prescribed method, students I have worked with have found this presentation helpful for visualizing interpretive inquiry as a 'formal' research process.

Central Themes in Hermeneutics

In any discussion of interpretive inquiry, it is worthwhile to begin with a revisiting of three themes which have been present in hermeneutics since Schleiermacher's work in 1819 (Smith, 1991). The first of these is a recognition of the inherently creative character of interpretation. The interpreter works holistically, rather than for example using classification systems, in an effort to discern the intent or meaning behind the expression of another.

The second theme has to do with the way 'good interpretation involves a playing back and forth between the specific and the general, the micro and the macro' (Smith, 1991, p. 190). Working holistically, 'good interpretation can only be pursued with a constant movement back and forth between the expression and the web of meanings within which that expression is lodged' (Smith, 1993, p. 16). To understand a part, requires an understanding of the whole, and to understand the whole, one must understand the individual parts. This movement back and forth between the part and the whole, a movement which has no natural starting or end point, is thought of as a circle and has come to be articulated as ' "the hermeneutic circle" at work in all human understanding' (Smith, 1991, p. 190).

The third theme is the pivotal role of language in human understanding. The language available to the interpreter both enables and limits the understanding that is possible. Since language arises from a community, reflects the influence of tradition, and marks a moment in history, history is linked with language in being understood as a condition of understanding.

Finding the Path in an Interpretive Inquiry

Students' experiences with interpretive inquiry projects have given real meaning to the expression that one 'makes the path by walking it'. Getting started was daunting for some course participants because of the feeling of not knowing where one was going, let alone how one would get there. Was it possible that one could end up nowhere? Might you bump into something frightening and strange because you couldn't see where you were going? Was there really no schedule or plan that was created in advance? What if it didn't get finished? How could one be sure in advance that one would 'do it right'? The apprehension of some students was palpable. As early starters began sharing stories of their projects and inviting our responses, more students came to appreciate the flow and unfolding quality of interpretive inquiry projects. I hope the discussions and examples provided in this chapter serve in the same way.

A Sample Study

Cory had been a secondary English teacher for three years when she learned that all grade 9 subjects were going to be de-streamed. She questioned whether this was a good idea given that teaching to more homogeneous ability levels seemed more efficient. She was also concerned that less able students would lose confidence in de-streamed classes. Cory read the government rationale for de-streaming, but unconvinced by it, decided to undertake her own inquiry.

As her first inquiry activity, Cory interviewed small groups of students from the 'basic', 'general', and 'advanced' classes. She was not surprised to learn that, like herself, the students also feared that in de-streamed classes, 'advanced program' students would be held back and 'basic program' students would feel intimidated. She did, however, encounter a number of surprises in her interviews and these new concerns or awarenesses gave direction and purpose to the remainder of her inquiry activities. Cory was very distressed to find that 'basic program' students currently referred to themselves as 'stupid' even without sharing classes with 'advanced program' students. She was surprised that even with differentiated curriculum, the 'basic program' students said they wanted material that would be more helpful to them in their lives right now as many had heavy care-giving responsibilites at home. Cory was startled by the 'worlds apart' life plans and expectations held by 'basic program' students vs. other students even at this young age. She noticed that the basic program students in her interviews came from lower income life situations and wondered if this was a general trend in the school.

As Cory's next 'data collection activity' she checked school records to see if this socio-economic pattern was pervasive for all the grade 9 students in basic programs. She began to appreciate that these students' parents might not have been as active and confident in students' placement decisions at the end of grade 8.

Next Cory looked for other researchers' findings on the questions of concern to her. She thought there would be little and was surprised to find over 20 years of research on ability grouping and the effects of tracking. The findings and critiques in this literature resonated with and often explained the phenomena she had found remarkable in her student interviews. She also found current reports on de-streamed classes and the models of teaching used to make these work. These approaches required a letting go of the teacher-centered, single lesson, 'common activity for all students' way of teaching. Instead, the teacher became a facilitator who introduced common material but then offered diverse cooperative learning activities. In demonstration sites, teachers received a great deal of support to restructure their courses in these ways.

Finally, Cory interviewed seasoned teachers at her school. Her literature review made her realize that long-time teachers would have dealt with ability grouping issues earlier in their careers. In the staff room, many teachers had spoken angrily and heatedly against the de-streaming that had been announced. She was surprised to find that, one-on-one, the teachers acknowledged that it would be better for the basic program students to be in de-streamed classes. Over their 17 or 20 years of teaching they had taught their courses in both streamed and non-streamed classes. They were too tired to change how they did things, yet one more time, and at someone else's initiative.

Cory had come full circle to the government rationale for de-streaming. She said that at first she had understood it but not believed it. Now she believed it. It was now also her rationale. She also understood what it would mean for teachers and was adamant and articulate in lobbying for the kind of support teachers and schools should have to make de-streaming work.

The Entry Question

Beginnings are always important. In interpretive inquiry projects one begins with an entry question. This starting place must be characterized by openness, humility, and genuine engagement. Cory's entry question was: 'Is de-streaming grade 9 a good idea?' The question posed has to be a real one rather than a point one wishes to prove. One has to genuinely begin from the humility of acknowledging that one doesn't know the answer or that one doesn't know what to do to be helpful to a situation one cares about. Useful entry questions are usually simple and open. They refrain from implying an expected answer to the question posed. Some examples are:

How should I work with the four 'special ed.' girls who now have to be mainstreamed in my grade 5 math?
Why are the students in this junior high so hostile to teachers in the hallways?
How can I help this high school teacher who is having trouble with her math class?

'Why is this happening?' and 'How can I or anyone help?' are often key components of entry questions. They generally reflect a relationship of care or responsibility and an attitude of openness and goodwill. Sometimes the questions have to do
with the researcher's desire to learn from something that apparently works well. In
these instances, the question often takes the form of 'How does this work?' And
sometimes the researcher wants to try using a new procedure, idea, or tool to
improve things in a particular situation. In this case the question takes the form of
'How might this help?'

As students have searched for entry questions for their interpretive inquiry
projects, I have encouraged them to seriously consider what it is that preoccupies
them, is mysterious or confusing to them, or most makes them wish that they could
be helpful or make a difference. Answers to these questions are important for at
least two reasons. For one, there must be a genuine engagement with the entry question to support the creativity and attentional energy required for a fruitful inquiry.
And secondly, if one's peace is disturbed by other preoccupying dilemmas, one
can't be fully available to the deliberation and reflection required in an interpretive
inquiry project. Consequently, I have not been surprised when students have chosen
to focus their interpretive inquiry projects on their children or even themselves.

It is also worth noting that entry questions begin from a practical concern.
While the studies themselves may draw upon, create, or elaborate theory, they
begin with a focus on a practical concern. It is perhaps worth considering at this
point that the Greek word for theory, *theoria*, means behold or contemplate. In
interpretive inquiry we begin with an openness to behold or contemplate life in its
wholeness an complexity.

The Spiral

As we think about the progress or development of an interpretive inquiry project, it
can be helpful to visualize it as a series of loops in a spiral. Each loop may
represent a separate activity that looks like 'data collection and interpretation'. In
Cory's study the four loops were: interviewing students; examining demographic data
in school records; searching research literature; and interviewing teachers. Altern-
ately, each loop may represent consecutive efforts to re-interpret one constant 'text'
or 'set of data'. I will return later to a discussion of the latter instance. First I would
like to discuss studies comprised of a series of explorations or 'data collections'
over time.

When a study is viewed as a series of loops in spiral, each loop represents
a different attempt to get closer to what you hope to understand. Each loop, or
separate inquiry, is entered with a question. What is learned in the loop provides
direction or a reframing of the question for the next loop. What is learned may in
fact change the direction of the study quite dramatically. This was evident in Cory's
study as her interviews with students led her to examine school records for socio-
economic patterns in tracking and gave her many concerns that focused her attention in her literature search. When her literature search informed her that ability

Figure 4.1   Interpretive Inquiry as an Unfolding Spiral

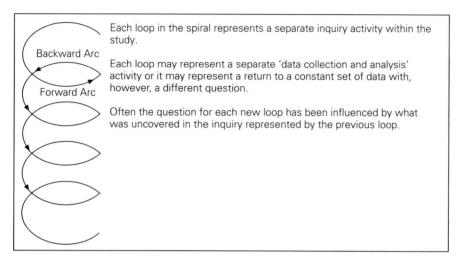

Each loop in the spiral represents a separate inquiry activity within the study.

Each loop may represent a separate 'data collection and analysis' activity or it may represent a return to a constant set of data with, however, a different question.

Often the question for each new loop has been influenced by what was uncovered in the inquiry represented by the previous loop.

grouping had been a recurring issue in education for many years, she became very interested in interviewing long-time teachers about their prior experiences. Shortly, I will describe two other sample studies showing the series of explorations in each. Before this, however, I would like to discuss the first loop, or the first activity one undertakes to get closer to what one wishes to understand.

The First Loop

Once an entry question is chosen and framed, the researcher proceeds by 'doing something' to get closer to the person or situation of interest. The 'doing something' as the first loop, can take a wide variety of forms, many of them seemingly global or unfocused. In Cory's study, the first loop was her small group interviewing with students from basic, general and advanced programs. The creativity I have observed in graduate students' choices of activities for the first loop indicates both their openness with their entry question and their desire to respect the way their entities of interest could show themselves. The following are examples of first activities in interpretive inquiry projects.

A grade 5 teacher who wondered how to include four 'special ed.' girls in her very sophisticated and complex grade 5 math program, began by interviewing one of the girls using the interview schedule provided in Chapter 3. In this interview she asked no questions about math but instead worked to understand the girl better as a whole person.

A secondary school principal, who had a second year teacher with a difficult class for math, sat in on her class, not with his usual checklist of teaching skills, but with two video cameras. Together with the teacher, he studied the videotapes to try to see the dynamics at work among the students.

A teacher who had completed a diploma program in reading instruction was eager to have parents use many of her new learnings to support their children's reading growth at home. As a first inquiry, she prepared and sent parents a small pamphlet of ideas about reading development. Soon after, when parents met with for parent–teacher conferences, she invited their thoughts or comments about the handout.

A teacher with a grade 1/2/3 developmentally delayed class wanted to know how well the children were dealing with the difficult life situations many of them had. Since they had just completed a unit on castles and so forth, she asked the children to each draw a picture of their ideal fantasy home and to indicate or label who they had in there with them. When these were completed she briefly conferenced with the children individually to have them tell her about their pictures.

As graduate students have shared their interpretive inquiry projects in our classes over the years I could not help but observe that the the biggest turning points in most studies came after the very first 'loop'. Very often two things happened in that first activity. For one, their understanding of the problem or question was often dramatically altered. For another, the relationship established with the other persons enabled further inquiry to take on an entirely different character. In the first loop of Cory's study, we saw her concerns about efficient teaching quickly replaced by her concerns about justice. When studies had such powerful first activities, they unfolded in directions that no-one could have predicted. When researchers did not have such potent first activities, they often felt stuck after the first loop and not sure where to go next. All of this has to do with the notion of 'uncovering' discussed in the next section.

Uncovering

Each loop or exploration, which can be understood as data collection and interpretation, will generate findings. Some of these may well be what the researcher would have expected. Others, however, may be surprises. In Cory's study, she found that the students also feared that basic program students would be intimidated in de-streamed classes. This was as expected. She also encountered many surprises however about the meaning and effects of streamed classes for basic program students. In hermeneutic terms, any unexpected dimensions that are revealed are called 'uncoverings'. While the uncoverings may not lead directly to a solution, they will often enable the researcher to understand the problem or question differently in order to reframe it usefully for planning the next step in the inquiry. Cory's uncoverings from her student interviews prompted her to examine demographic data in school records and gave focus and purpose to her attention as she studied related literature.

The notion of uncovering, developed by Heidigger in *Being and Time* (1927/ 1962, p. 56, cited by Packer and Addison, 1989, p. 278) is an important one in interpretive inquiry. Packer and Addison remind us that the Greek word for 'truth', *aletheia* can be translated as unconcealed, unhidden or uncovered. If something about an entity has been hidden from our awareness, our research works to 'let it show itself, not forcing our perspective on it. And we must do this in a way that respects the way it shows itself' (Packer and Addison, 1989, p. 278). The uncovering of an entity is the return arc of the hermeneutic circle and it is the response to our inquiry.Thus, if there are no surprises, we either do not yet 'see' what can be uncovered, or we have not yet approached the entity in a way that respects the way it can show itself. It became a matter of some humor and anxiety in our courses to recognize that if one hadn't encountered any surprises yet, the research wasn't happening.

Two Sample Studies

Next I would like to briefly describe two more studies to illustrate the conversational nature that interpretive inquiry can have. Both studies have easily discernible separate loops in the spiral of the interpretive inquiry. One can see examples of questions reframed by one uncovering leading to the next step in the inquiry. One can also see a variety of approaches used to allow entities to show themselves.

Example 1: Teenager–Adult Relationships
Mary taught health and science in a junior high school. While her interactions with students in class were agreeable, she was confused by the change in the students in the hallways. They would never say hello or acknowledge her as she passed their way. They appeared withdrawn from and hostile towards all adults they encountered in hallways. In this map or outline of Mary's inquiry I have used italics for emphasis to show the connections or linkages between one inquiry activity and the one following it.

As the first activity in her research, Mary asked a small group of students to help her preview a film for possible use in health class. As she listened to their discussion of the film she heard their *general grief about their location in life as teenagers.*

As the next loop in the spiral of her inquiry, she asked two classes to complete a brief questionnaire. The questions invited completion of statements such as '*Being a teenager is . . .*', 'I am happiest when . . .' and so forth.

Mary identified *recurring themes*, expressions, and complaints in the questionnaire responses and as the third loop *brought these back to the classes for discussion* and elaboration. By listening to the students talk she heard their discouragement with the *futility of interactions with adults.* They felt extremely frustrated in their communication and negotiation with adults, especially their parents.

As the fourth loop, Mary approached *resource people and literature to search for ideas* about ways to help the students with their trouble. She found a program package that introduced students to the notion of communication in the role of 'child', 'parent', and 'adult'. The package had many role plays for students to practice with. Mary had begun using the package in her classes and some students were already reporting on their efforts with these new awarenesses at home when she wrote her report for the course.

Example 2: The New Nurse

As part of her hospital management duties, Janet was responsible for the nursing staff in an ICU. Jim, a recently graduated male nurse had been part of the staff for some time when many of the nurses began to complain that they didn't want to be assigned to work with him. None of them could articulate any specific reasons why or specify anything in particular that he had done wrong.

As the first step in her inquiry, Janet followed routine procedures by conducting a standardized interview with Jim to assess his general knowledge. His general knowledge was fine. She still had no way to understand the discomfort of the other nurses.

As the second inquiry activity, Janet conducted a simulation exercise with Jim in an empty hospital room, describing the conditions of imaginary patients in beds A, B, C, and D. At a certain point in the simulation, she indicated that patient B was starting to have an emergency and she asked Jim what he would do. He said that he would sit and talk with patient A who was depressed. When Janet expressed surprise at this he explained that all of the other nurses would always go to an emergency but they wouldn't take time for the patient who was depressed. Through lengthy conversation they clarified both that he had a strong desire to continue working in an ICU rather than a different ward and that it was understandable that other nurses wouldn't feel comfortable working with someone whose response to an emergency wasn't predictable and desirable.

As the final loop of her inquiry, Janet observed the work of a team of nurses with Jim as a member of the team. There she noticed two things. First she observed that none of the nurses were mentoring Jim. Nobody was saying, 'Here, you try it this time.' Second, she 'saw' for the first time that there was nothing about his appearance or personna that invited mentoring. There was nothing 'junior-looking' about him. He looked strong and large, had held an administrative position in a previous career, and he carried himself with authority. Janet later advised nursing staff that they would have to make a conscious effort to start doing all the mentoring things one does with a new graduate and staff member.

In each of the separate inquiries Janet made, we can see her efforts to get closer and closer to understanding how Jim experiences being a nurse in their ward and how other nurses experience working with Jim. Ideas for inquiry activities come out of knowing the context and the opportunities for inquiry afforded by the context.

Both of these studies show interpretive inquiry as part of a conversation that is ongoing. Although the written accounts were completed and shared, Mary and her students would remain in the school and she would continue to try to be helpful to them in ways that make sense. Janet and Jim and the other nurses would continue to find their way together. Both Mary and Janet had collected only as much 'data' in their explorations as they could manageably study, learn from, and act upon in furthering their inquiry. Within the constraints of available time and energy, they had both taken a variety of approaches to enable their 'entities' to 'show themselves'. The activities they used help one to see more concretely how a fusion of horizons is accomplished through a dialogue of questions and answers with the entity or 'text'. In both of these studies, the researchers' discoveries and expanded understandings enabled them to identify promising directions for helpful action. So often, many solution strategies are well within our repertoires; it is mainly our understanding of the problem that requires growth.

'Single-loop' Studies

In the two examples of interpretive inquiries just described, the researchers had little difficulty 'seeing' what was uncovered. It isn't always so easy. In these 'multi-loop' studies, the researchers had a variety of opportunities for dialogic engagement with their entities. Some studies look more like a single loop in that there is only one 'data collection' activity or the 'data' for the study already exist in some sort of textual form.

In these instances, the researcher often makes repeated 'loops' with the same set of data, revisiting the data each time with a question that has been reframed from what was learned in the previous set of deliberations. In studies of this form, the researcher's experience of the forward and backward arcs of the hermeneutic circle becomes even more pronounced.

Many thesis studies are often a combination of both 'multi-loop' and apparently 'single-loop' inquiries. When a study entails a series of interviews and observations, what is learned in each activity provides a focus or reframed question for the next inquiry activity. At the end of the data collection activities, the researcher then works again with all transcripts, field notes, research notes, and artifacts as a single text. Although the researcher has been making sense of things all along the way, the task at the end is to articulate the most coherent and comprehensive account of what can be learned from the inquiry. Each of the transcripts and field notes have become parts of a whole and the meaning of each can now be reconsidered in relation to the whole. I will describe an example of a brief 'single-loop' study after the following discussion of the forward and backward arc of the hermeneutic circle.

The Forward and Backward Arc

Packer and Addison (1989) explain that in the forward arc of the hermeneutic circle, projection, we use our fore-structure to initially make sense of the entity, text, or data. That is, we use our existing preconceptions, pre-understandings or prejudices including purposes, interests, and values to interpret; this is unavoidable. It is in the backward arc that we evaluate our initial interpretation and attempt to see what we did not see before. In this evaluation process, the researcher reconsiders the interpretation by re-examining the data for confirmation, contradictions, gaps,

Figure 4.2   The Hermeneutic Circle

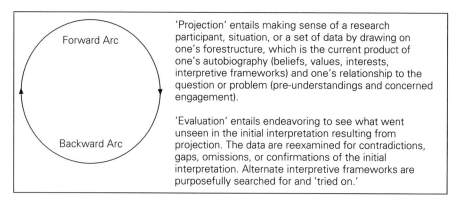

'Projection' entails making sense of a research participant, situation, or a set of data by drawing on one's forestructure, which is the current product of one's autobiography (beliefs, values, interests, interpretive frameworks) and one's relationship to the question or problem (pre-understandings and concerned engagement).

'Evaluation' entails endeavoring to see what went unseen in the initial interpretation resulting from projection. The data are reexamined for contradictions, gaps, omissions, or confirmations of the initial interpretation. Alternate interpretive frameworks are purposefully searched for and 'tried on.'

or inconsistencies. This may entail making charts or summaries or lists in order to uncover possible patterns or relationships which are not easily discernible when considering a large amount of information simultaneously. In this process it is just as important to ask what is absent in the data as what is present. Re-examining the data is a very deliberative process. In the effort to see what was not seen before, the researcher's question must be genuine and the researcher must search for the coherence and reasonableness in the behavior of others.

The researcher does not seek a uniquely correct or 'accurate' interpretation, but rather the most adequate one that can be arrived at at that time. In this search, the researcher will often try out other conceptual frameworks for their interpretive power. The search is for an interpretation that is as coherent, comprehensive, and comprehensible as possible (Packer and Addison, 1989).

A 'Single-loop' Study Example

Ann was a drama expert. One would be hard-pressed to find a drama book she hadn't read or a drama course she hadn't taken or taught. Her full-time job was teaching drama in a secondary school and she wanted to use her interpretive inquiry project to advance her understanding about teaching drama there. The drama department in her school was required to give a departmental exam and so all grade 12 drama students were asked to write a paper about the benefits they had derived from their drama course. Ann decided that instead of just marking her students' papers she would study them for her interpretive inquiry project.

For a long time, Ann found herself spinning her wheels in the backward arc. It was hard for her to see anything she had not already seen before. For every benefit that students reported, Ann could cite the page, author, and title of a book that had described such benefits from drama instruction. Our whole class was sympathetic. Ann knew so much about drama. What could she possibly learn from the grade 12 students?

Finally, in her deliberations, Ann did come to see something she hadn't noticed before. There was a pattern or relationship that intrigued her. The students who reported the greatest number of benefits were also the students who were the most self-disclosing. Ann had frequently used debriefing discussions after activities or exercises in her drama class. She recognized that the students who were the least self-disclosing in their papers (and who also claimed the fewest number of benefits from drama) had also been the least active participants in the oral debriefing sessions in class. Given that the senior drama course had not been a forced choice for students, that is, she had every reason to believe they all wanted to be there, Ann planned to pursue the reflection aspect of the drama course with greater attention the following year.

The example of Ann's study illustrates the generativity of interpretive inquiry. The study opened up a new question and focus for continuing inquiry with her drama teaching. She found a rich starting point for thinking about how to get more out of what was happening in the classroom. Ann's experience with the interpretive inquiry process is also an example of how difficult it can be to move beyond one's usual categories to see what one hasn't seen before. One has to believe that there are patterns or relationships to be discovered. And one has to actively search for the coherence and reasonableness in the behavior of others.

Evaluating an Interpretive Account

Ann's research story demonstrated the kinds of outcomes that one expects from an interpretive inquiry. As Packer and Addison (1989) have articulated them, these expected outcomes are:

- Ideas for helpful action are identified (fruitfulness or generativity of the research)
- New questions or concerns are brought to the researchers' awareness.
- The researchers are changed by the research (self-reflexivity), that is, the researchers have discovered inadequacies in their own initial pre-understandings.

In evaluating an interpretive account, Packer and Addison have clarified that validity is not the issue in terms of proving an interpretation true or false. 'Validation' would imply the possibility of interpretation-free norms or standards. Instead, the question is whether the interpretive account can be clarified or made more comprehensive or comprehensible.

Concerns about 'validity' stem from the fear that without 'validation procedures' interpretive accounts might be viewed as mere opinion or speculation. The impulse towards the grammar of validation originated in the natural sciences paradigm where hypotheses were treated as guesses which needed to be tested. An interpretive account is not a guess or speculation. It is instead 'the working out of possibilities that have become apparent in a preliminary, dim understanding of events' (Packer and Addison, 1989, p. 277). Packer and Addison emphasize that the fore-structure or pre-understanding of the researcher who has entered the circle in the right way, in the right manner, will embody a particular concern, a kind of caring, which facilitates a perspective or way of reading which might otherwise not be possible. Thus the interpretation is ordered and organized by the fore-structure and further guided by 'a sense of the complexity of the human relationship between researcher and research participant' (Packer and Addison, 1989, p. 277). In other words, the concerned engagement the researcher brings to the question and the human solidarity that is sought through the inquiry give direction and guidance to the interpretation.

Some may fear that the hermeneutic circle is a vicious one in that we can only understand in terms of what we already know. Packer and Addison remind us that the circularity of understanding is essential and that the real test of an inquiry or interpretation is whether or not we uncover a solution to the difficulty that motivated the inquiry. They suggest that a 'true interpretive account' will help us and the people we study and will further our concerns. They note that 'concerned engagement' distinguishes interpretive inquiry from other forms of human inquiry which seek only to describe or just understand human phenomena.

Thus, when we evaluate an interpretive account, we are not trying to determine whether it has provided validated knowledge or timeless truth, but rather we are asking whether our concern has been answered. Packer and Addison reviewed the four general approaches to evaluating interpretive accounts: requiring that an interpretive account be coherent; examining its relationship to external evidence; seeking consensus among various groups; and assessing the account's relationship to future events. Their discussions clarified that while these approaches do not make interpretation-free validation possible, they are reasonable approaches to use in that they direct our attention and discussions to considerations we value when asking whether 'what has been uncovered in an interpretive inquiry answers the practical, concernful question that directed that inquiry' (p. 289). They also caution us however that all four approaches may not reasonably support an interpretation, and that in fact, sometimes none will as when an interpretation that brings a solution to a practical problem may at first seem implausible and unconnected.

In summary, evaluation of an interpretive account should not be confused with objective validation from traditional approaches to inquiry. To evaluate an account we ask whether the concern which motivated the inquiry has been answered. To judge whether an answer has been uncovered by an interpretive account, the following questions can direct our attention to considerations we value.

Is it plausible, convincing?
Does it fit with other material we know?
Does it have the power to change practice?
Has the researcher's understanding been transformed?
Has a solution been uncovered?
Have new possibilities been opened up for the researcher, research participants, and the structure of the context?

Writing the Interpretive Account

There seem to be as many ways to write interpretive accounts as there are interpretive inquiries. Each research story is different and invites a different mode of telling. And each time we tell the story we may tell it from a changed perspective.

When students have written interpretive accounts as course assignments, I have encouraged them to begin as though writing in a journal, starting with how they came to be concerned, interested in, or knowledgeable about their entry question. If students had already studied literature that was pertinent to their question, I invited them to either present some of the key ideas or theories that now influenced their thinking or to simply interweave these ideas conversationally where it informed their consideration of findings during the study. In the same way that they mentioned theoretical literature which informed their interpretations, I also encouraged them to relate autobiographical material which predisposed their responses to or interpretations of people, events, or texts during their study. This practice encourages self-consciousness about one's fore-structure and helps the researcher to become aware of taken-for-granted assumptions held about the way life is or should be.

When students have had a more generous time frame, as when working on a thesis rather than a course assignment, I have encouraged them to begin their writing with a personal story which can help us understand their concerned engagement with their question. I remember once having a lengthy conference with a graduate student who was concerned about the way many boys drop out of hockey at the age of 10 or 11. At the end of our meeting we stood chatting in the hallway where he told me about going home to Ottawa for Christmas and how much he looked forward to skating down the river with his friends. Of course they would take their hockey sticks and pass a puck back and forth because that just made it better. Then he told me childhood stories about being the first one out of the classroom at the end of each day in order to race home and complete homework so that he could go to the neighborhood rink, plough off any new snow, and play hockey in -30 Farenheit weather. Until he told me all of these stories I really didn't understand what he meant by the word 'fun' in his thesis or why he was so concerned about 10-year-olds putting their skates away.

The personal story at the beginning of an interpretive account is a powerful way to support a reader's fusion of horizons with the text. The personal story allows access to the writers' perspective and the meanings that words and events hold for them. Creating an opportunity for more shared meanings at the beginning of the text can only make the interpretive account more comprehensible.

Regardless of the format, components, or sequence of the interpretive account, there is a way in which it must function as a well argued essay. One way or another, the writer is offering interpretations or arguments and these must be supported by enough illustrative material to enable readers with different perspectives to form their own interpretations. The readers should have enough illustrative material to make sense of the research from their own standpoints while still being able to see how the researchers could see things the way that they do.

Finally, a particular signature of interpretive inquiry is self-reflexivity. Writers often make a point of identifying places in their studies where they have become aware of inadequacies of their pre-understandings. Sometimes this is reported as part of the movement in the study. Sometimes there is a special reflection section where the writers examine how their understandings have been transformed by the research. Wherever it occurs, this reflection is the thread that holds the research story together.

Acknowledgement

This essay is taken from Ellis, J. (1998) *Teaching for Understanding*, New York: Garland Publishing.

References

PACKER, M.J. and ADDISON, R.B. (eds) (1989) *Entering the Circle: Hermeneutic Investigation in Psychology*, Albany: SUNY Press.

SMITH, D.G. (1991) 'Hermeneutic inquiry: The hermeneutic imagination and the pedagogic text', in SHORT, E.C. (ed.) *Forms of Curriculum Inquiry*, Albany: SUNY Press, pp. 187–210.

SMITH, J.K. (1993) *After the Demise of Empiricism: The Problem of Judging Social and Educational Inquiry*, Norwood, NJ: Ablex Publishing Corporation.

Part Two

Pedagogy and Student Research

Chapter 5

Writing and Passing Notes: Resistance, Identity and Pleasure in the Lives of Teenage Girls

Sandra Spickard Prettyman

Introduction

> I suspect that the difference between personal and impersonal knowledge, or practical and impractical knowledge is not a difference in what it is we know, but how we tell it and to whom. (Grumet, 1987, p. 319)

Many of us have memories of the notewriting/passing that went on when we were in school and can probably remember exact passages from some of the notes we sent or received. We wrote about ourselves, and about others, and in doing so helped to construct what Valerie Walkerdine has called the 'fictions' of our lives. Reading the notes which I have been collecting for this study has brought back many memories, both joyful and painful, from my own high school days and I often find myself reminiscing about what these notes meant for me as a young girl. I remember the secrecy and intimacy of writing and passing a note to a friend, the camaraderie that this implied. I remember that giddy feeling when someone wrote that Bobby liked me. I remember writing a note during English class and having the teacher take it and read it to the whole class, sinking down further and further into my seat with every word. I remember how left out I felt when Trisha, my best friend, wrote a note to another friend and seemed to forget about me. All of this and more floods my consciousness as I read these notes and talk with these young women about their current experiences.

I this essay I will be investigating the role that notewriting/passing plays in the lives of young girls at school and I will argue that, for girls, it carries out a variety of functions, only one of which is communication. Themes of resistance, identity and pleasure surface throughout the stories and experiences of the girls that participated in this study, liking them through the bond of this specific cultural practice. I will be using notes, interviews and classroom observations in order to gain a better understanding of what this practice means to the girls who engage in it and how they use it to create resistance, identity and pleasure. I will also look at the implications that the practice of notewriting/passing has in the context of schooling and girls' place in it.

Notewriting/passing plays an important role in popular school culture and we must begin to look critically at the function(s) which it serves and the meaning(s) and significance that it has in order to better understand the fictions which girls create about themselves and their place in the institution of schooling. By more closely examining such intimate processes as notewriting/passing we can better understand how girls participate in the school culture and construct their identities in the context of schooling.

Boys Write Notes Too, Don't They?

Shortchanging Girls, Shortchanging America concentrated on the ways in which the education system-often unwittingly-inhibits, restricts, diminishes, and denies girls' experience . . . It seemed to me that the girls in the AAUW survey were telling us that, at adolescence, at the moment of transformation from girlhood to womanhood, they learn that boys are still central in every aspect of the culture. I began to wonder, if girls feel a reduced sense of self, how is that expressed in their attitudes toward all the vital threads of their lives? (Orenstein, 1994, xxiii)

Notewriting/passing is not a cultural practice which is specific to only one gender. However, the notes, interviews and observations which I used for this study suggest that boys and girls use the practice in very different ways and for very different purposes. The notes that boys write are much shorter and to the point than the notes which girls write. They communicate specific information and rarely contain information about feelings and emotions. Boys write most often to their girlfriends and rarely to other boys and the notes are passed between classes, not in class. Girls, on the other hand, often write lengthy notes in which they reveal feelings and emotion. Direct information is sometimes given, but usually in the context of the telling of a story.

I'll meet you at 3 clock by the back lot. (Josh)

I don't know what I'm wearing Friday and what diff is it? My parents won't be home tonight so I'll pick you up at 8 and we can go to my house. (Zach)

So what are you doing tonight? I can't wait to see Jason so I'm going to go over right after school. What do you think I should wear? I was going to wear the blue skirt, but now I don't know? I want to look nice, but not too preppy. (Erin)

Can you believe Mr __? What a joke!!! Anyway, I don't care too much. Do you have to take the quiz tomorrow? I can't believe that those guys fooled around so much that now we're all screwed. It makes me crazy. Like I have other things to do, ya know? (Liz)

I was most intrigued by how girls used notewriting/passing to express themselves and their feelings, often constructing their identities (and those of others) in the process. This was not as evident with the boys and I thus chose to focus most specifically on the notewriting/passing practices of girls. In addition, I believe that all too often the voices and experiences of girls are left out of research and theory, which is one of the ways that they come to see that 'boys are still central in every aspect of the culture'. (Orenstein, 1994, xxiii) My goal here is to give recognition and space to girls' voices and experiences in an attempt to better understand and promote their place in society at large, and in education in particular.

Studying the Insignificant

What is needed then . . . is a research mode which prioritizes multiple levels of experience, including the ongoing relations which connect everyday life with cultural forms. (McRobbie, 1994, p. 184)

This chapter looks at one particular cultural practice which takes place in schools, that of notewriting/passing, and attempts to make sense of it as discourse, as a cultural text or practice. I am searching for alternative explanations for this practice, since it seems that there is more here than initially meets the eye. I want to investigate how this discursive practice is linked to the production of knowledge and identity, social constructs which are embedded in power relations. Much has been written about the dynamics of classroom life, but little focus has been given to this particular practice, even though the interviews which I conducted with students show it to be a very prevalent one. In fact, it seems that little has been written about any of the cultural practices which students engage in while at school and the production of meaning and pleasure which accompany them. In this paper I hope to move beyond a mere acceptance of this practice as 'the way things are' to an understanding of notewriting/passing as a cultural text and some of the implications that this has for both students and teachers.

The data which I have used for this study includes notes which I have collected from high school students, interviews about notewriting/passing conducted with students and teachers, and classroom observations. The notes, interviews, and observations were collected and conducted between January 1995 through March 1996 in a small community in South-eastern Michigan. I have analyzed over 100 notes from girls and boys ranging in age from 13–18 years old and have conducted 20 interviews with students and six with teachers regarding their thoughts on the process and implications of notewriting/passing in their lives. I have also conducted six day-long classroom observations in order to get a better feeling for the community of students and teachers which were being interviewed.

My analysis will draw upon the works of Angela McRobbie, John Fiske and Henry Giroux, as well as other post-modernists who have written at length about the issue of popular culture and its relation to pedagogy. I will be using many of the concepts and theories which they have put forth in my analysis of what notewriting/passing might mean to the students who engage in it. Especially important will be their definition of what constitutes popular culture, the resistance which is often contained within its production, and the pleasure and meaning which is produced from it.

I will also be drawing on the works of Valerie Walkerdine, Jennifer Gore, Patti Lather and others in order to examine the function which notewriting/passing plays in the construction of identity for young girls. The works of these writers will provide insight into how girls might use notes as a form of writing the self and as a vehicle for self-expression. I will also use the works of Carol Gilligan and Peggy Orenstein to think about the adolescent development of girls and how notewriting/passing might be a way for them to cope with the pressures of growing up in a male dominated society, of which schooling is a part.

Subjectively Speaking

> I was unprepared for how much the journey into gender would become a journey into myself, how much the voices of the AAUW survey echoed my own. While writing this book, I began to look at myself in the way I looked at many of these girls: with a kind of double vision. (Orenstein, 1994, xxvi)

Before beginning, I must locate myself in this study, for I am not an unbiased, objective observer, but rather a woman who has written, passed and received her share of notes in the past and has actively participated in this particular form of popular school culture. I feel very close to the subject of notewriting/passing and also very close to the students and teachers whom I interviewed, since I have much in common with many of them. Many of the feelings and emotions which are present in my memories of high school resurfaced in the interviews and observations which I conducted. The voices of these girls often seemed to echo my own and I am now able to recognize how the themes of resistance, identity, and pleasure were present in my own schooling experiences, coloring and constructing my reality and my future. I do not pretend detachment, but rather hope that my attachment will give rise to a greater level of critical insight and reflection as well as a form of self-expression that will enhance this work.

Notes on/as Popular Culture

> To see culture as neither fixed nor finite but as dynamic, expansive and intrinsically shaped by power and the struggle against it is to occupy a very different position in this 'crisis' of authority over what is to counts as legitimate knowledge. (Lather, 1991, xvi)

Popular culture is a process where meanings and pleasure are created within a structure of unequal power relations. 'The politics of popular culture is that of everyday life' (Fiske, 1989, p. 56). This definition is based on two important premises: that popular culture is a process, not a product and that power is a force, not a possession. This chapter looks at the act of notewriting/passing as one of the ways that students create and circulate meaning and pleasure in their lives, a process which contains contradictions and resistance and which serves to help students deal with the subordinate position in which they find themselves, both in our society as a whole and more specifically in the social system of education.

If we view popular culture as a process, we see that it is an active, evolving entity rather than a static object or product. It is not a product created by the mass culture industry for use by the people, but rather a process which is created and developed by those who use it. It cannot be imposed by others, but must grow from within, nurtured by those who create and use it. Students use many things in order to produce their own culture, including the time, space, and resources of the class-room. This is one of the contradictions which is inherent in the creation of popular culture: the use of dominant culture resources to produce meaning and pleasure for the subordinated, in this case the students. The subordinated students take the resources provided for them (paper, pencil and classroom time) and create some-thing quite different than what was anticipated. They are making do with what they have in order to create their own meaning and pleasure.

The process by which popular culture is created is a dynamic one which operates within a system of social relations of dominance and subordination. It is an attempt by the subordinated to make sense of and deal with their subordination, while trying to oppose or resist it. This locates power as a force which operates within relationships and which can be either positive or negative. It is something which can be exercised rather than posessed and we are all constantly working to (re)negotiate the terms of this power. Michel Foucault has said that 'individuals are the vehicles of power' and that it is important to determine 'how things work at the level of on-going subjugation, at the level of those continuous and un-interrupted processes which subject our bodies, govern our gestures, dictate our behaviors, etc.' (1976, pp. 97–8). The classroom can be seen as the site of various discourses, some of which create relations of power and resistance and that help to create different positions which can be occupied by the participants. It is a space where students are sometimes able to contest the cultural and pedagogical domination which they face everyday and where they are able to exercise power and create their own meanings and pleasures. This is how popular culture grows and flourishes, as a result of the everyday tactics of the subordinated.

Writing as Resistance

> . . . the definition and construction of reality, that is how knowledge and meaning
> are constructed and organized, are always being challenged and struggled over.
> (Gotfrit, 1991, p. 182)

I remember being in Spanish class and writing notes to a friend during lab time, when we were supposed to be working on listening skills. I remember American History when I would pretend to listen and take notes about what the teacher was saying, all the time writing long notes to my friends, some of them detailing just how boring the class and the teacher were. The situation does not seem to have changed much over the years; students state over and over again in notes and interviews how little they care about class, how bored they are, how terrible the teacher is, etc. The most common answer to the question 'Why do you usually write notes?' is 'Because I'm bored.' Alfred Alschuler has written about 'the battle for students' attention and the "war games" which occur in classrooms'. (Alschuler, 1980) He describes various tactics which students use in order to avoid and resist attending to instructional material; I would add notewriting/passing to his list and say that they serve as a discourse of student resistance in the classroom.

The initial response that many people have to 'Why do students write notes?' is that it is simply a way for them to communicate with their friends. Yet students have many other opportunities for communication: lunchtime, between classes, before and after school, etc. In addition, many notes that are written are not passed until after class or between classes, when the students could also talk to each other, and probably do. All of the teachers that I interviewed said that notewriting/passing was strictly a form of communication between students. Yet, most of the students saw it very differently.

> First of all I don't think this is a very common practice at all, if students do write notes it's just to tell someone something. We don't allow them to talk in class, so we shouldn't allow them to write notes. (English Teacher)

> Sometimes students need to get a message to a friend and won't see them in class so they might write a note to get information to them. (Biology Teacher)

> Kids don't write notes to get out of class, they do it to be cool. (Health Teacher)

> I write notes because it's a way to get out of class. Like why should I pay attention when it has nothing to do with me or when it's stupid? (Erin)

> It's a good way to get out of class without sleeping and getting in trouble. (Jenny)

> Sure I could talk to Jenny after class, but if I write a note then I don't have to pay attention. (Liz)

These students seem to be resisting in some way what their teachers are attempting to do, which is to keep their attention and facilitate learning. In addition, there was a large discrepancy between the perceptions of teachers and students about how many students actually engage in this behavior during the course of any given day. Teacher estimates ranged from 5 to 20 percent, while students guessed that anywhere between 65 and 75 percent of the students wrote/passed notes. The observations I made showed that about 60 percent of the students wrote/passed notes during the course of a school day. While this is a bit lower than the estimates given by students, it is much closer than those given by teachers.

The resistance also seems to give the girls great pleasure, which fuels their desire to continue the behavior. Subverting the system and those who dominate in it produces a sense of accomplishment for these girls. The girls often spoke of their pleasure, but it was also obvious in the classroom observations that I did. With every note that Liz passed in English class there were smiles and low giggles, but when the teacher turned to her she had a straight face and seemed to be paying close attention to the discussion. After class I often saw Liz and her friends give each other a high-five for having successfully passed the note (or notes) and pulled one off over the teacher. Their words also show this same pleasure.

> I like to pass notes in class because it's more fun, like there's no challenge in giving someoneone a note in the hall. ([laughing] Liz)

> Part of the fun is getting away with it, like if the teachers are that stupid then we must be smarter than them. I think that's it, like we try to be smarter than them and it makes us feel good. ([gleefully, smiling] Erin)

The classroom can be a site of resistance and contestation between dominant and subordinant, teacher and student. The students use material and space provided by the dominant culture to construct their own texts, texts which serve to resist and sometimes disrupt the very same dominant culture. This practice can be seen as disruptive to the extent that it questions the prevailing notions about what education is for and what should happen in classrooms. Students should be using classroom time, space, and resources to learn, not to create meaning and pleasure by writing/passing notes, shouldn't they?

Why Resist?

Almost all of the notes which I analyzed made some negative reference to teachers and schooling.

> Can you believe how stupid he is. I can't believe he's making us do this stupid stuff. I'm just gonna write you cause there's no way I'm working on this dumb project. (Erin)

> I hate this class. Mrs _____ thinks I'm taking notes. Yeah, right! Not in this lifetime. (Jenny)

> Mr _____ is soooooo boooooring! I can't wait to get out of this class and back to the real world. I need to make it look like I'm working though, so I have a really studious look on my face. (Liz)

These quotes, from notes that girls wrote in class, show their disdain for teachers and schooling. But why do they resist in this way, why do they feel the need to disengage in this way? Is it because they do not or cannot connect with certain classes or texts or methodologies? Is it lack of interest or a feeling that none of it is relevant to their lives? Or is it that it is not as important for them to succeed academically and so teachers allow them to write and pass notes?

The days that I spent in classrooms with these students showed their notewriting/passing to take place in many different types of classrooms with many different types of teachers. I would see Liz, a bright, well-liked student, writing a note in History class, nodding her head all the time to show the teacher that she was paying attention. I would likewise see her in French class, passing a note to Erin as she was moving around the room doing oral exercises. When I asked her later if she didn't like these classes or these teachers she said: 'No, I really like History and French, especially Mrs _____. But that doesn't mean I always want to pay attention. Boys act out in certain ways and girls act out in certain ways. Only ours (girls') are usually less disruptive, maybe quieter is the word, so we write notes instead of being physical jerks like the guys.' Liz, and many of the other girls that I interviewed and observed, talked about how their teachers reacted to them writing/passing notes in class, most saying that it was not a problem.

> Teachers don't really care too much, ya know. Most of the time they don't even know though. Stupid, huh? (Erin)

> If you're not disrupting class, they don't really care. (Meg)

> It's just something we (girls) all do and they can't really stop it, so they just let us. (Liz)

This differed from what teachers told me, most of them saying that students shouldn't be allowed to write notes and that if it became a problem they would deal with it like any other discipline problem.

> I don't think kids write notes really that much, but maybe it's just in my class that I don't see it because it's such an advanced class and they need to pay attention. But if I saw it a lot I would have to do something, we can't just let them do whatever they want. (AP English Teacher)

> If students are going to write notes then I'll send them down to the office, like I would any other discipline problem. Sometimes I've read them outloud or sometimes I throw them away. But it just doesn't happen very often. (Algebra Teacher)

Yet in my classroom observations I only once saw a teacher discipline a student for notewriting, taking the note away and throwing in the garbage. This was interesting because after class I saw some other students go up to the garbage can and retrieve the note, much to the dismay of the girl who had written it, who was trying desperately to get it back. Do teachers not see the notewriting/passing activity that is going on, or do they decide to allow it since it is less disruptive than other forms of student resistance? Is this one of the ways that Peggy Orenstein would say girls lose out in the educational setting? Girls are quiet, keep to themselves, and pretend to pay attention. Teachers recognize and approve of their behavior and therefore do not look any further into how these girls might be resisting and disrupting in their own quiet way.

The classroom is a site where various discourses compete and where student consent and cooperation is marked by moments of resistance. These discourses do not exist in a vacuum, but rather in a system of power relations. Students can be seen as active agents in this process and the discursive practices in which they engage as a way of taking control of their lives and their knowledge and in some small way resisting the forces of dominant culture, in this case the institution of schooling.

The practice of notewriting/passing also intrigued me for the multiplicity of meanings that it encompassed. I was amazed by the fact that there are now numerous ways to fold notes and that different folds can indicate the content of notes and different ways that they should be passed. There is currently a book out which is a top seller at school book fairs that talks about all the different ways to fold notes. Is this a way for the dominant culture to incorporate some of this student resistance and therefore neutralize some of the impact that it has? Students also use codes for different words and different things that they want to say, so that outsiders will not be able to understand. Liz told me at one point that if I had any questions about what the notes said I should call her, because 'sometimes we use a lot of words for other words and you might need me to translate like, if you know what I mean'. Folding and code using add depth and complexity to the discursive practice of notewriting/passing and offer students a way to create a multiplicity of meaning, an overflow and abundance. It also gives them the space for self-expression and a way to control their experiences and remain outside of the dominant culture. Creating meaning gives pleasure which drives resistance and is one way to upset the power relations which usually serve to control.

Writing Themselves and Their Discontent

> It is not that we are filled with roles and stereotypes of passive femininity so that we become what society has set out for us. Rather, I am suggesting that femininity and maculinity are fictions, linked to fantasies deeply embedded in the social world which can take on the status of fact when inscribed in the powerful practices, like schooling, through which we are regulated. (Walkerdine, 1990, xiii)

Adolescence was, for me, a painful time filled with humiliation and self-doubt, a time when I clearly felt myself to be different, to be the 'Other', yet I was always trying to please and fit into the normative expectations which would define me as accepted and acceptable. I was trying to figure out who 'I' was and why I was so different, or felt so different, or had been set up to be so different. The notewriting/passing that I engaged in as a student was a way for me to be the 'Other' and still be accepted, to live the fictions of my life as reality. The data which I have collected for this study shows much the same thing: girls using notewriting/passing in order to present themselves as 'Other', while at the same time as accepted and acceptable. Yet another contradiction of popular culture. We can't resist too much.

Notewriting/passing can be seen as a tactical maneuver used by girls to create alternative subject positions for themselves. It is one of the ways that they position themselves, both in and out of the classroom and one of the ways that they construct and are constructed by the fictions which are their lives. While pretending to *take* notes in class, a girl is really writing *notes*. She is a 'good' student and an imposter at the same time, masking her resistance with an outward mask of studiousness. The subject positions that girls hold in the classroom are based on bipolarities created and constructed in the classroom by the discursive practices in which they engage, notewriting/passing being one of them.

Speaking about School
I'm so sick of school. I hate it!!!
> *but later*

I need to get an A on this biology test so I can go to the game this weekend. (Jill)

This class sucks. I hope I never end up like Mrs —. She's so stupid.
> *but later*

I hope she likes my paper. I'm pretending to work on it now. (Liz)

Speaking about Boys
As soon as you start he'll want to be with you again and all that. *That's out!* If he can't fucking stand by you now, then what's he going to do later?
> *but later*

But, I know that you want to get back with him and be cool again, so I hope it works out, since it's what you want. (Jenny)

He said he'll stay with her until college, but he's a jerk. He only stays with her because he knows you won't go back.
> *but later*

You will be the *only* one he keeps in the end. You watch. (Liz)

I'm going to fill you in on everything . . . I was afraid he'd hit or something and now I'm not upset that we broke up.
> *but later*

I just don't know how I'll do it. I mean, who's gonna take me to the prom? (Erin)

These quotes illustrate some of the contradictions that girls feel about their lives, both in and out of the classroom, and who they are in relation to them. They resist learning, but they want to do well; they want to fit in, but they challenge the status quo; they desire normativity, but they write against it; they want/need/like boys, but they 'trash' them. Is notewriting/passing a way for girls to silently speak about their subordinate place, a way for them to tell their 'real' stories? Does notewriting/passing help these girls move from a subordinate subject position as student/girl to a more powerful one as a writer? Leslie Gotfrit says that, 'We make sense of our experiences in ways that attempt to resolve the contradictions of the self that are created and lived within dominant forms' (1991, p. 182). Yet, these girls seem to embody these very contradictions in their production of this particular form of popular culture. The notes that girls write and pass often seem to position them as different than both boys and teachers, the 'Other' in many ways.

Carol Gilligan has done research on adolescent girls and the loss of voice and connection that they experience as they approach adolescence. Is notewriting/passing a way for girls to keep their voice and to stay in connection with other girls? Most of the girls which I interviewed and observed wrote to other girls, although some wrote to boyfriends, and they often talked about how notes let them stay close to their friends.

> Ya know, we don't get to see each other as much as we used to now that everyone has boyfriends and stuff. So we write notes and then tell everything, and it's kinda like it was before. (Leslie)

> I like being close to my friends, I guess I might even love some of them, but you can't really say that, ya know? It wouldn't be cool. So we write and stay in touch and that's ok. (Liz)

> I don't know what I would do if I couldn't write to my friends, it's like therapy I guess. Sometimes we write about unimportant stuff, just what's happening, but sometimes we write about what bothers us or is like hurting us or what pisses us off and it's good, great even, to get it out and know that it's someone who understands and cares and is there. (Erin)

Notewriting seems to be one way that girls stay in connection with one another, even if they can't do it in other ways at this age. Research on adolescent development shows that by late adolescence the crowd or 'clique' has changed shape and begins to disintegrate into loosely grouped sets of couples that are 'going together'. (Cobb, 1995, p. 274) This coincides with Gilligan's findings that as adolescence proceeds girls tend to give up relationships (like those with girlfriends) for 'Relationship'. Yet the girls that I spoke with and observed seemed to need and want the continued closeness with other girls, and they got pleasure from their continued relationships with other them. But it is part of their identity that must be kept hidden to a certain extent, they're not supposed to need or want same-sex relationships at this time in their lives. Their relationships become voiceless, expressed mainly in the written notes passed surreptitiously to friends.

> How are you girl? I haven't talked to you in soooooo long. Like we have been so busy with everything and everybody else, but there all shit. I really need to talk to you, so I'm just gonna write today cause I know we'll never get a chance to like really talk, everybody else is always around and it's never the same. But it is sometimes. I need you so much. Life is such shit. But I can be me with you and I need that now, even if it's just in a note. You treat me like me and accept me and like me. You always know how to make me feel good and writing this note will help I hope. So here goes. (taken from a 2 page note written by Jessie)

Madeleine Grumet has written that, 'Our stories are the masks through which we can be seen, and with every telling we stop the flood and swirl of thought so someone can get a glimpse of us, and maybe catch us if they can' (1987, p. 322). Do the notes that girls write/pass give us a glimpse into their lives, or are we still only seeing the mask? Or has this mask become so enmeshed that we (and they) are no longer able to 'unmask' them? How can we help girls like Jessie, Liz, Erin and others to feel more connected with each other, so that their communication and relationships don't have to be 'voiceless' and underground? And what does all of this mean for education and our attempts to help these girls learn?

Implications for Education

> Certainly the common conception of pedagogy is blind to the ways in which broader social relationships are embodied in the teaching/learning process. (Gore, 1992, p. 140)

I believe that notewriting/passing can offer us some insight into the experiences of girls in the classroom, experiences which can only be understood in terms of the complicated and often contradictory ways in which resistance, identity, and pleasure are socially produced and constructed. These themes are reflected in their words, both written and oral, as well as their actions, and they give us an important glimpse into how girls oftentimes resist the explicit curriculum which we try to teach. Yet how much of their notewriting/passing represents the learned behavior of a hidden curriculum? Lessons which they have learned all too well: that girls should be quiet, passive, and non-disruptive; that girls should begin to sever their relationships with other girls in order to pursue 'Relationships'; that their voices are not worth being heard. Much of who they are (or who they are expected to be) is reflected in these lessons and I wonder how much of their notewriting/passing is aimed at resisting these hidden lessons of identity.

It is important for us to begin to look at the ways in which relations of power operate in the classroom, for we can never move outside of them. And we must begin to recognize how students resist, how their identities are often constructed as a result of this resistance, and how they gain pleasure from all of it. Perhaps this is what these girls are doing when they write/pass notes, they are attempting to make sense of and 'write' a place for themselves within the relations of power that exist in the classroom, between teachers and students, between boys and girls. If girls are not paying attention in class, what does that tell us about the material and perhaps the method of teaching? Do they feel it isn't important, do they feel excluded and disconnected, do they feel teachers don't care?

We, as educators, need to take seriously the experiences of girls in the class-room in order to better understand how resistance, identity, and pleasure are both created for and by these girls. If we look seriously at notewriting/passing as a cultural practice, what does it tell us about girls and their place in schools? What would happen if teachers, especially English teachers, began to take seriously this form of writing and expression? Or would this just be another way to incorporate the resistance? These questions and more come to mind when I begin to think of ways to help students and teachers move toward an educational system which recognizes and respects the lives and experiences of all of its participants.

References

ALSCHULER, A. (1980) *School Discipline: A Socially Literate Solution*, New York: McGraw Hill.

COBB, N. (1995) *Adolescence: Continuity, Change and Diversity*, 2nd edition. Mountain View, CA: Mayfield Publishing Company.

FISKE, J. (1989) *Understanding Popular Culture*, London, New York: Routledge.

FOUCAULT, M. (1976) 'Lecture two: 14 January 1976', *Power/Knowledge: Selected Interviews and Other Writings 1972–1977*, GORDON, C. (ed.), New York: Pantheon Books.

GILLIGAN, C. (1992) *Meeting at the Crossroads: Women's Psychology and Girls' Development*, Cambridge: Harvard University Press.

GIROUX, H. (1989) 'Popular culture as a pedagogy of pleasure and meaning', *Popular Culture, Schooling and Everyday Life*, GIROUX, H. et al. (eds) Granby, MA: Bergin and Garvey.

GORE, J. (1992) *Feminisms and Critical Pedagogy*, New York: Routledge.

GOTFRIT, L. (1991) 'Women dancing back: Disruption and the politics of pleasure,' *Postmodernism, Feminism, and Cultural Politics: Redrawing Educational Boundaries*, GIROUX, H. (ed.) Albany, NY: State University of New York Press.

GRUMET, M. (1987) 'The politics of personal knowledge', *Curriculum Inquiry*, **17**, 3.

GRUMET, M. (1988) *Bitter Milk: Women and Teaching*, Amherst, MA: University of Massachusetts Press.

LATHER, P. (1990) *Getting Smart: Feminist Research and Pedagogy with/in the Postmodern*, London, New York: Routledge.

McROBBIE, A. (1994) *Postmodernism and Popular Culture*, London, New York: Routledge.

ORENSTEIN, P. (1994) *Schoolgirls: Young Women, Self-esteem, and the Confidence Gap*, New York: Anchor Books.

WALKERDINE, V. (1990) *Schoolgirl Fictions*, London, New York: Verso Publications.

Chapter 6

Mentoring Authorship in the Elementary School Classroom Through the Writing Process

Nina Zaragoza

Traditional writing instruction focuses on skills and corrections. Children are given prompts and then expected to write on them with creativity and fluency. They are collected by the teacher, red inked, handed back for corrections and usually filed away forever. Writing in this way becomes static, tedious and meaningless. If we want children to become real writers who want and need to write we need to set up a writing program that mentors young authors.

Let's talk about some of the underlying basic principles of a writing process program. First of all, this program works children through a process that *all* authors experience. Whether an author is 6 years old or 60 years old they go through the same process as they create a piece of writing. Therefore, when we implement process writing in the classroom we need to understand that all children need to be treated and seen as authors. The job of an author is to write. Sometimes authors might write for themselves as in diary writing but more frequently an author writes for an audience. To reach this audience an author needs to publish work so that it can be read by readers within and beyond the immediate community. An integral part of a writing process program implemented in the classroom, then, is publication. With various forms of publication available children begin to realize they are authors. Without publication creative writing is denied one of its inherent purposes-communicating to others.

Now let's begin to examine the specific details of implementing a process writing program in an elementary school classroom.

Elements of a Writing Process Program

1 Time to write

Children must be given time to write every day. A 20–30 minute daily writing period instills in children the habit of writing and gives them the necessary time to develop fluency and practice skills. This is the minimal time period necessary for children to work on first drafts, to edit and revise drafts, and to publish finished drafts as hard-covered books. This time period also allows children the time to confer with their friends and teacher, to absorb new ideas, and to participate in editing, revising, publishing and sharing. This daily commitment to writing communicates to the children the significance of writing in the curriculum and provides them with the time to integrate and automate writing skills.

2   Control of topic choice

If children are allowed considerable freedom in choosing their topic, they realize that what they have to say, not only what the teacher assigns, is important. While initially some students might show great frustration when faced with the task of choosing their own topic, generation of ideas will become easier through sharing, peer/teacher questioning and opportunity to co-author. Development of topic ideas will also be easier as children listen to literature and discuss the material from an author's perspective.

3   Active student control

When children are given the time and opportunity to choose and develop personal topics, they begin to feel control over the writing process. This feeling of control is essential for through this they learn that the influence of their choices extend beyond their work to the classroom environment. When they see that their work and opinions are accepted in a supportive atmosphere, they are more willing to take active risks and their writing skills become more fully developed. Writing becomes connected to their personal work, activities and social interactions. Students become less passive, more independent, and begin to make their own decisions. Their control over decisions produces the desire and motivation to learn and be active participants in the writing process.

4   Integration of skills

Giving children the freedom to focus on one aspect of writing at a time enables them to feel less overwhelmed as they are allowed to concentrate on the skills at the time in the process when they are most meaningful.

- *The first draft.* In writing first drafts, children are taught to focus on their ideas and not to be concerned about spelling, grammar, handwriting. Invented spelling is encouraged and priority is given to exploring thoughts, ideas, and feelings. When children begin to feel safe about using words and realize that invented spelling helps with writing down their ideas they become confident writers who willingly take appropriate risks for continued writing growth.
- *Revision of the draft.* During the revision stage the children continue work on their content by sharing with their peers/teacher and clarifying and receiving ideas for draft development. In this stage the main idea (i.e., selection of a title), the sequence, and the concept of reality/fantasy are developed and refined. Community members contribute ideas to aid in the revision of the draft.
- *Editing.* It is within the editing stage, when the draft is being prepared for publication, that instruction in mechanical skills takes place. Spelling is

standardized, punctuation is corrected, and capitalization is discussed and corrected. With this type of instruction children begin to learn these skills in the context of their own work. They begin to understand that the purpose of such skills is to develop a piece of effective communication.

- *Publication.* During the publication stage, the children cut and fold paper to the measurement of pre-made covers, and transfer their corrected draft onto the pages of their new book. At this point, handwriting skills are taught and reinforced, and children learn that legible handwriting is another necessary part of effective communication. When handwriting is not an issue children can also publish computer generated copy.

5   The right to an audience

When children are given the opportunity to share their work with an audience, they learn that the essence of writing is communication; writing skills become meaningful and children feel in control as they help themselves and others.

TAG (Zaragoza, 1987, 1997; Zaragoza and Vaughn, 1992, 1995) is an acronym that can be used at the beginning of the year to help children positively receive the work of others. This acronym helps the children remember the following rules: 1) T-Tell what you like, 2) A-Ask questions, and 3) G-Give ideas. The effect produced with TAG is so positive that it continues even after active reinforcement of the strategy is stopped.

6   Conferences

Another element of the writing process is conferences. These can take place during the creation of the first draft, revising, editing or sharing. They should last from about three to seven minutes and should concentrate on one specific skill at a time. Therefore, if the child is working on the initial draft or its revision, the conference should only address questions of content. When the child is involved with editing, conversation should revolve around the mechanics. At the publication stage of the process, comments should be directed towards handwriting. This conference behavior enables the student and teacher to focus on one skill at a time and avoid being overwhelmed by dealing with too many corrections at once.

The type of questions that teachers use during conferences is very important. Questions should exhibit the teacher's trust in the child's own judgment. Questions such as 'What are your concerns?' and 'Could you tell me a little more?' are appropriate because they encourage the pupil, not the teacher to talk. Such questions also demonstrate the teacher's genuine belief in and respect for the child.

First Day: Introduction of Writing Process to Full Class

T   We are going to write about anything we want. What do we call people who write stories?

Ss   Authors.

T   Where do authors get their ideas?

Ss From looking around; from things in our family; from things we do . . . from other people.

T That reminds me . . . There is one word that we can use to talk about 'things that happen to us' It starts with 'ex'.

Ss Exercises . . .

T Those are really good tries. I was thinking about the word 'experiences'. Authors write about their experiences. Some authors write make up pretend experiences, too.

S Yes, people can write about their childhood . . . when you are adults you can write about your childhood.

T That's right. We can write about our memories sometimes. OK. Now when we begin to write . . . when you get an idea . . . what do you do when you don't know how to spell a word?

Ss Sound it out.

T Well, what if when you sound it out, you still can't think of the first letter, what are you going to do?

Ss Ask somebody.

T That's true you can ask somebody. In the first draft, what is important are your ideas. If you get up and ask somebody you may forget your ideas . . . Now give me a big word . . .

S Massachusetts.

T Massachusetts . . . \M\ . . . Oh, great! I have a great idea and I don't want to stop to think of all those letters, so I'll put an 'M' then what can I do if I don't want to write any of the other letters?

S Leave a blank.

T That's right! That's what I do when I don't want to worry about spelling, you can leave a blank. Let's all write. All of us are going to write because all people write.

All students and teacher write. During implementation on the first day, the teacher, whilst writing, sits within the community of student writers. After about five minutes or so the teacher should get up and go to every single child and give them each a positive/encouraging comment such as:

— I see you have already started writing.
— You have a lot to say.
— Don't worry about handwriting.
— Oh, you don't need to erase. Just cross it out and go on. We are not worried about how it looks.
— I see you aren't worried about spelling. You just put a blank right there.
— I like how you are not afraid to write this word.
[To Mandy who drew a house]
— Now tell me something about this house.

The teacher continues to circulate and then comes back to Mandy who has written something in invented spelling:

T Wow, Mandy, you've written something. Tell me what it says.

S A man lives in this house.

T   That's great. The story goes with your picture.

[**T** picked up a student's draft and asked:]

T   'Everyone listen for one minute. Marco is looking right at me. I know that he is ready to listen. Now I see that everyone is listening. What do we call this? This is what we first work on when we begin to write.

Ss A rough draft.

T   I call it a first draft, but some people call it a rough draft. Where did you hear that language?

Ss From my other teacher.

T   That's good. What is most important when we do a first draft?

[**Ss** No response.]

T   OK, what is not important when we write a first draft? Remember, what don't we worry about when we write a first draft?

Ss Spelling.

T   That's right. And another thing we don't worry about is handwriting. Now what is important in a first draft?

Ss Your story

T   That's right. What is most important is your idea, your story. Go back to writing. Thank you for letting me interrupt you.

The children write for about five more minutes as the teacher continues to individually talk to each child.

T   Let's get back together as a class.

S   Wait. I'm not finished.

T   Oh, let's talk about what authors do. What authors do you read?

S   Amelia Bedelia.

T   Good! I read a lot of Amelia Bedelia too.

S   *Ralph and the Motorcycle* (the Beverly Cleary book)

T   How long do you think it took Beverly Cleary to write that book?

Ss A year. . . . five years . . . five months.

T   Yes, different authors take different amounts of time to do their writing. I am a very slow writer. So it takes me a long time to write. So do you think we need to finish our story today?

Ss No.

T   What are we going to do with our drafts?

S   Save them.

T   That's right. Authors save their drafts so they can work on them the next day. Since you all are authors now we are going to write everyday so we need to save our drafts. I'm going to give each one of you a notebook to write your drafts in this way your drafts won't get lost and you'll be able to look back on your writing. This will be your writing process notebook. Tomorrow when it is writing time the first thing you'll do is take it out and begin writing.

Discussion of First Day

While some of the dialogue and amount of time spent in writing on the first day will change according to the age of the children, the foundational principles remain the same. As I have said previously, a writer is a writer no matter how old or how young. Therefore, we use the same vocabulary that all writers use. If you notice in this transcript of the first day I do not lecture on the writing process but begin to teach it within the context of the children's work. So for example, the children learned the word 'draft' during the time they were actually working on a draft. In this way, the vocabulary is introduced within the context of meaningful use. Now, my goal on the first day of writing is not to have students memorize the process it is to give them a feel for what they will be doing everyday in our class and help them feel safe and excited about writing. On the first day I do want them to feel like authors, though, so I consciously make sure I do a number of things. If you notice, I automatically begin to talk to them as authors, connect to professional authors and encourage active response and personal control through broad questions. Notice that I work them through the *whole* process, including sharing and publication so the purpose of writing is clear. Therefore, on the first day I adjust my schedule so that time for sharing is assured. I also make sure that empty hard covers are visible so that children can immediately put their writing piece into published form. In fact, during the first class I make sure I get at least one child to publish a book. I do not, though, show them an already published book because I do not want to inhibit their work. Many believe that showing samples will help children but in fact the message we give when we show samples too early is 'This is the way your book should look.' We do not want to send this message because the length of each publication would vary, according to the student and we want all children to feel successful. For example, a published book for one kindergartner could easily be 'I love my Mommy.' The product is not important here — what *is* important is that this child feels like an author and that the written work is published. Once students see this first completed publication they become *very* motivated to get their own work published as quickly as possible!!

Let me make something clear: The first written piece of an author should be responded to with great care. We want all children to feel safe and accepted. Therefore, their written work must be received with the utmost respect. Students need to understand that what they say and write is important and valued. To do this I make sure that all children publish their first piece — no matter what it might be. Remember, authors write every day and there will be plenty of time to edit, refine and develop detailed stories.

The first day or week or, for some children, month is *not* the time to be overly critical or perfectionistic. It is the time to help all your students feel like authors as they publish their first books. What follow is one way in which I make book covers.

Publication: Book Covers

I *urge* you not to underestimate the power of these book covers. Some teachers decide not to introduce publication until their children can write 'complete stories'. In these classrooms, then, students don't get a full view of the process and the motivational push that publication gives is lost. I suggest that before you introduce writing process to your class you take the time to make these covers. The harder the cardboard you use the more effective since the closer the resemblance student authored books will have to the books of professional authors. Some teachers decide to take the easier path and use construction paper or manila cardboard to make covers. I guarantee that these covers are not as effective or motivational. It is worth the extra time and work to make hard-backed covers. In this way, too, you will more easily be able to place your students books within your regular class library. When their work is included with the work of the professional authors their personal perception of authorship continues to be strengthened.

To make hard cardboard books covers the procedure is as follows:

Materials
- 17″ × 12″ piece of wallpaper/contact paper
- Two 6″ × 9″ pieces of hard cardboard
- Scissors
- Glue (Glue stick is easiest, neatest)
- Book writing paper

Procedure
1 Place wallpaper/contact paper backside/sticky side up and glue the two pieces of cardboard, side by side in the center. Use a finger space between the two boards.
2 Cut the corners of the wallpaper off and fold (glue) sides over onto the cardboard.

Inside of book
1 Fold two blank sheets of paper under three sheets of writing paper.
2 Fold in half and sew along the fold. (Staple if sewing machine is not available)

Inside and cover
1 Put glue on the back flap inside the cover previously made.
2 Place folded (stapled) inside sheets, inside the cover and close the cover. Open and adjust papers for opening and closing the book.

Sharing the Work

After children become confident about themselves as authors I begin to introduce other ways to publish. I do not do this usually until the second half of the year when I know that all have truly internalized the identity of author. At this point, children are encouraged to type their final copies or, if resources allow, even begin their drafts right on the computer. At around this time, too, children start to design their own ways of publication as they scrounge around the classroom for needed supplies!

The following is a transcript of an initial sharing session. This session is usually scheduled after children have written for at least 15 to 20 minutes. On the first day I will ask for volunteers to share in front of the room. From the second day onward children sign up to share their work. Children are encouraged to share no matter where they are in the process. Therefore, an initial draft might be shared, a title might be shared or a published work could also be shared. Teachers who only allow published copy to be shared in front of an audience give a number of dangerous messages. First, that the *product* is most important, not the process (remember this is *process* writing). Also, when only a publication is permitted to be shared the author's natural use of the audience is denied. An author needs an audience to help with the refinement of the piece of writing. When a work is already published ideas given by the audience become meaningless since they cannot be used to revised the already published piece. Finally, children need to share first before the teacher shows a sample of previous student work or their own piece of writing. When children are shown other work too early there is a real danger that their writing will become inhibited as they take on the traditional message that this must be the way their work should look. After awhile, when all children feel safe as authors, the teachers should share their work since they, too, are members of the writing community.

T Now that we all have our folders/notebooks for our drafts let's come together as a class so we can share our work. Who would like to share?
[No response.]

T I know sometimes it might be a little scary to share but in this class it won't be because we do something called **TAG**. This helps people feel comfortable about sharing. Who can guess what T stands for?
[No response.]

T It's 'Tell'. What would we tell someone about their story so they feel good about it?

S Something nice.

T That's right! We are going to tell them what we liked about the story. Tell what you like. [Teacher writes this on the board after the letter T] Good! Now what do you think A might stand for?
[No Response.]

T When we want to find out about something what do we do?

S We ask.

T Good and that's what we do after we listen to someone's story. We ask them about things in the story. A stands for 'Ask questions.' [Teacher writes this on the board after the letter A] Now can anyone guess what G stands for?
[No Response.]

T When we want to help someone with their writing we can give them what?

S Ideas.

T Yes, and that's what G means. After we listen to our friend's story we can 'Give them ideas or suggestions.' [Teacher writes this on the board after the letter G] to help them with the story. Now everyone let's say this. [Children repeat after teacher: 'T: Tell what you like; A: Ask questions; G: Give ideas'.]

T Good. Now who would like to share?

[A few students raise their hands; the teacher chooses one randomly and says:] You know today I will choose a student but after this I am not going to choose anymore. We're going to have a sign up notebook so that when you want to share you can sign your name under the day you want to share.

T So now whenever you want to share you sign-up where there is space and if there is no space that's OK because we'll be sharing every day and we'll all get a chance. You can sign up whenever you want but do you think everyone can be at the sign up sheet all at once?

S No.

T Why not? It will get too crowded. That's right. So the rule is only three people at one time. Let's begin sharing. Come on up Derek. Now before you start reading your story I want you to look around and make sure everyone is looking at you. Recognize someone who looks ready to listen.
[No response.]

T Who is sitting nicely and ready to listen?

D Chris.

T Good. Now say 'Chris is sitting nicely.'

D Chris is sitting nicely.

T Good. Now tell someone else.

D Amy is sitting nicely.

T Excellent! Now begin sharing.

D [reading from his draft] I like Jessica. I like Randy. I like my Mommy.

T [Claps] Everyone give Derek a hand. Good. Now let's do T A G. What does T stand for?

S Tell what you like.

T That's right. Now someone raise your hand and tell Derek what you liked about his story. [Hands go up]. Now Derek you choose someone.

D Jessica

J I liked your whole story.

T Good, Jessica. What part did you like the best?

J When he said my name.

T Oh! It is nice to hear your name. Does anyone have any questions for Derek about his story?
[No Response.]
[Teacher puts her hand up and Derek picks her.]

T Why do you like the people in your story?

D Because they're my friends.

T Oh, good. Maybe tomorrow you can add that to your story 'because they are my friends'. Give Derek a hand for sharing, everyone. Derek, thank you for being the first one to share. Now you choose someone else to share. Raise your hand if you'd like to be the next one to share. Derek now you choose.

Usually I will allow about three children to share during the first session. If the class as a whole is attentive and eager I might allow more than three. I also would try to include a child who has published the first day so that the class gets a good view of the book cover. I find that after the first child shares and the students see how positive the work is received through TAG most children clamor to share and become upset when sharing time is over. Because writing is every day children realize quickly that they will have many opportunities to share. As you noticed, too, I quickly helped children take over the session and run it themselves. Notice, how I specifically guided their responses. Not only did I guide them in TAG but also in how they responded to their peers' work (applause) and how they positively recognize each other ('_____ is ready to listen.'). I also immediately allowed the first child to choose the next child to share. These techniques are a powerful way to create a supportive classroom and allow children to positively recognize each other. The only 'problem' might become that everyone wants to recognize everyone. An easy way to curtail this is say 'Recognize three people for the way they are sitting/looking at you/ready.'

As you heard in the dialogue above, many of the sharing rules were briefly touched upon. These rules will be elaborated upon and reinforced during the whole first week so that all children become comfortable with them.

As time passes and children are secure with the process schedule I am more flexible with the order of the different parts of the process. So for example, if for some reason on one day we did not have time for all the children to share that were signed up the next day we might start with full class sharing before breaking up to work on our writing pieces. Other days when we fall behind in the full class sharing we might extend the time in order to catch up. This flexibility is possible when students feel secure and safe as authors. One thing they will never let you forget is sharing time!

Writing Process Rules

It is crucial that the rules of writing process are clear and consistent. With this consistency children are enabled to become independent and feel secure with all expectations. During the first week of writing process rules are created together as a full class. As with all class created rules the teacher should know the foundational principles the rules are based upon and guide the children to create the specific corresponding rules. What follows are the general writing process rules that guide us.

1 Write three different first drafts. (This rule is not enforced until the child has published at least the first piece.)
2 Pick one draft to publish.
3 Read your draft to revise/edit. (Beginning writers initially skip over revision and edit immediately and some writers do both simultaneously.)
4 Have a friend help you revise/edit your draft.
5 Sign up for an adult to revise/edit your draft.
6 Write edited copy on publishing paper.
7 Proofread your final copy.
8 Give a friend your final copy to proofread.
9 Sign up for an adult to proofread your final copy.
10 Put your final copy in a cover.
11 Share, help others revise, edit, proofread, illustrate, go back to step 1.

Note that there are three times to sign up. I have already mentioned that one is for sharing. The others are for adult editing/revising of draft and for proofreading of final copy before child places it into a cover. I use three separate notebooks and they are invaluable for keeping children in power and for ensuring that children are not forming a line next to the teacher as they wait for feedback. With the notebooks I can easily review who has shared and requested help consistently and who needs to be encouraged to sign up more frequently.

Writing process cannot be separated from the rest of the community since a positive supportive environment throughout the day is necessary to help children feel safe, successful and respected. These feelings need to be fostered throughout the day by all community members so that children feel comfortable telling their stories and receiving positive guidance. (For further detail about the full classroom community see Zaragoza, 1997.)

Before we begin to discuss the intricacies of teaching and evaluation through the writing process here is a checklist to help you mentor true authorship.

Writing Process Checklist

- Children choose their own topics.
- Children are given sustained and consistent time for daily process writing.
- Children have a separate notebook just for their drafts.
- Children have daily access to sign-up sheets for editing, proofreading and full class sharing.
- Children share their work in all stages of the process (draft or publication).
- Children use T-Tell what you like, A-Ask questions G-Give ideas (TAG) during small group and full class sharing.
- Children self revise/edit/proofread and revise/edit/proofread work of their peers.
- Children have daily access to book covers and publishing paper to publish individual stories.
- Children put their published books within the classroom library for peers to read.
- Teacher writes and shares at least once a week to model the importance of writing.
- Teacher conducts skills lessons to full class within the context of a child's writing and during the appropriate stage of the process (i.e. handwriting spoken about during publication).
- Teacher/revises/edits/proofreads together with child after child has self-revised/edited/proofread and had a peer revise/edit/proofread.
- Teacher keeps a log to note individual child progress.
- Teacher encourages co-authorship.
- Teacher makes sure that book covers, sign-up notebooks publishing paper and an audience are always available to children.

You now have a complete overview of the program including some samples of the initial individual and full class interactions. The following sections will provide some detailed discussion on individual teacher/student conferences, full class contexualized skills lessons and assessment techniques.

Examples of Class Interactions

Josef During Full Class Sharing

Josef shares his story (at around the end of the first month of implementation) and the class responds with TAG (Tell what you like, ask questions, give ideas)

T	How can Josef give us more information?
S	More detail.
T	That's good. How else?

[No response.]

T	What about his friends? What could he do to give us more information?
S	They could say something.
T	That's right. His friends could talk. That's called dialogue. Josef what could your friends say when they walk in your house?
Josef	Hi.
T	Good, that's dialogue.

Here I am working with Josef on revision of his draft. Notice that we are not talking about the mechanics of the piece but about its content. Here I am pushing Josef to be more fluent in his writing by adding more details and dialogue. I would make sure that during the next writing session I would hold Josef accountable to making these revisions on this piece. Either I would conference with him directly or I would ask a student to work with him, i.e. 'Jessica, since you have had dialogue in your story would you help Josef with his tomorrow?'

Another way I do this is ask Josef who he would like to have help him tomorrow. In this way Josef still remains in control. If he happens to choose someone who has not had much experience with this type of revision I would say 'Josef, I know that you like to work with __ but for this skill you need to choose someone that has already used it in their own writing.'

Full Class Lesson

T	Jessica I really liked how your story was complete. (to the class) What are some of the reasons that I say her story is complete? What does her story have?

[No response.]

T	Does her story have a beginning?
Ss	Yes

T	What else . . . a story has a beginning . . . Alvin?
Alvin	and an end.
T	That's right. It has an end. And what else does it have?
Mike	middle.
T	Good. Jessica's story has a beginning, middle and end. What's the beginning?
Ss	She has a teacher.
T	Good. What's the middle?
Ss	He leaves.
T	What's the end?
S	He comes back.
T	Jessica also has something in her story that most complete stories have . . . a problem and a _____?
	[No response.]
T	What word goes along with problem? When we solve a problem what is that called?
Nate	Solution.
T	That's right. Jessica's story has a problem and a solution. What's the problem?
Ss	The teacher leaves.
T	Good. What's the solution?
Ss	The teacher comes back.
T	That's right. They go to complain to the principal and the teacher they like comes back. What an excellent story, Jessica.

This is a clear example of a contextualized lesson. Here I use Jessica's story as a vehicle to teach basic aspects of a narrative piece: beginning, middle end and problem and solution. Notice that my lesson emerges through questioning. First I start with an open-ended question and then if children need more support narrow the questioning until a child comes up with the answer. Throughout the lesson I continue to connect the major concepts to Jessica's story, i.e. 'Good. Jessica's story has a beginning, middle, and end. What's the beginning?' In this way the instruction is kept within the context of meaningful written work.

In subsequent individual writing conferences I will connect to this full class lesson as I move children to include these basic elements in their own story. During full class sharing, too, these concepts will be reinforced as we listen to other pieces and talk about their beginning, middle, end. Questions to encourage such reflection might be: 'What is the problem of your story? Have you thought about a solution, yet? Maybe when you think about a solution it will be easier for you to get to an end of your story.'

Timothy: Idea for Draft

Timothy had a hard time writing — no ideas — I stopped the class and asked each child what they were working on.

As the period went on Timothy still hadn't marked the paper:

> **T**   I want to see you write something. I'll be back in three minutes.

The teacher left him and on returning noted that he had written his name.

> **T**   OK. Now you need to continue to write. Mark your paper.

About ten minutes later the teacher approached him again

Timothy	I have an idea.
T	What?
Timothy	My friends.
T	Good. What letter do you think you should write to begin the word 'My'?
Timothy	Z.
T	Good. Write it down. Now what letter for friend?

Timothy hesitates then struggles to make the letter 'T'. After that he writes a few more letters and stops.

T	Now tell me what that says?
Timothy	My friends are nice. I play with my friends.
T	That's great. Are you finished?
Timothy	Yes. I want to share.
T	Do you want to practice reading it first?
Timothy	Yes. [He begins to read.]

Timothy, like many writers, got stuck on an idea. To help Timothy with ideas I stopped the class and asked each child what they were working on. This sends a clear message to Timothy that he does not need to only depend on me, his teacher, for ideas but can get help from his friends. Here I was also working to get Timothy less afraid to mark the paper. He was very hesitant and so needed direct instructions to 'mark the paper'. Allowing him the time to do this and not doing it for him is extremely important so that he learns that is his work, he is the author, and it is his job to write. Therefore, I continued to push him to write something. If you notice, I did not correct him when he said 'Z' for 'My' because at this point what was important was his marking the paper — no matter what he wrote. Of course, in publication standard spelling would be addressed. The minute Timothy was finished with his story I asked him to tell me about it. When he did I wrote down the words he dictated. Notice, that I did not mark his paper until he did! In this way the message is loud and clear that he is the author and I am only the editor.

Timothy in Publication

> **T**   Let's go Timothy, pick up your pencil and start writing now. Here, write the 'F'. Good, line down, now make the lines across. Hurry up now, and concentrate. Make your 'r' now . . . right next to the 'F'. Good, now make the 'i'. You do that letter well. Now, write the 'e'.

Timothy listened and performed the tasks exactly as directed. At times the teacher talked briefly about letter formation.

T   Start at the top line then go down. Good. Now make the circle.

Sometimes the teacher guided his pencil. Other times I formed the letters for him. She was firm and her directions continued to be short and to the point. Timothy finished his book and then read his story into the tape. The teacher quickly got a cover for him and stapled his finished publication in.

Here Timothy is putting his edited draft into publication. It is here, and only here, where we talk about handwriting. Handwriting is important in the publication because this is what others will read and therefore it must be legible. Some young children are able to copy the whole edited draft on publication while others need more guidance. Here I had Timothy write some letters but so as not to negatively frustrate him I wrote some of the letters. We need to make sure that while we facilitate children's progress we do it in such a way that the child feels positively accomplished. Timothy was given time to practice his writing. This is to ensure that when he shared in front of the class he felt successful and proud.

April

April was having a difficult time starting a new draft. The teacher encouraged her to get up and walk around to see what others were doing. Then the teacher realized she had already got an idea from Tory for her last poem:

T   Oh, you know how to get ideas from your friends. You're good at that. Remember you got that idea to start your poem from Tory?

April nodded yes. A while later the teacher looked over and she had written a good amount of text.

T   You're really writing! You look really happy!
Tory   She's happy because I'm drawing her pictures for her.

April was an author who had great difficulty with getting ideas and frequently tried to push the teacher for ideas. Here April is positively recognized for seeking ideas from her peers. This constant recognition and reinforcement will develop a true community of writers not dependent only on the teacher but willing and able to ask for guidance from their classmates. In this way, too, the teacher is not the only one responsible for writing process but all community members become active and responsible participants.

Assessment Issues

Assessment/evaluation during the writing process revolves around two major principles:

1   We evaluate a skill during the stage of writing where it is most meaning-ful; and

2   Student writers are evaluated according to their own individual growth and are not compared to other writers.

Therefore, as mentioned earlier, handwriting is never spoken about nor as-sessed when a child is working on a draft. This would be quite inappropriate since what the child needs to focus on in a draft is the content. Handwriting *is* spoken about and evaluated during the time of publication since this is the place where legibility is meaningful. Discussion of standard spelling and other features of lan-guage such as punctuation marks, verb agreement is most meaningful as the child edits so it is here where assessment of these language skills should be assessed. If such skills are assessed during the creation of the draft creativity is inhibited.

Children should be assessed according to their own individual progress and not compared to others. Therefore, formal 'grade collection' cannot take place until you know each child and what they can do. After you have a few pieces of writing you can begin to monitor progress over time as you look back and look ahead during the process of writing. Evaluation in writing process should always have the purpose of encouraging and moving writers along in their own development.

Draft

Here I can evaluate fluency as I look at the length of drafts over time for each individual writer. A child who goes from a two-sentence draft to a five-sentence draft in two weeks has made good personal progress in fluency.

I can also evaluate the range of topics written upon over time and get various grades from this. Therefore, a child who has written about dogs for three weeks and then moves on to another subject has shown progress as they work with different topics and genres.

Revision

During revision since ideas are expanded upon with the use of dialogue, adjectives, details, etc. a child's use of these techniques can be monitored over time and evalu-ated in the context of growth. Grades can also be obtained as we watch children revise with each other and listen to the advice they give to their peers.

Editing

Here we concentrate on standard spelling and other language features such as punc-tuation marks, tense forms, etc. As children self-edit their work grades can be obtained from what they add and what they delete. The editing stage is where I help children work on specific skills. For example, if I feel a child needs to work on punctuation at the end of a sentence I will help correct all other aspects of the draft and then have the child try to punctuate each sentence individually. For example, 'Derek, now I want you to go and read each sentence and try to put all the periods where they belong.' I can therefore, obtain a grade from within the context of personal writing.

Unless I am required by my administration to give formal spelling tests I do not since during draft creation (invented spelling) and editing spelling is naturally addressed. If I must give traditional spelling tests I ensure meaningful work by allowing students to choose their own words from their writing and reading. (For details about 'individualized spelling' see Zaragoza, 1997.)

Sharing

During sharing an oral development grade can easily be taken as the child's expression, voice quality, confidence is monitored over time. Again, each child is evaluated within the context of their own progress and not compared to others. In this way, children remains successful as they grow in writing ability.

Publication

As mentioned earlier, handwriting and final presentation (i.e. neatness of book cover; illustrations) can be used to obtain grades. We need to be careful about what 'standard' we use to decide what is legible. For one child it might be appropriate to be pushed to rewrite a publication for legibility two times but another child might be pushed to a negative frustration point. This is where, again, your knowledge of your children and their individual strengths and abilities will help you to be successful in appropriately assessing your young authors. In this way, too, your students will continue to feel successful as you mentor them into authorship through the writing process.

References

ZARAGOZA, N. (1987) 'Process writing for high risk and learning disabled students', *Reading Research and Instruction*, **26**, 4, pp. 290–301.

ZARAGOZA, N. (1997) *Rethinking Language Arts: Passion and Practice*, NY: Garland.

ZARAGOZA, N. and VAUGHN, S. (1992) 'The effects of writing process instruction on three second grade students with different achievement profiles,' *Learning Disabilities Research and Practice*, **7**, 4, pp. 184–93.

ZARAGOZA, N. and VAUGHN, S. (1995) 'Children teach us to teach writing', *The Reading Teacher*, **49**, 1, pp. 42–7.

Chapter 7

Negotiating Place: The Importance of Children's Realities

Melissa A. Butler

When I first asked the question, 'What can you tell me about your lives?', I never expected such a profound set of answers from my second graders. I went into my classroom located in the Robert Taylor Homes anticipating self-examination.[1] I realized I was crossing a border that many people fear and/or refuse to cross, and I knew I had much to learn. I was prepared for anything. What I found were the most amazing children, more wondrous than I could have ever imagined. They were gentle, precise in their thinking, and open with their hearts. We talked. We talked a lot. As we were reading and writing and painting and dancing we discussed their world and we told each other stories.[2] These stories reflected such a deep understanding of their lived experiences, an understanding that stemmed from multiple sources and different perspectives. As I listened I discovered many things, but much of what I discovered did not make sense at the time. Sometimes when I'm closely involved in a context I get enveloped in the contradictions and end up having a difficult time seeing and making sense of them. My classroom was such a place.

I have recently begun to reflect back on my students' stories and I think they hold levels of significance beyond what I (and my students) originally thought. Their stories are profoundly telling of their realities and dramatically revealing of their experiences and perceptions of the world. In this paper I will share some of my students' stories and try to uncover the knowledges and experiences at work within the specific contexts of their lives. I want to delineate some possible purposes for (and behind) these knowledges and explain the importance of recognizing these understandings within the site of the school and using them as the basis of curricula. Lastly, I hope to offer some pedagogical possibilities regarding these knowledges so our insights from these knowledges can merge with an emancipatory discourse in order to work for projects of social justice both within and outside of the school.[3]

Our story sharing started in the classroom simply as a talking time. We would discuss what was taking place in our lives. After I started realizing the magnitude of some of the things the students knew I decided that their experiences needed to be the basis of our curriculum; our main purpose in school would be to talk and think about the negotiation that took place daily in their lives. We would work towards critical, emancipatory understandings of the world. This had to happen if the children were to feel comfortable talking about their lives. This had to happen if things in the world were to change. We could not be immersed within a 'discipline, content-centered' curriculum and find ourselves enough space to understand our lived worlds.[4] Thus, the stories of experience became the foundation for our investigations into ideas of power, justice, unity, respect, resistance, oppression and change. Our conversations were almost never exclusively descriptive, they were descriptive within a framework calling for change and action. The space we created within our classroom for free, trusting talk had a lot to do with the kind of conversational stories we experienced.

All knowledge, including mine and the students', can never be explained in a stationary way. Our space was complex, full of overlap, re-articulation and contradiction. The origins of our understandings are and forever will be unknown. I do not wish to spend my efforts trying to explain the exact nature of any of our understandings. That would be impossible and ridiculous. What I do want to do is tie together themes of understanding and lay out possible purposes for these understandings. In this regard I hope to provide some new insights about the importance of my students' knowledges and how they, and other knowledges like theirs, need to be taken seriously within the contexts of school.[5] Thus, this paper will serve to legitimize my students and their experiences while also working for a theorized discussion about knowledge that might allow for transference to other pedagogical sites.[6]

As our pool of discussions grew in the classroom, the more I realized the inconsistencies within the students' stories. Sometimes their stories seemed fictitious, other times factual. Students sometimes made a statement in complete contradiction to something they said yesterday. Students would retell certain stories over and over in different ways under the guise of being 'real'. At times, they would add imagined characters or places to their accounts and blend them into the 'real' story. They also sometimes placed themselves as part of a particular story when they were not 'actually' there. They occasionally would talk about something in the future as if it had already happened. There were all sorts of overlaps and contradictions; I had difficulty distinguishing between what was and was not 'real'. When I was confused by the content of their stories I sometimes asked clarification questions. At times this led to clarity (for me), but other times it led to a break in the story and a time of confusion for the storyteller and the other children. I began to realize that perhaps there were different realities at work within these stories. The students' messages could not be separated simply along the lines of fiction or fact. There was something important going on, but I could not name it. Thus, I tended to take their realities for what they were: *the* realities. I questioned the content in private and sometimes with individual children, but generally I simply went with the flow of the class; if they said something was true or that something happened, I believed them and we discussed the world through their eyes. This is certainly not to say that we did not question the world and its realities, for that was the basis of most all of our work. It is the content of their realities that tended to go unquestioned because I did not completely understand the complexities or know how to question those realities without stifling the discussion of them.

Now, as I reflect back on our discussions I have new insights that may help with an understanding about what was going on within the stories and realities of my students.[7] Some questions I have are: Why was I trying to frame the discussions in terms of my own understandings? Why is consistency important, anyway? Why were the students retelling and overlapping their stories? What did they gain from this? What explains this? Were they conscious of their contradictions? Why was I so aware of these contradictions? Why did they enjoy and need to tell about their experiences in this way? What was going on? How important were these constructed realities to their lives?

As I came to understand the way my students put together their own realities I noticed that they had different purposes for their explanations depending on what they wanted and/or needed. There was quite an art to their storytelling and their tellings allowed them to negotiate their lives in different ways. In my current sense of the contexts, I see five main themes which come out of their knowledges in terms of how they *used* them in the classroom and in the community. Most of their stories were told in order

1 to invent what they wished was true (a way of coping);
2 to show off and impress other children (be 'cool');
3 to fit into their consistent understandings of the world;
4 to live within the complexities of hyperreality; or
5 to develop goals and practice ideas for empowerment.

I will now try to show the complexities within these knowledges and how my students' realities seemed to be a compilation of memories, imagination, lived experience, and dreams.

Inventive Knowledge as a Means of Coping

Anytime anyone in the class mentioned moving from the buildings there was an immediate rush of conversation, 'I'm moving too', 'Ah, uh, my mama say we be moving soon', 'Yep, we gonna move to the suburbs'. If I asked when they were moving they would respond by saying anywhere from 'next week' to 'in five years'. Sometimes they would just pick a month and say that was the month they were moving. Their moving stories included much fantasy and imagination. I am quite certain that they heard many stories in their homes about the possibility if moving. I myself heard many a parent say 'we need to move outta here soon' or 'it's ok, baby, we'll be moving soon'. The desire for students to move was so great that they would find every opportunity to talk about this desire in terms of a reality. When they heard someone else speak of the possibility of moving they were reminded that it did, indeed, have potential in their lives. These stories were so important to their understanding of what 'could happen' or what could eventually solve their lives' problems. These individualist dreams were appealing to hold. Even when we would talk and put the community's oppression in a broader perspective and discuss possibilities for change within the community, they still held strongly to the dream of moving.

It is interesting to note that all of my students told moving stories, not just a select few. They rarely called one another on the 'truth' of their stories. If someone in the class said they were moving, we said we would miss them and that would be that. Actually, no individual moving story was ever very long because it inevitably spurred a moving story from someone else. There would be a long spiraling string of brief stories until everyone had gotten a chance to speak on the subject. This kind of discussion was very similar to the talks about the buildings and where people lived. If a certain building was mentioned in conversation, '5041', anyone who knew *anyone* in that building would immediately state that they knew that information. The information about building 5041 would spiral into talk about 5100, 5135, and 5201. Again, there was no lengthy discussion about any of the buildings, they just wanted to state that they knew what they knew. The building talks seemed to be for the purpose of 'showing off' and looking informed. They were also quite fun for the children since they got to talk about something of which they knew so much. The moving stories were a bit different because although there wasn't much substance to the talks and they were fun for the children, they seemed to serve a purpose of 'coping' with immediate lived circumstances. Living the daily struggle of poverty was temporarily lifted by discussing the reality of moving, as temporary as that reality may have been. Since all the children were living in poverty and experiencing similar oppressions, there was collective solidarity in their avoidance of calling each other on the 'truth' of their statements.

Another place where their stories seemed to be for the purpose of coping with lived circumstance was with regards to their fathers. They would often tell stories about their daddies coming to visit around their birthdays and the holidays, especially Christmas. The mood of the class was quite different when discussing their fathers than it was when talking about moving or buildings. Often, only one or two people would tell a story about dads and then the subject would be changed. It seemed that they could only handle talking about their dads for a short period of time.

Many times the talk about daddies would change into a discussion about the birthday or holiday that was upcoming. Birthdays, especially, led to intense sharings about Chuckie Cheese.[8] These talks might start with 'my daddy say he gonna take me and my sisters to Chuckie Cheese.' Other kids would say 'my daddy took me to Chuckie Cheese' and 'So is my daddy — he's gonna give my mama money so she can take all of us to Chuckie Cheese.' They sometimes spiraled into talks about what it was like at Chuckie Cheese and how they were going to (or did) have so much fun. They would go on and on about the pizza they ate and who was at the party and what games they played. These talks would flow like contests; 'I ate two whole pizzas', 'Yeah, but we played all the games *and* ate pizza', 'My mama say next time we gonna get to play all the games we want.' The stories would be clearly fictitious, but extremely fun. Sometimes they would even say they had been to Chuckie Cheese the night before while also earlier saying that they had watched a certain television show we had been discussing. Sometimes I'd say something like, 'Golly, you sure were busy being in all those places at once?!' This teasing would be followed by a coy smile on their part, but never a denial of previous statements; the fantasy was understood and accepted as a different form of reality.

Many of them had, indeed, been to Chuckie Cheese. They did not go as often as they said they did, but they had enough of a history that they could explain the setting of the restaurant, but with obvious creative embellishments. They liked it so much and they, like most children, wanted to go back. If there was a time when they actually got to *go* to Chuckie Cheese they would always make sure that they emphasized the reality if the situation to me. I remember Xavier saying, 'No, Ms. Butler, I mean we *really* get to go to Chuckie Cheese this time — *really*!!' It was important that he emphasize the actuality if the situation because one of his dreams was going to come true. Though the children did not call one another on the 'truth' of these stories either, it was obvious they all knew that the realities they were explaining were indeed 'make-believe'. This is evidenced by their emphasis on '*really*' when they actually did get to go and their ability to be teased about some of their playful inconsistencies. This was fine. They loved telling stories about Chuckie Cheese; it was great fun for them. Since the reality was allowed to become so 'real' in the classroom through many people buying into and participating in the stories, the stories served an important function for the children. Our talks were a wonderful outlet for dealing with disappointment. It seemed that the students needed these stories in order to deal with the lived reality of not getting to go to Chuckie Cheese as often as they wished.

It may seem rather typical for children, no matter where they live, to make up stories about going to a fun place. However, I feel there is a big distinction between my students' stories and similar stories that I may have told when growing up. My students' stories were almost always linked to 'family togetherness', 'reunions with their fathers' or 'spending time and money on friends that they couldn't always see'. They spoke of these things through the discussion of a particular place (e.g. Chuckie Cheese) because they had spent time with family and friends together there before. Similar stories were told about holiday times and birthday parties. They would fixate on the place because it provided the 'easy and collective' story. These stories could rally the excitement in the classroom and create temporary believability for all involved students.

It is important to note that the stories were not only about the future, but also the past. After a holiday time in which there was much disappointment, the students would tell similar stories, but instead of proclaiming what might be, they spoke of what 'had been'. It is here where the collectiveness and safety of the class was so important. They took great personal risk by discussing their 'realities' in these terms. If someone called them on their 'honesty', there could be even more hurt. Talk time was a significant space for dealing with some painful lived experiences. In the context of our classroom which also spent much time discussing the socio-economic, cultural and political explanations of poverty, black-male imprisonment, community violence, police brutality, and other limits to agency, the stories had a synergistic influence. Not only could students playfully deal with some of their disappointments, but they could also gain a critical sense of agency through situating their disappointments as part of larger struggles.

The magnitude and frequency of the 'coping' stories was intense. These stories came and went quickly and often throughout the day. The tellings about birthdays and moving, especially, would come during lunch time and more 'informal' classroom times. Stories such as these could be told without much emotional affect; they could just roll off the tongue like playing the dozens.[9] I considered these stories as much a part of our classroom ritual as our after lunch bathroom break and reading time. They were constant, continuous, charming moments.

Unfortunately, recognition of these stories and their place was not uniformly appreciated by all the teachers in the school. I remember being in the teachers' lunchroom once when I overheard a group of white teachers talking about the 'laziness and irresponsibility' of the children and their parents. They were saying, as they often did, 'They give them birthday parties, Nike shoes, and trips to Chuckie Cheese, why can't they pay for this field trip?' I also remember talking to the other second grade teachers about our students and birthdays. One of the teachers was telling us that all of her students had *big* parties with lots of friends and cake and food. She simply thought that her students were different than mine. 'Your students don't get birthday parties? Well, mine do,' this was the same teacher who said her students 'don't know much about guns and gangs and all that violence stuff'. I wonder if she actually ever listened to her students. They were living in the same buildings as my students, many were even blood-related. Or, maybe this proves how convincing their stories really were. Regardless, the stories were very much a part of the culture of the children in our school. The students' imaginations, memories of past 'good' times, and needs to cope with their disappointments all played an important role in the situation of these stories.

'Coolness' as a Function of Knowledge

Another theme that I saw playing a role in the students' stories was the need to impress other children and to 'be cool'.[10] Of course, this is almost always a function of children's behavior and certainly played a role in the aforementioned stories. However, there were times when the story tellings became even more acutely related to the need to be 'cool'. Again, even though this desire to impress other children can be found in other children's contexts, it becomes much more profound when the desire is directly linked to a need that specifically relates to quality of life and sometimes to life itself. In the lives of my students, being 'cool' was constantly changing and was definitely not simply about image; there was nothing simple about the nature of 'cool' in their contexts.[11]

Much of our classroom discussions revolved around the goings-on in the community and therefore, much of our talks dealt with shootings, funerals, drugs, gangs, police brutality and guns.[12] This is certainly not to say that these were the main things going on in the community. They were, however, the things that the children brought up most frequently for discussion. We spent the entire year discussing these issues in relation to justice, power, unity and change. We never tired of our talks; they were essential to working for community change and social justice. In this context, students' knowledge about particular violent happenings allowed them important speaking space when we were having conversations about working for change. Talking about guns, shootings, drugs, gangs or police and situating the discussion within a question or statement of injustice got excellent attention from the other students in the class. The Sisterhood and Brotherhood of the class depended on the constant interrogation of important community occurrences in relation to our larger emancipatory project. If a student wanted to talk about ants or rocks or something interesting, but seemingly irrelevant to justice, the other students in the class would stop her or him. 'What does that have to do with peace and power?', 'How you gonna help your Brothers and Sisters by talking about that?' and 'That's nice, but what does it have to do with us and *our* People?' were constant comments students made to one another. I must admit I was a bit surprised when they started to focus all of our conversations around our larger project, but they did and I was not going to stop them.[13] It was exciting.

In the context of our classroom, though, 'cool' was defined in stark opposition to how it was otherwise defined in the community. The negotiation between contradictory 'cools' was a constant problem for the students to handle. When talking about the shooting in the community, for example, there was a continuous string of contradictions between the 'coolness' associated with being in a gang and the 'coolness' of speaking out against gangs in the classroom. Nothing would cause a backlash from classroom Brothers and Sisters more than a child saying she or he wanted to be in a gang. Thus, their descriptions about gangs, drugs, and shootings consisted of 'cool' impressions they received from the street, messages they learned from older siblings, images they got from the media, and ideas they were discussing in school.

When I first started talking with students I quickly realized that they would try to out do one another with stories about recent shootings and funerals. 'There was a boy — he got shot', 'Yep, he be my cousin's friend', 'Ah, uh, my mama say we gonna go to the funeral', 'Yep, we gonna go too and my uncle know the boy, the boy was his friend', 'I heard the guns and I saw the body, now the body's in the hospital.' The stories would continue until all who wanted to speak on the matter had a chance. These stories were not necessarily consistent as evidenced by the discussion of both going to the hospital and the funeral. This frequently happened, but it seemed not to matter to the students. The talk time provided an important space for reflection about the violence in their lives as well as providing a bit of a 'spectator outlet' for them to show off what they knew. The children with the most information got the most talk time. It was exciting to have something important to say and to have the forum for people to listen. This kind of 'cool' took place both inside and outside of the classroom.[14]

Much of what the students knew was not only learned from the community in terms of its articulated meaning, but was also learned in terms of its performance. I witnessed much performance on the part of my students once they stepped out of the classroom.[15] They could perform 'toughness' and show certain gang affiliations. They could talk about guns and drugs and funerals as if they were not bothered by them. They could show affects that would change depending on who was watching them; affects were subtly different with parents than they were with teenage acquaintances in the buildings or police working in the streets. I am not certain if they could have articulated what they were doing upon request. Their understandings about how to act outside of school was visceral and instinctive.[16] The purpose of these understandings was for survival which was inextricably linked to the nature of being 'cool' in different contexts.

In contrast to the understandings outside the classroom, the negotiation of 'cool' within the classroom was quite different. Examples of negotiation can be evidenced through much of our discussions about gangs and guns. Guns were 'cool' in many ways. My students, though they would say things like 'put down the guns and pick up the books', would also easily slip into a hand gesture we called the 'gun move'.[17] The boys would also fold intricate, paper guns, like I used to fold notes. In addition, if the visual art was not abstract and related to a project we were doing, the boys would almost inevitably draw people who were 'the gangsta cool' guy equipped with Nike shoes, a side-ways hat, and a gun in hand.[18] These things happened almost instinctively. If I or other classroom Brothers and Sisters questioned the students, they would act as if they were surprised they had produced such art or made such a gun signal. No one ever got 'in trouble' for doing these things, we just raised questions about them and tried to put these actions within a broader context. When Gerald once pointed his finger like a gun to Christopher's head, Ebony asked: 'What do you mean by that? Are you trying to kill your beautiful, Black Brother?' Gerald was taken back and said '*no!*' and then looked confused.

When dialogues like this took place and I tried to push further and ask questions such as: 'Why do you think Ebony asked you that question? Was it an important question? Have you seen other kids make the 'gun move'? What is it that makes that move 'fun'? Why do you like to do that? Gerald, especially, would try to deny that he liked it. He would act as if he was getting in trouble and try to deny that he wanted to make such a 'gun move' in the first place. However, some of the other boys, especially the ones who used the 'gangsta cool pose' frequently, had their thinking and agency extended by being allowed to discuss the desire behind their felt contradictions.[19] They would identify where they had seen certain images and styles and say that they liked the images because they made them feel good (in varied ways). Because they could identify some origins of their desires and attempt to articulate them, the conversation about the consequences of their actions went deeper than it otherwise would have gone.[20] By creating awareness of the 'gun move' and other 'gangsta cool poses', and relating these actions to larger community struggles, the students became more conscious of their actions and better able to feel and articulate why these actions might be harmful for them and the community.

Discussions along these lines seemed to be due to multiple factors. The students liked to discuss what they lived, and they held onto and utilized certain understandings in order to function in their world; most importantly, though, these discussions seemed to revolve around their desires to be 'cool' in whatever contexts they might find themselves. Whether it was inside or outside the school, children were concerned with how they were perceived and this notion strongly influenced their practices of certain knowledges. Again, the importance of how they were perceived goes beyond style. The purpose of focusing on 'coolness' was, for them, a survival skill. To be able to slide into a pose in order to fit in, but to balance the pose so as not to fit in too well was the art of being 'cool'.[21] The fact that 'cools' ran in direct contradiction in certain contexts made things all the more problematic and all the more necessary to learn. Students needed to understand their place in the community and the school and be able to negotiate their safety and identity in both locations.

The classroom dynamics, though problematic in their contradictions, almost served to liberate the students' ideas of 'cool'.[22] By eventually discussing the purposes and appearances of certain 'cools' the students found some agency within their performances, instead of simply acting on instinct. The students became the source of their 'cools' instead of merely acting within certain prescribed 'cool' roles; this allowed them some control over their lived situations. 'Cool' became a strategy they could employ in different contexts. They could articulate what the dangers were in their lives, they knew how they needed to handle them individually (act 'cool'), and they could also place their struggles with larger contexts of injustice. It is within this overlap that their lived knowledges merged with their ideologies and combined with a pedagogy of hope within the classroom, thus allowing students to embrace a more liberatory perspective about their worlds.

False Consistencies of Understanding

One of the biggest challenges I faced as a teacher was getting children to move their thinking beyond 'yes vs. no' and 'good vs. bad'. This was often frustrating because even when students understood certain complex phenomenon, they had difficulty expressing the complexities.[23] I remember being so struck by some of their descriptions; guns are bad, drugs are bad, gangs are bad, police are good. They would make quick statements like this, yet most every detailed story they told would run counter (or skewed) to these stipulations. Why? Where were they learning these 'good-bad' ideas? Why were their statements running in contradiction to their understandings and otherwise stated ideas? What was the need for such simple statements?

Students would often call gang bangers 'bad'.[24] They would say, 'he used to be good, now he be bad all the time', 'those gang bangers be killin' all our people,' 'guns be hurting us all the time'. This analysis would also extend to statements about drugs. 'Drugs kill your brain and are making your head turn upside down'. 'The drug man at the store — he be mean', 'Those are the boys who be selling drugs — they don't care about us.' They would also write poems about these issues and often tint issues in the community in this negative light. Police, too, seemed to be frequently explained within the dominant paradigm of 'safety'.[25] Students would sometimes say, 'I would call the police' or 'I want to be a police' as their 'solutions' to problems. A few times when police would be walking down our hallways, some of my students would smile the blindest, most cheery smiles and exclaim 'Hi!'[26]

There were elements of truth within the students' statements, yet there was something quite off about them. We could have just had a powerful discussion about police brutality where certain students shared stories about family members getting beaten up by the police.[27] Students could have just explained how the police and the gang bangers trade guns and drugs or how the security in their buildings lets the drugs be sold anywhere.[28] Even after their own articulation of such events, they would still resort back to oversimplified, dominant viewpoints. This did not always happen, and there were certain students who never allowed themselves to speak in the dominant discourse or within its paradigm. The fact that many of the students did, however, is still quite problematic.

I can only speculate as to the need for these concordant, simple explanations of reality. First, the students are children and many of the adults in their lives encouraged them to repeat and chant phrases over and over.[29] There is a level of routine in their talk at times; they say things just because they are *supposed* to say them. Also, the media has a strong influence on children. Even though we spoke and questioned as much as we could, there were so many images and assumptions that we missed in the process. Negotiating *New York Undercover*, alone, was a difficult task.[30] How could we have possibly uncovered all the assumptions that the students embrace through watching their typical six to seven hours of TV per day? They were constantly seeing commercials, movies, and TV shows where police saved the day, drugs were the result of the 'evil' gang members, and guns were only held by 'mean' people. The discourses within the media were exhaustively fortified within the students' world views.

Another dynamic at work within the students' understandings of 'good' and 'bad' was their parents and care takers. I heard many parents, some involved with drug trade themselves, flat out saying to their children, 'you ain't gonna get yourself messed up with them people or they drugs!' and 'you stay away from those boys, you hear, they be gettin in trouble and bein bad.'[31] I think the parents were so concerned about protecting their children from the shooting, trading, and using surrounding drugs that they said, candidly, 'drugs are bad, people that use drugs are bad, and you stay away — I don't want you killed.' This is most likely due to both the extremeness of the situation (the felt danger was profound), as well as the fact that parents felt they needed to speak 'simply' to children. The result of this parental talk, whatever its specific reason, had penetrating effects on the students' articulated understandings.

To revisit the idea of 'coping' once again, this too played a role in the students' need for simple dichotomies. It was difficult for them to deal with their lives' placement in the world. Why wasn't their community like the ones they saw on TV? Why were the police violent and unreasonable when the messages from TV kept saying the police are there for protection and safety? How come people who sell and use drugs are 'bad' when some of the people they love most in the world sell and use drugs? How come guns are 'bad' when the police give guns to people in the community? How come selling drugs is 'bad' when the money from them is what provides for clothes and food? The contradictions were endless. My students were told one thing, but saw and felt another. How could the result be anything other than feeling 'bad' about themselves? They were living within what every-one(thing) around them was telling them not to *do* and not to *be*. The most obvious way for them to make sense of things was to declare individual convictions contrary to everything in the community. This made things simple and easy. They would be 'good'; they would not use drugs, they would not be in a gang, they would not touch a gun, and they would smile at the police. Everything would be fine, right?

Quite to the contrary, everything would not be fine. Though this world view was seemingly comfortable for the students, it in no way addressed the larger social contexts at work within the students' lives.[32] This is where classroom pedagogy played such a considerable role. The students needed a space to articulate their understandings, talk about their desires, fears, and hopes and realistically probe the world through a critical, liberatory lens.

It is meaningful to point out that though many of the parents verbalized much of the same 'simple, dichotomous' discourse as the children, their understandings were seemingly different. The parents with whom I spoke very much grasped the social dynamics at work within the larger world. Many could speak about the complexities of their situations and point blame outside of the community to larger social structures. The distinction, I think, between their role as parents and mine as a teacher living outside the community, is that they *lived* there. Their lived experiences dictated a different agenda. I often ask myself, 'how could people living under the conditions of day to day poverty and violence articulate anything other than an individualistic agenda of escape?' There were huge limits to their personal agency, let alone the collective agency of the community. They could not hope to change the structures influencing the community. They could only see getting themselves out of the situation and perhaps getting a few family members out with them. This is not to say that all of the parents I knew wanted to 'get out'; there were multiple viewpoints as there are anywhere. Some parents seemed to think this was just the way it *was*. Others knew it shouldn't be this way, but also knew there was not much of a possibility for them to leave. Still others saw their oppression as staying with them no matter where, geographically, they lived. Regardless of the variance of thinking, the mentality of individual escape and individual discipline about 'staying' clean' permeated the discourse and understandings of the children.

The curriculum of our classroom directly addressed this individualistic discourse and tried at every turn to question and dismantle it. I saw huge changes in the children due to these questions and discussions. Their abilities to make sense of their lives while not having to ignore the inconsistencies was so empowering.[33] Their agencies grew from the refocusing of blame away from themselves and the people they loved; we were able to focus our attention to broader, more complex explanations of oppression. Their need for false consistency was no longer necessary for their understanding of the world. They still voiced certain dichotomies and acted uncritically at times, but generally, the critical groundwork had been built for them to use as a means to liberate both themselves, their community, and their world.[34]

Hyperreality and Contexts of Contradiction

One of the most strongly visible attributes of my students' understandings was their contradictory nature. These inconsistencies, as previously stated, were used in order to cope, be 'cool', and fit into certain prescribed ideas of the world. Through all of these areas, though, there seems to be an underlying hyperreality for the students.[35] Many times the students were conscious of the argumentative 'flaws' within their stories, but many times it seemed that the overlap of their stories was beyond their grasp.[36] The students were seeing so much from so many different places that they seemed to almost be experiencing vertigo. The overwhelming nature of their lives caused them to locate themselves within certain contexts in adaptive ways. However, through this adaptation, there seemed to be a lot of confusion and uncomfortability in the process. This caused them to not always 'know' when something was or was not 'real'. It went beyond their constructions of varied realities at different times; there were moments when hyperreality seemed to overwhelm them and they had little control over what they 'knew'.[37]

For example, the students would have many new stories each week about who was shot and who was involved, but the data surrounding the discussions was always a bit fuzzy. It was never quite clear if the shooting victim died, if the victim was in the hospital, who heard the shots or what exactly led up to the incident. It was extremely difficult to tell how much violence there actually was in the community. There would be times that students would talk a lot about shooting, but this did not always correspond with the stories I was hearing from the parents in the community. I remember a time when parents told me there had not been shooting for over two weeks, though the students had been discussing a shooting incident just the day before. Did this mean that the children were lying? Did this mean that the violence in their lives was so felt and deeply understood that it was difficult for them to distinguish between fantasy and 'reality?' After all, if there was always the fear of shooting because lived experience proved it could happen at any time, why does it matter if it 'really' just happened or not? For children who have memories of violence, watch it on TV, dream about it, and constantly discuss it in and out of school, why wouldn't it seem like it 'just happened' or 'always happened?' Their realities were so caught up in their fantasies of what 'should be' and the bombardment of images of 'what is' and 'could be' that it all seemed to be a jumble of stories that were told through permutations in different contexts. This created times of deep confusion and sadness for the children; there were moments when no sense could be made of anything.[38]

A specific example of the confusion that was sometimes felt by myself and the students can be found with Derrick. Derrick came to school one day and was very upset. He had been scatter-brained for a few days; he was always playing in his desk and was thinking about something else during our discussions. He seemed to be floating somewhere beyond where we were. He said, 'My mama, Sharon, and me got to move or else they gonna kill us — they after my daddy and they can't find him.' I tried to think about what I should do. I asked him if he wanted me to call his mom and take them someplace safe. He said, 'My mama said I can't tell no-one or else I'll get it.' I was frantic, yet he seemed so calm. I asked what he needed and he said he didn't know.[39] He seemed calm, but still understandably unsettled. The next day he came to school and I asked what happened and he said, 'I don't know.' He retold some of the same story, but didn't seem as upset; I couldn't figure it out. That day at lunch I talked with Sharon (his fourth grade sister). I asked her about the situation; she knew nothing about it.[40] She looked at Derrick and he then looked down at his food. She told me more about her story of the situation, but she seemed to be confused about Derrick's story.[41] She went over to him, hugged him and whispered something in his ear. Later, when I talked to Derrick, he still seemed confused. I don't think he purposely told a 'lie'; he did not seem to completely understand the situation. He was floating around with all sorts of possibilities in his head and he was scared. Later in the summer I spoke with Derrick's father about his story.[42] There turned out to be some 'truth' to Derrick's story, but he seemed to organize the situation differently than it happened. Derrick has an amazing imagination; his thoughts are extremely profound and he definitely overlaps many ideas within his thoughts. I think he was overwhelmed with his situation and a bit confused. In order to escape from the whole situation and try to make sense of it, he went into his imagination and came out with his story which was very real to him. His realities were always so distant, but yet so profound.[43] He would periodically 'leave' the reality of the world in order to deal with his pain. This did not necessarily help him make sense of his life, but it allowed him to become numb to its painful effects.[44]

The students did their best to discern things, but sometimes they could not and thus, things got scary. Sometimes there wasn't much we could do, but the classroom space allowed freedom for mistakes, jumbled thoughts, unclear conclusions, and questions. The children were always trying to make sense of their lives through making connections and striving to articulate their ideas and feelings. Since our classroom was safe and solely for the purpose of working for liberatory understandings, much of what might have otherwise gone unquestioned, was discussed. This allowed students to at least feel comfortable within temporary moments of confusion.

Imagination as Empowerment

I recently called Whitnesha on the phone. She was telling me about her 'dancing job' downtown. She said her teacher, 'You know, Ms Chicago', fired her because she was speaking the truth about her black people. Whitnesha said, 'The white kids were telling me about their school and they ask about mine. I just said that we learn peace and power and they just told up on me. Ms Chicago didn't want me telling those white kids about the projects and about other black kids.' Whitnesha went on at length about her power and how she is trying to spread peace to everyone. 'You know, Ms Butler, they is resisting me! Now, what am I going to do? They need to know the truth!' It is quite exciting to hear Whitnesha talk. She seems to be practicing her powerful strategies by talking about them as if they were 'real'.[45] Her memories of a particular context are merging with her imagination and lived experience and are facilitating her vision for the world. For her, this appears to be quite liberating.[46]

Other occurrences such as this happened in the classroom, especially towards the end of the year. Students would choreograph confrontations in order to talk about resistance, power and respect. They would also dramatize daily experiences and have intense conversations within their dramatizations.[47] I was completely amazed by their detail and discussion about collective strategy. What was happening? Were they escaping their 'realities' in a new way? Had they moved beyond 'coping?' Were they really enacting possibilities for systemic change?

The students appear, now, to be moving into a new form of understanding. They are incorporating all of their knowledges (and their functions), but it appears that their focus is *towards* something, instead of simply *against* something. This growth and understanding of purpose both in school and in the community has strongly influenced their senses of agency. It is here where their knowledges are merging with their sense of purpose and resulting in the most fantastic of stories. They are starting to prepare themselves for action; their goals for the world are starting to surface through their explanations of reality. It seems that this focus is encouraging them to view more possibilities within the world.[48]

My students' realities are an interwoven package of stories. The knowledge which creates these stories is negotiated through a combination of memory fragments, lived experience, imagination and future goals. The students construct their realities in relation to the contexts in which they find themselves. Sometimes the contexts are playful, other times they are threatening. Their negotiations occur on the edges of these contexts. The children are attempting to find their places in the world, a world which feels unjust, yet one in which they want to find hope.

The knowledges which create their stories are inextricably tied to their personal needs for survival;[49] there are pragmatic aspects to their survival as well as a need for collective struggle which affords them much endurance in their quests for survival.[50] In what places do the students see themselves as needing to persevere? What kind of sustenance is needed? How can this best be attained? What strategies do the children use in order to deal with their particular contexts? These questions are revealing. Sometimes they need to be playful and dream away their disappointments. Other times, they need to blend in and work around certain constraints. They can adapt their 'coolness' in multiple ways to assure their security, or they can use it to probe new liberatory understandings. At times the children embrace simple ideas without thinking; much has been entrenched within their minds. They may cling to particular notions in order to simplify their lives and create more 'certain' understandings. They may, in some contexts, have no articulate understanding of their situation; the confusion may result in a moment of paralysis. Most all the children living in the context in which my students find themselves experience many lived contradictions between the realities in the media, the realities at school, the realities on the street and the desired realities in their minds.[51] The question, for me, is not to prove or disprove whether these negotiated realities exist for all children in all contexts, but rather, to look at how we can work to assist students in finding places of possibility within their places of contradiction.[52]

The way students understand their own lives is significant.[53] It is the way they come to know their own identities in relation to others and the world. It is the means by which they negotiate their own agencies in places where limits to agency are profound. Recognizing the depth of their stories is essential. Legitimization of their knowledge affirms their lived experience and encourages their power to examine the world. If taken seriously, their knowledges can serve as a basis for them to begin to collectivize their struggles and work *towards* something; if ignored, their negotiations will stay at an individual level and serve purely functional purposes of survival.

Too often the school is a place where these knowledges are ignored and/or intentionally shut out. The dark cloud of the school bruises the brightness of hope and possibility within its children. This results in children losing interest in school and, many times, also losing interest in themselves and their worldly purposes. We need to find ways to make student knowledges the basis of school direction and curricula. The pedagogical space of the classroom provides a safe location where agencies can be exercised in relation to an emancipatory project. If we care about larger issues of justice and liberation, we must listen to our students. They have voices of possibility and hope.

As I was finishing this paper, I spoke with Whitnesha on the phone. She asked me what I was doing and I told her I was writing this paper. She asked me to explain what I was writing. I told her the paper was about knowledge. I said I was writing about all of the things she and her classroom Brothers and Sisters knew. I said, 'I'm trying to prove how much you know and how smart you are.' She said, 'Ms Butler, you don't have to prove that, but we could show it.' I asked, 'What do you mean?' She replied, '*all* they got to do is *come* visit and see us, then they *all* would know.'

I think Whitnesha is precise; it is not difficult to hear and learn about children's thoughts. I believe students' knowledges need to be better understood within the framework of their realities. We must discern the purposes of their stories so we can provide opportune spaces for them to extend their thinking and better negotiate their places in the world.

Notes

1 The Robert Taylor Homes is a housing project consisting of 28 buildings on the South Side of Chicago. The housing is completely segregated; the tenants are exclusively African American.

2 In this paper, stories are defined as tellings about life, descriptions about day to day experiences.

3 The cultural work of social justice is my larger project; it influences many of my assumptions regarding both research and teaching.

4 We were/are working within a poststructuralist, post-modern view of curriculum. For more analysis about this paradigm, see William F. Pinar (1995) Chapter 9.

5 I am most concerned with the action and collective work that could be inspired by this research.

6 By pedagogical sites I mean more than just schools; spaces exist in myriad places and contexts.

7 The type of research I am doing runs counter to the positivistic notions of the scientific method and objective, controlled investigation; for more theorized analysis about this type of research, see Joe L. Kincheloe (1991) Chapter 3.

8 Chuckie Cheese is a pizza restaurant chain where there is both pizza and games!

9 For an excellent description of 'playing the dozens' and its situation within a context of 'coping', see Richard Majors and Janet Maucini Billson (1992), pp. 101–2.

10 My understanding of the term 'cool' has been strongly influenced by *Cool Pose, What Is Cool?: Understanding Black Manhood in America* by Marlene Kim Conner (1995) and much music, including music by Ice T, Ice Cube, Arrested Development, A Tribe Called Quest and Miles Davis.

11 *Cool Pose*, p. 5.

12 The basis of all of our work was descriptive and then interpretive about the community. Our writing workshop time, especially, was spent writing essays and poems all about the community, what the students saw, heard, smelled, felt, or in any other way, knew.

13 I recognize that this pedagogy might be disturbing to some people, since it directly avoids focusing the instruction on content about specific 'classic' fields of study. My work as a teacher was not to fill my students with content knowledge that someone else determined. My cultural work had the aim of working for a liberatory discourse that my students could create, embrace, and use in fighting for their lives and a broader social justice.

14 I often heard children talking about 'recent' events in the lunchroom, hallways, and bath-rooms. When this type of talk happened outside the classroom there was no mediating force or placement within a particular politics. When the discussions took place inside of the classroom, there was much room for us to talk about these experiences in terms of their collectivity and contextual meaning. In both contexts, 'cool' played a strong role.

15 The significance of this performance is further explained in *What is Cool?*, pp. 30–2.

16 At times we talked about the issue of what their 'performances' meant. For instance, we had much discussion about Maya Angelou's *Life Doesn't Frighten Me* (1978 1993) in which the students realized that there were many ways to deal with being frightened. Some said they would 'let things roll off their back', 'act tough', 'sit straight' or 'be still and don't say a word'. These discussions helped them articulate what their bodies per-formed in certain contexts.

17 The 'gun move' refers to the pointing of the fore finger and thumb like a side-ways 'L' to mimic a gun being held to someone's head.

18 The boys were the students who did this type of art almost exclusively. When the girls did non-abstract art they tended to draw rainbows, hearts, and friends. There were large gender gaps with regards to what students expressed about their community. The boys spoke much more vividly and graphically of the violence. The boys, too, had a much more difficult time negotiating their desires when they ran contradictory to what they 'thought was "right"'.

19 For a more thorough analysis of the dialectic between pleasure and ideology, see Henry Giroux and Roger I. Simon (1989), pp. 14–19.

20 It is here where students often show outward resistance since though they may under-stand that guns are harmful to the community, they may feel that their voice is being shut out by not allowing space for them to make sense their visceral feelings.

21 I will never forget D'Angelo. He was the coolest of the 'cool'. He was a strong part of the classroom, giving important ideas and feelings, yet he never took complete control

and became 'the leader'. In the hallways, all the older kids knew who he was (which could be extremely dangerous since older kids want the younger ones to follow in their footsteps without question). Outside of the school, D'Angelo amazed me even more. He would look around and seemingly understand all the dynamics at work. He would seem shy, yet would speak out strongly if someone spoke to him. He didn't draw attention to himself, yet he always made his presence known. He could adapt to any situation with ease.

22 Our discussions about 'cool' were not easy at first. It was also not easy for students to almost 'become different people' when they were in the classroom. Their lived experience about 'cool' did not help them perform in the classroom; their experience helped them talk and formulate ideas, but the 'cool' performance in the classroom was quite different and had to be learned anew.

23 Some people may argue that children of the age that I taught were not 'developmentally' ready for such thinking. I do not buy into any systematized order of learning stages; each child is different and experience is often the biggest indicator of such 'readiness'. My students' experiences were certainly much different than any of the children studied for official reports of 'developmentally appropriate learning and teaching'. Also, the most exciting aspect of teaching is getting children to express what they 'know' in multiple ways. The fact that this area was frustrating for us is more telling of my students' experience than it is about their developmental stage.

24 Here I am not confusing 'bad' with its meanings of 'cool' or 'down' or 'good'. I am using 'bad' in its traditional sense, not something the students wanted or liked.

25 I am using 'dominant paradigm' as the set of viewpoints that is most readily heard and embraced by mainstream media, corporate business, and 'functional' schooling.

26 When students said 'Hi!' it was not a mocking resistance. Eventually, they thought about their actions and some of their 'hellos' became a reversal of respect and thus, a form of resistance. Initially, though, the greetings were out of blind, unquestioned, respect'.

27 I vividly remember when Derrick calmly, yet passionately told us how the police came and hit his Daddy 'up side the head with a long, hard stick until he was down on the ground bleeding' and then how the police took his brother and 'pushed him against the car and hit him over and over until he cried and got into the police car'. The students and I listened and we knew; we understood.

28 This frequently happens in order for the police to get information out of certain gang members. They will also ask for drugs in exchange for guns and visa versa, depending on what kind of 'collection' is being encouraged by the city or the 'community police team' at the time.

29 This is extremely scary to witness within a classroom. I have gone into many classrooms where students are all seated and uniformly chant 'Good morning, how are you?' or if asked a question, all say 'Yes!' with the same tone and pitch of voice. It is as if students are encouraged to answer questions without thinking about them and say things just because it is 'polite' or 'right'.

30 NYU is a TV police drama which airs Thursday nights on FOX. The police are extremely 'cool' on the show at the same time the show deals with things of which the students easily relate. It is confusing for the kids because it seems to 'true', yet the police characters are not at all what they personally experience.

31 This phrase was often followed by an affectionate, but stern look and bop upside the head.

32 This view would in no way help the students to 'survive'. There needs to be a move beyond individual explanations for poverty and violence; the systemic causes need to be addressed in order for lived conditions of oppression to change.

33 Wow! The students created the most amazing things. They would write poetry raising the most profound questions, paint abstract pictures that uncovered the hidden feelings in their lives, and develop dances that spoke to the audience with a gentle honesty and intense hope. Their work encompassed everything in their lives. They not only knew they were going to change the world when they got older, they knew they were in the process of changing it *now*! It was magical to witness.

34 Without this pedagogical space, students would simply re-articulate 'consistencies' that they were told to speak in order to fit themselves into the dominant paradigm of the world. For this to work and make their lives less oppressive, the dominant paradigm must actually fulfill its promise of equal, individual opportunity, fairness, and justice. However, the entire context in which my students found themselves disproves this possibility.

35 I am using this term to explain the phenomenon of realities having no literal grounding; ideas and images which come from multiple angles all at once and overlap with their inconsistencies to create contexts which are *hyper*-real.

36 As evidenced by the game playing stories — stories about buildings, Chuckie Cheese, etc.

37 It is not that they ever completely lost their power of agency, but at times it seemed like they were spiraling out of 'grounded' understanding and their methods of coping and finding consistencies did not work.

38 I can vividly remember times of us sitting together talking and having nothing make any sense. Someone would ask the question 'why?' about something and we just would not know. At times we cried, other times we spoke to each other through our eyes and there were moments when we simply let the mass of confusion wash over us and pass as quickly as it came.

39 I gave him my phone number (though he already had it) written largely on a piece of paper and told him to call me at any time and I would come pick them up and take them wherever they needed to go.

40 Sharon and I already trust for one another, so I knew that she would respect that Derrick had told me in confidence and she would understand my position.

41 She said that she did not know where her Daddy was. When I asked if he could be in trouble, she said, 'Yes.' She said her mama was alright, but that they were trying to move because her older brother kept getting in trouble. The older brother was a largely affiliated gang member. She seemed quietly concerned about the situation (their family situation was often in flux).

42 Derrick's father had been in and out of jail. After his last release, he was 'straight', but then got back into 'selling' in order to make some money; the selling led to using which explained Derrick's flux of behavior. He said he had gotten in trouble with the gang, but it had blown over. However, he wanted to move the oldest son out of the neighborhood so they could be safer. He said they were never in danger.

43 He would always float in and out of the classroom discussion and was at his best when he could freely paint, dance, and write. His thoughts were always the most amazing; out of the blue he could create and articulate thoughts that held such intense insight.

44 This is, in a way, a sense making practice. It makes sense because it allows temporary 'survival'.

45 Though Whitnesha has, in the past, had a dance class, she has never had a dancing job and does not currently attend any classes.

46 I speak with her often on the phone. Every time I call she is playing 'dance class' or 'school'; she tells me what she is teaching and how she plans to have her students change the world. She is full of spirit and spunk and could talk for hours about her ideas about how to 'help her black brothers and sisters.'

47   I particularly remember Ronald and Xavier dramatizing a store owner and a man who was stealing something from the store. They went on for at least 20 minutes, acting out the stealing, the chasing, the police that put the man in jail, then the man escaping from jail thus inspiring another chase. The skit became a cycle with commentary throughout. All of us sat and watched in amazement. There was so much to their story; it was profoundly telling of their thoughts about current injustice and what they wish could happen. It was brilliant.

48   All of my students are now being taught by my friend and thus, I keep in contact with their new insights. Their work is currently quite focused on the possibilities for changes within the world; they are mentally preparing themselves more and more for collective resistance against systemic oppressions.

49   Again, survival does not just mean protection *from* something; there is also the working for collective survival *towards* something.

50   These can be found through their performances on the street and in their buildings.

51   Here I am generalizing based on my experience with a small group of children. I have spoken with enough children in the area to feel confident that much of their knowledge and constructed realities have underlying parallels.

52   This focuses the research work towards what *can be done*, and is not merely a re-articulation of what *is*. I am not trying to speak for my students in a different language. My purpose is to elucidate the children's voices to the best of my ability in order to encourage that their knowledges be taken seriously.

53   I recognize that even though this is important, it is difficult to grasp what children do and do not understand. It is also hard to distinguish between what they know and what they have come to know through investigations. The human being as subject is constantly changing and thus, the process of identifying knowledge is also a process of creating new knowledge. It is a never-ending process.

References

ANGELOU, M. (1978/1993) *Life Doesn't Frighten Me*, New York: Stewart, Tabori and Chang.

CONNER, M.K. (1995) *Cool Pose, What Is Cool?: Understanding Black Manhood in America*, New York: Crown Publishers.

GIROUX, H. and SIMON, R.I. (1989) 'Popular culture as a pedagogy of pleasure and meaning', *Popular Culture, Schooling and Everyday Life*, New York: Bergin and Garvey.

KINCHELOE, J.L. (1991) 'Exploring assumptions behind educational research: The nature of Positivism', *Teachers as Researchers: Qualitative Inquiry as a Path to Empowerment*, London: Falmer Press.

MAJORS, R. and BILLSON, J.M. (1992) *Good Pose: The Dilemmas of Black Manhood in America*, New York: Simon and Schuster.

PINAR, W.F. (1995) 'Understanding curriculum as poststructuralist, deconstructed, post-modern text', *Understanding Curriculum*, New York: Peter Lang.

The names of the children have been changed in order to protect their privacy.

Chapter 8

Using Dramaturgy in Educational Research

Ellen Swartz

Introduction

Within the last two decades, numerous and trenchant critiques of curriculum and pedagogy have revealed the Eurocentric character of 'standard' school knowledge.[1,2] Specifically, critiques from the fields of multiculturalism, culturally relevant studies, and Afrocentrism have provided theoretical and practical alternatives to this 'standard' (Asante, 1991, 1991/1992; Banks, 1992; Fox-Keller, 1985; Goodwin, 1996; Harris, 1992; King, 1991; Nieto, 1992; Tedla, 1995; Thompson, 1986; Wynter, 1990a and b).[3] In the classroom ecology tradition of research, ethnographic approaches have been successfully used to gather rich 'life-like' data and findings about many of these alternatives which are often called emancipatory (Anyon, 1981; Grant and Sleeter, 1986; Ladson-Billings, 1994; Lampert, 1990; McLaren, 1986/1993; Shakes, 1995).[4]

In a recent ethnographic case study that examined the use of emancipatory concepts in teaching and learning (Swartz, 1996b), Erving Goffman's concept of dramaturgy (1959) was used as a way to frame data collection, analysis, and findings. In this framework, the voices and actions of a study's participants are represented (and re-presented) as a way for them to consistently speak for themselves rather than only be spoken about by a researcher. Recounting what occurs as classroom drama or performance wherein the voices of all participants are 'cast' as roles that *will* be heard by readers, avoids the typical reduction of ethnographic accounts to brief excerpts of the researcher's choice. In this way, dramaturgy has the potential to democratize ethnography by more fully representing the voices of those present.

This article re-enacts and critiques sections of fifth grade social studies lessons that exemplify emancipatory concepts. This demonstrates how a dramaturgical approach to case study research allows both researcher and reader to make their own interpretations and meanings. It also shows how dramaturgy is well suited to the examination of emancipatory concepts such as those found in the fields of multiculturality, culturally relevant teaching and learning, and Afrocentrism.

Emancipatory Concepts

In studying the emancipatory theories and practices of multiculturality, culturally relevant teaching and learning, and Afrocentrism, I have observed a number of
broad characteristics that are common and compatible among them. Knowledge
from these fields demonstrates that effective teaching and learning are based on
high expectations of students and an approach to knowing that requires the use of
inclusive and indigenous scholarship (Asante, 1994; Banks, 1992, 1995; Harris,
1992; Keto, 1989; Ladson-Billings, 1994; Swartz, 1992a).[5] Teachers and students
are encouraged to expand their knowledge and ways of knowing, become authors
of ideas and questions, solve problems, and act with critical agency (Freire, 1970;
Goodwin, 1996). They are invited to build upon what they know, and to ask questions and take positions that 'standard' curriculum and pedagogy don't — about
the vantage point of narration, the subjectivities and inter-subjectivities of all those
who were and are present, about the role of power relations in who leads (hierarchy/
heterarchy) and whose interests are served (Fox-Keller, 1985; Giroux, 1992; hooks,
1989, 1991, 1992; Morrison, 1992a).[6,7] In these fields of study, teachers and students
are centered in their own learning and encouraged to think with consciousness, care,
and responsibility about the relationship between what they are teaching and learning and their own individual and collective lives (Hilliard III, 1986; King, 1991;
Noddings, 1991/1992; Underwood, 1991). Following are nine specific emancipatory
concepts drawn from these broad characteristics to use when examining pedagogy.[8]

1 Problem-posing pedagogy
   Student 'ownership' of, and engagement with, curriculum is enhanced
   when a teacher facilitates an instructional process that asks questions or
   poses problems. When students are invited to participate in this way, their
   responses are part of creating the content of curriculum.
2 Student-centering
   Students are centered in instruction when discussion and dialogue occur
   that acknowledge and build upon their personal characteristics and multiple
   and overlapping group identities.
3 Relevance of community and culture
   Familiarity with students' culture(s) is essential because the selection of
   pedagogical approaches is affected by teachers' perceptions of the community and culture(s) of their students.
4 Critical thinking
   Pedagogy that asks students to answer open-ended, critical questions requires them to use higher levels of thinking (e.g. interpretation, analysis,
   synthesis). Relying on only recall and 'right–wrong' questions is avoided
   because it creates student passivity and alienation from the learning process.
5 Active learning
   Active learning occurs when students discover knowledge in ways similar
   to doing what practitioners such as historians, scientists, and mathematicians do. Students are invited to think about their own and others' questions

or assumptions in order to develop concepts for further exploration and research.

6   Indigenous knowledge and accurate scholarship
    Voicing the indigenous narratives and knowledge bases of all cultures and groups, including those that have been historically silenced and misrepresented, avoids the inaccuracies that occur when knowledge and knowing are seen as the proprietary space of privileged groups. Using indigenous knowledge centers specific groups as the subjects of their own narratives. When these narrative are combined, a more comprehensive account is produced.

7   Validity of students' knowledge
    Beginning where students are and building on what they already know through questions that connect their personal, family, and community lives to curricular content, invites them to value what they know as a foundation for further exploration.

8   Addressing issues of justice
    Taking stands against inhuman, criminal, and unjust practices (e.g. enslavement, genocide, colonization, child- and wage-labor exploitation) avoids the selective valuing of life based on race, class, gender, and other supremacies. This curricular practice reflects a commitment to fairness and equity.

9   Multiple ways of knowing
    Ways of knowing such as reason, personal and group experience, logic, intuition, the scientific method, authority, and empathic understanding and caring are positioned in heterarchal rather than hierarchal relation to each other in curriculum and pedagogy. This means that each way of knowing may 'lead' (in the sense of being the most effective way to know something in a particular context), and that no way of knowing is innately superior to others.

This study's examination of pedagogy for the presence and use of emancipatory concepts in a classroom produced re-enactments and critiques of teaching and learning that can be studied by preservice teachers and practitioners. Before presenting these, the following section more fully explains how drama has been used in the research practices of other educators, and how dramaturgy can be viewed as a validity practice in ethnography.

Drama and Ethnography

Drama has an obvious metaphoric relation to teaching and learning because it uses language, gestures, signs, and symbols to create a context for communication and engagement. Peter McLaren has critically examined the performance nature of school practices and rituals (e.g. the bells, the pledge, the regimented movement of groups, the disciplinary routines, the instructional protocols) in a working class school (1986/1993). In one example, he described how student behaviors changed upon entering school in the morning and moving '... "offstage" ... where they must write their student roles and scenario in conformity to the teacher's master script. ...' (90). Within this trope, his ethnographic research described school as a multiply-staged, ideology-wielding series of dramas with characters, roles, scenes, and scripts.

Madeleine R. Grumet provides another 'take' on drama and schooling by suggesting that dramatization can help to rework inequitable power relations in classrooms (1978). By conceptualizing curriculum and pedagogy as dramas, teachers and students can come together to create knowledge — to collectively make what is abstract concrete. This coming together of different characters to share the stage(s) — whether their roles are large or small — uses a dramaturgical form to value all voices equitably — to make a way for all voices to be heard on multiple levels.

Constructing yet another 'take', the eminent anthropologist Victor W. Turner conceptualized ethnography as performance almost three decades ago (Turner and Turner, 1982). As a teacher of anthropology he involved his students in developing performances of ethnographic data in order to give them an 'inside view' of other cultures that would transcend their mere cognitive understanding. Turner and Turner reported that they also gained insights from viewing and participating in these performances — insights that they were able to turn into hypotheses for future field testing. Their dramaturgical approach to ethnographic data brought participants and researchers closer to knowing and understanding that which occurred in the original. It is this closeness or 'closer-ness' to the original that can facilitate pedagogical analysis as well.

Dramaturgy can also be seen as a way to create a credible and trustworthy portrayal of what occurred in the field — a description that participants reading it later could say, 'Yes, that's what happened ... I remember that ... that's what I said. ...' As Goffman explains, theatrical re-enactment also acknowledges the dramaturgical structure of all social interaction in the sense that such interactions are remembered and recorded (in our minds and other ways) as vignettes, narratives, accounts, stories, etc. with numerous ways to 're-play' them. In this way, dramaturgy can be seen as a validity practice that also shapes the final form of data presentation.

In traditional ethnography, the word 'record' means 'to set down in writing or the like as for the purpose of preserving evidence'. The etymology of the word 'record' reveals root meanings that further support the idea of dramaturgy as another way to represent or 're-present' ethnographic findings. 'Record' (or 're-cord') is a combination of the Latin *recordari* (to remember), *re-* ('again and again' to indicate repetition), and the Greek root *chorde* (gut) which is a string or thin rope made of several strands braided, twisted, or woven together. Thus, the social interaction that is 're-corded' is 're-membered' (much in the way that Barbara Christian uses this hyphenated version 're-member' to mean putting the parts back together, 1995), meaning that the members (constituent parts of any structural or composite whole) are able to be put together again and again. The 'cord', which is made of gut (intestinal tissue or fiber used to make tough strings; basic and essential) represents (and 're-presents') the significant members or constituent parts that are the braided-together strands of what occurred.

In the lessons presented below, the original 'performance' was made by those who observed it because they were its participants (i.e. students, teachers, researcher), and it was 're-corded' (or 're-braided') as a 're-performance' by weaving back together the actual (taped and written words) and remembered (observations) social interactions in the form of scenes in a play. Participants' meanings and interpretations of what occurred were made around and through their own and others' roles in the form of critical commentary. Each dramatic performance differed from non-ethnographic drama in that the 'script' and the thoughts of its author were continuously informed and re-informed by the 'actors' as they lived the actual events of their real lives. These 'actors' appear in each lesson through a remaking of events that intends to let their voices and mine come together to do the directing. All ethnographic accounts have implicit dramaturgical qualities; these 'performances' make such qualities explicit.

Pedagogical Examples of Emancipatory Concepts: Students as Researchers

The classroom examples that follow were selected because they demonstrate the nine emancipatory concepts above. They were selected from lessons about the pre-Columbian African presence in the Americas, Taino culture before the arrival of the Spaniards, the meeting of the Taino and Spaniards, and ways of working toward equality and justice given a 500 year history of colonialism in the Americas. Most of the examples were drawn from lessons taught by practitioner Susan Goodwin of Rochester, New York who was invited into the study to teach a class of fifth grade students. A few examples were taken from my interactions with the same students on related topics. Ms Goodwin is an experienced teacher whose practice is based on emancipatory concepts which she consistently and artfully demonstrated in this study. As the action researcher studying these concepts, I also tried to use them as I interacted with students. While future research is needed, the excepts that reflect these attempts suggest that emancipatory concepts can be effectively used by inexperienced teachers if they are familiar with the concepts and are exposed to classroom demonstrations of them.

Each example was selected because it demonstrates the concept under which it is listed, it may also demonstrate other emancipatory concepts — all of which are identified in brackets and bold type where they appear.

1   Problem-posing pedagogy

Student 'ownership' of, and engagement with, curriculum is enhanced when a teacher facilitates an instructional process that asks questions or poses problems. When students are invited to participate in this way, their responses are part of creating the content of curriculum.

Ms Goodwin was teaching a lesson on the pre-Columbian African presence in the Americas. After reading about the fourteenth century emperor of Mali, Abubakar II, she discussed Abubakar's 2000 ship ocean voyage with students.

Ms Goodwin
2000 ships? How many people do you think it took to sail all those ships? [*emancipatory concepts one and four*]
Brandon
A million?
Karen
10 000
Ms Goodwin
Well, maybe not a million but many thousands [*emancipatory concept six*]. So, do you think they got there?

Ms Swartz — observer
Here is the critical problem posed again — now in a way where students have enough indigenous content to think about it and perhaps 'solve' it [*emancipatory concepts one and four*].

I think a couple got there and most of them sank.
Ms Goodwin
Why do you think that? [*emancipatory concepts one and four*]
Jamal
Some would be able to make it.
Ms Goodwin
Does anyone have anything to add to that? [No response.] Columbus — how many ships did he have?
Roland
Three.
Ms Goodwin
Did they all make it?
Several students
Yes.
Ms Goodwin
Well, so if Abubakar lost even 10 ships, how many would be left? [*emancipatory concepts one, four, and nine*]
Danisha
1990 ships.
Roland
Maybe they split up.
Ms Goodwin
Oh, that's a good idea! Maybe some went to Puerto Rico, some to Mexico, and some to other places in the Caribbean [*emancipatory concepts seven and nine*].
Jamal
I agree with you now.
Ms Goodwin
You do? [smiling and pausing] Well, that's *nice*. I need all the help I can get! Well, we see their bones, sculptures, and portraits, so we *know* they got here.

Ms Swartz — observer
This section reflects a problem-posing pedagogy that poses problems by asking students open-ended and critical questions. 'So do you think they got here?' is the whole point of the lesson or the problem posed by the lesson — to voice the indigenous narrative and knowledge base of the Mandinka as part of the evidence for the early presence of African people in the Americas, and to involve students as historical detectives in deciding what they think [*emancipatory concepts five and six*]. Ms Goodwin asked students to reflect on what they thought about this possibility based on what they had just learned — from using the methods of knowing the past that Ms Goodwin had previously discussed with them. By asking students (some of whom doubted if too many of Abubakar's ships made it to the Americas) to compare the Columbus voyage to Abubakar's voyage, she asked them to analyze, interpret, and synthesize what they knew, which involved reason, logic, and personal experience [*emancipatory concept nine*]. Building on Roland's comment that maybe the ships split up, used Roland's response — based on what he already knew from personal experience — to 'create' the content of the curriculum by using his voice [*emancipatory concepts seven and nine*].

2 Student centering

Students are centered in instruction when discussion and dialogue occur that acknowledge and build upon their personal characteristics and multiple and overlapping group identities.

Ms Goodwin showed students several slides of Olmec Heads and asked questions that considered the identities (e.g. cultural, personal), experiences, and knowledge of her African American students.

Ms Goodwin
What's the picture on the right? [a back view of an Olmec Collossus Head] Monica? [shaking her head as if she didn't know] I see at least two on your head. Regina? [not picking up on the clue either] I'm looking at them *all* around *your* head [*emancipatory concepts two, three, six, and nine*].
Danisha
[raising her hand and finally calling out] Braids, braids, braids.
Ms Goodwin
Yes, and there are beads at the ends of each braid. [students looking back at the picture again] And who traditionally wears braids in their cultures? [students not seeming sure] African people! As a matter of fact, they [archaeologists] have found that the seven braids carved on Olmec heads matched the hair-braiding styles worn in Nubia and Egypt, which are in East Africa. So the Olmec heads might even be portraits of East African people [*emancipatory concept six*].

Ms Swartz — observer
Several students began to say who was wearing braids and counting the students wearing braids. The number was six until Mr Baker, the classroom teacher, pointed out that Arthur — who also wore breads — had not been counted.

3 Relevance of community and culture

Familiarity with students' culture(s) is essential because the selection of pedagogical approaches is affected by teachers' perceptions of the community and culture(s) of their students.

In a lesson about the similarities between the Taino culture and students' families and cultures, we talked about the ways in which cooperation was part of the Taino way of life as well as a part of our own. Because I was familiar with some of the cooperative activities that go on at church, I was able to build on students' group experiences and knowledge.

Ms Swartz
Who goes to church? [many students raising their hands] Ok, so sometimes you go to church and there's a special day where everyone comes together and does certain activities. What are some of the special days days in your church. [*emancipatory concepts one, three, four, and seven*]
several students
Sunday.
Martin
First Sunday.
Cassandra
First Sunday is Women's Day.
Ms Swartz
So what do women do on Women's Day? [*emancipatory concepts one and seven*]
Nicolas
Go to church.
Danisha
They do a program.
James
They go shopping.
Ms Swartz
OK, so to do the Women's Day program, women have to go shopping to get some things, they have to plan, they have to cooperate, they have to work together to make a successful program. That's communal, that's working as a community. So that might be one thing that is similar between your culture and the Taino culture. [*emancipatory concepts six and seven*]

4 Critical thinking

Pedagogy that asks students to answer open-ended, critical questions requires them to use higher levels of thinking (e.g. interpretation, analysis, synthesis). Relying on only recall and 'right–wrong' questions is avoided because it creates student passivity and alienation from the learning process.

This excerpt is from a lesson on the arrival and meeting of the Spaniards and the Taino, and the ensuing conquest of the Taino by the Spaniards. While several emancipatory concepts are used in this example, Ms Goodwin's use of open-ended and critical questions is consistent throughout and encourages students to interpret, analyze, and synthesize information.

Ms Goodwin
[showing a slide of a Taino cacique wearing a guanin or gold symbol of power around his neck] What is the cacique wearing around his neck?
Roland
Gold.
Ms Goodwin
So what do you think the Spaniards thought when they saw this large piece of gold? [*emancipatory concept four*] [No response.] Well if I take out two hundred dollars worth of bills to buy a bag of potato chips, what would you think? [*emancipatory concept one, four, seven, and nine*]
Karen
That you're rich.
Ms Goodwin
Yes, and what else? [*emancipatory concepts four and seven*]
Ali
That you crazy.
Ms Goodwin
Well, what do you think the Spaniards thought? [*emancipatory concepts one, four, and seven*]
Mr Baker
That you might be willing to share it.
Nicolas
Someone might try to take the 200 dollars from you.
Ms Goodwin
When the Spaniards saw the gold that caciques wore, they thought that they had a lot of gold and they wanted it. They took so much gold and other resoures from the Caribbean and Mexico and South America that Spain became the richest country in Europe [*emancipatory concept six*]. And what do you think happened to the people that they took all this from? [*emancipatory concepts one, four, seven, and nine*]
Janet
They got poor.
Ms Goodwin
Yes, and what else? [*emancipatory concept four*]

Ms Swartz — observer
These cultures were changed.

Ms Goodwin
[continuing to show slides of the Spaniards with guns and attack dogs, their invasion and torture of the Taino, and their resistance] So how were their cultures changed? [*emancipatory concepts one, four, five, six, and nine*]
Sholanda
People were killed.
Ms Goodwin
Yes and they were enslaved by the Spaniards who came with an agenda to take their land and to force them to work. We have two different value systems operating at the same time. [*emancipatory concept six*]

Mr Baker

What is an agenda?

James

Something you're going to do.

Mr Baker

Yes. Do you think that the Spaniards wanted to share?

Several students

No.

Ms Swartz — observer

Mr Baker reflected the focus of the lesson as he asked students to think about and interpret the meaning of the definition he had just asked for in the context of the lesson, which invited their voices into the lesson to be part of creating the curriculum [*emancipatory concepts one and four*]. He also reflected the indigenous voice when he asked about the Spaniards sharing as an example of the term 'agenda' [*emancipatory concept six*].

Ms Goodwin

What happened in this period of history affected what history was going to be like for the next 500 years — what it was going to be like for Indigenous people, for African people, for European people. It tells us about Resistance, Rebellion, and Revolution, and it's 1995 and we still have Resistance, Rebellion, and Revolution [*emancipatory concept six*]. So who was enslaved before African people in the Americas?

Karen

The Taino.

Ms Goodwin

Yes, now I'm going to ask you a few questions to see who's paying attention. This is a question I ask my students. What grade are my students?

Kisha

Eighth grade.

Ms Goodwin

No, tenth grade. But do you have to be in a certain grade to be able to think?

Several students

No.

Ms Goodwin

Where does thinking come from? [*emancipatory concept four*]

Ali

Your head.

Ms Goodwin

Yes, from your mind. So how does the history of the last 500 years still affect us today? When you're considering the answer you're thinking about the Indigenous people, African people, and European people.

Ms Swartz — observer

This way of introducing a lesson summary engaged students, some who had not been paying attention, by referencing her tenth grade students and asking these students whether you had to be in a certain grade to be able to think. This let them know that they could use their minds to come up with an answer, and that Ms Goodwin was using their knowledge as part of the content material of the lesson [*emancipatory concept seven*]. This is another example of how Ms Goodwin posed questions that engaged students [*emancipatory concept one*]. She constructed know-ing as possible by making students aware that she saw them as thinkers and as learners whose understanding was related to paying attention. This strengthened her relationship with students by centering them in instruction [*emancipatory con-cept two*]. It also asked them to respond to an open-ended, critical question that required higher levels of thinking such as interpretation, analysis, and synthesis [*emancipatory concept four*], and to pursue knowledge through discovery and active learning [*emancipatory concept five*].

5 Active learning

Active learning occurs when students discover knowledge in ways similar to doing what practitioners such as historians, scientists, and mathematicians do. Students are invited to think about their own or others' questions or assumptions in order to develop concepts for further exploration and research.

Ms Goodwin showed slides of Olmec heads and asked students to reflect upon what they saw through discovery and active learning.

Ms Goodwin
What's he wearing on his head?
Maxine
A hat.
Martin
A helmet.
Ms Goodwin
What's the difference? Who wears a helmet? [*emancipatory concepts one and four*]
Joshua
Soldiers wear helmets.
Janet
Soldiers.
Ms Goodwin
So if an emperor were going exploring, might he take soldiers or guards with him? [*emancipatory concept one*]
Several students
Yes. Yeah. Yes.

Ms Swartz — observer
This use of archaeological evidence to form an assumption and reflect on its possibility represents active learning in that this is how historians develop concepts that they then research. [*emancipatory concept five*]

6 Indigenous knowledge and accurate scholarship

Voicing the indigenous narratives and knowledge bases of those groups that have been historically silenced and misrepresented avoids the inaccuracies that occur when knowledge and knowing are seen as the proprietary space of privileged groups. Using indigenous knowledge centers specific groups as the subjects of their own narratives. When these narratives are combined, a more comprehensive account is produced.

Ms Goodwin
(explaining how the same currents that may have brought Abubakar II to the Caribbean also brought Columbus) So what do you think happened when Columbus arrived? [*emancipatory concepts one, four, and five*]
Jamal
I think it wasn't too friendly.
Ms Goodwin
Why? [*emancipatory concepts one and four*]
Jamal
If somebody tried to come over here and take my land, I'd be pretty mad.
Ms Goodwin
Do you think that the Taino were upset as soon as they saw Columbus and the Spaniards, or do you think that they waited to see what these newcomers were about? Had they met strangers before? [*emancipatory concepts four and six*]
Several students
Yes.
Ms Goodwin
Who?
Sholanda
The Mandinka.
Ms Goodwin
Yes, we learned about the Mandinka coming, so the Taino had met people from other places before. But what happened when the Spaniards came? [*emancipatory concepts five and six*]

Ms Swartz — observer
Even though the question about whether the Taino were initially upset with the Spaniards or waited to see what they were about posed only two options, its narrower construction seemed necessary to guide students past a typical Eurocentric pitfall that suggests that hostility may have been a two-way street, or an inherent response to the arrival of strangers. This master-scripted suggestion or implication avoids the reality of a friendly Indigenous welcome, which is central to an indigenous account, responded to by Spanish aggression and invasion. [*emancipatory concept six*]

7 Validity of students' knowledge

Beginning where students are and building on what they already know through questions that connect their personal, family, and community lives to curricular content, invites them to value what they know as a foundation for further exploration.
Ms Swartz
[after showing slides about Taino life] The Taino had a communal way of life which was one of their traditions. What does that mean — a communal way of life?

Cassandra
They worked together.

Ms Swartz
Yes, they worked together as a community. They shared the land, and they worked together for the benefit of everyone. They were cooperative. Do we live in a community?

Several students
Yes.

Ms Swartz
This classroom is also a type of community. And sometimes we work together, we're cooperative. What does that remind you of — the word cooperative? [*emancipatory concepts one and nine*]

James
Together.

Ms Swartz
When you get in groups to do projects what is that called? [*emancipatory concepts seven and nine*]

Jamal
Cooperative learning.

Ms Swartz
Yes, cooperative learning.

Martin
What is going to be the first notes?

Ms Swartz
Thanks, Martin for reminding me. Cooperative learning is your first note, because we're seeing something about the Taino people from a couple thousand years ago that we're doing today. In other words, we're learning this from our ancestors — from the people who came before us. [*emancipatory concepts two and seven*]

Ms Swartz — observer
Building upon students' knowledge of their classroom as a community and on their experience with cooperative learning gave them a valid way to connect their own knowledge and experiences to something similar in Taino culture.

8 Addressing issues of justice

Taking stands against inhuman, criminal, and unjust practices (e.g. enslavement, genocide, colonization, child- and wage-labor exploitation) avoids the selective valuing of life based on race, class, gender, and other supremacies. This curricular practice reflects a commitment to fairness and equity.

During a lesson on the Spanish invasion and conquest of the Taino, Ms Goodwin suggested that what happened 500 years ago in the history of the Americas is still affecting us today. She introduced the concepts of Resistance, Rebellion, and Revolution, and James later added a fourth — Research. Ms Goodwin suggested one way to fix the situation is to work for justice and equality, and then she asked us to think about how we could do this. On the following day, I facilitated a discussion with the class on this topic.

Ms Swartz

Yesterday we talked a lot about what happened 500 years ago and how that's still affecting us today, and when Ms Goodwin asked us to think about this, we talked about the three R's — Resistance, Rebellion, and Revolution, and then later James added a fourth 'R' which was Research. Ms Goodwin suggested that one way to fix the situation was to work for justice and equality, and then she asked us *how* we would do this. . . .

Kareem

[calling out] Forget the past.

Ms Swartz

Kareem, how would that help us to work for justice and equality? [*emancipatory concept four*]

Kareem

I would just forget about it.

Ms Swartz

So are you saying that we have equality and justice in this country now? [*emancipatory concept four*]

Kareem

Yeah.

Ms Swartz

You do? [*emancipatory concept nine*]

Kareem

No.

Ms Swartz

OK, if you don't, are you saying that there isn't equality and justice in this country? [turning to the class] What do you think? Can knowing about the past deal with this — with not having justice and equality? [*emancipatory concepts one and four*]

Jamal

I think that we should never forget the past because the past is what makes us what we are today.

Ms Swartz

Can you say a little more about that? How does the past make us what we are today? [*emancipatory concepts five and nine*]

Jamal

We don't live in a perfect would . . .

Ms Swartz

[several students talking to each other] Is everyone listening . . . Joshua did you hear what Jamal said?

Joshua

[shrugging his shoulders]

Ms Swartz

Let's listen to what he is saying. [nodding to Jamal to continue]

Jamal

We don't live in a perfect world but we can improve by learning from the mistakes of the past.

Ms Swartz

OK, learning from the mistakes of the past. Kareem, what do you think about that? Could we learn from the mistakes of the past? [*emancipatory concepts one and two*]

Kareem

Yeah.

Ms Swartz

Yeah, I would think we could. Who would like to read their ideas from their homework paper about how we can work for justice and equality? OK, you have to speak in a loud voice so everyone can hear.

Tina

We can work together.

Ms Swartz

Yes, if we want to have justice and equality, we have to work together. Any other ideas? [No response.] Let's talk about what is justice. What does justice mean? [*emancipatory concept one*]

Janet

Peace.

Ms Swartz

OK, peace is a part of justice because if there was justice, there'd probably be more peace. What else is justice? Yes, Martin. [*emancipatory concepts one and four*]

Martin

Kindness.

Ms Swartz

Kindness? Well yes, if people were kinder to each other then there'd be more fairness and there'd be more justice. That's a good idea. Any other ideas? [*emancipatory concepts one and two*]

Kareem

Freedom.

Ms Swartz

Freedom, tell me a little more about it. I *know* freedom is a part of justice, tell me how. [*emancipatory concepts one and nine*]

Kareem

They should have did their work their own self instead of having slaves do it.

Ms Swartz

Yes, they shouldn't have made other people work for them and not pay them anything. That wasn't fair and it wasn't just. So for there to be justice, there has to be freedom and fairness. [*emancipatory concepts seven and eight*]

Ms Swartz — observer

As we discussed how to work toward justice and equality, students were using and building upon personal and cultural experiences to reflect their awareness of the 'do unto others' concept and its relationship to having peace, kindness, and fairness. Taking a stand about what I saw as unfair or wrong opened the door for students to use their own knowledge and experiences in the discussion. [*emancipatory concepts two, three, four, seven, eight, and nine*]

Brandon

There won't be no war.

Ms Swartz

All right, so if there was justice, it might be a way to avoid war, it might be a way to have peace, which was Janet's suggestion. Kareem, one thing I got from what

you were saying is that if people treat other people the way they want to be treated
... [*emancipatory concepts two, five, and seven*]

Kareem

[finishing my sentence] ... they treat us the same.

Ms Swartz

Yes! So if you're trying to work toward justice, then you would probably treat
people the way you want to be treated. So that might also mean that you wouldn't
participate in anything that you thought was wrong. It also might mean that you'd
be fair to yourself. What does it mean to be fair to yourself? [No response.] How
would that bring about more fairness in the world if you were fair to yourself? Any
ideas on that? [No response.] What does that mean, fair to yourself? Roland?
[*emancipatory concepts one, four, seven, and nine*]

Roland

You want to do things that you think are right.

Ms Swartz

OK, that's how you'd be fair to yourself?

Roland

[nodding yes]

Ms Swartz

You'd be *thinking* about what was right and trying to do that. [*emancipatory
concept seven*]

Joshua

Never put yourself down.

Ms Swartz

Thank you very much! That's good Joshua! Never put yourself down. Be good to
yourself. Now how does that help us have fairness in the world — being good to
yourself and not putting yourself down? Yes? [*emancipatory concepts one, four,
and seven*]

Cassandra

Like if somebody treats you wrong and you think it's not right for them to treat
you wrong, you can tell the person and you can say like why people should treat
other people right — the way they want to be treated.

Ms Swartz

OK, Joshua, did you want to build on that?

Joshua

You shouldn't pick on somebody else because somebody picks on you.

Ms Swartz

OK, so if somebody picks on you, what are you going to do? [*emancipatory
concept one*]

Brandon

Tell 'em you don't want to be picked on.

Ms Swartz

What if that doesn't work? [*emancipatory concept one*]

Arthur

Walk away.

Mr Baker

What if it doesn't work?

Brandon

You could talk to 'em.

Ms Swartz
You could talk . . . you could walk away . . .
Mr Baker
Remember your drug resistance education.
Joshua
Or you could fight back.
Ms Swartz
Sometimes you might have to fight . . .
Martin
And if you don't want nobody else to put you down, don't put them down.
Ms Swartz
Right. Who heard what Martin said? Anybody can repeat it. [No response.] See, part of learning and being in a community is that we have to listen to each other. Martin, will you say it again? [*emancipatory concept nine*]
Martin
If you don't want nobody to put you down, don't put them down.
Kareem
That's what I was going to say.
Ms Swartz
Good!
Mr Baker
Treat them as you want them to treat you.
Ms Swartz
Right, so, getting back to Kareem and Jamal's point, how can we learn from the past? [*emancipatory concept four*]
Janet
Whenever you make a mistake in the past, don't make it in the future.
Ms Swartz
So, if you make a mistake, and you know it's a mistake, then one way to fix it would be don't repeat it in the future. I think we've come up with a method or a way to work toward justice and equality: Don't repeat the things that you know are a mistake or wrong. So the kinds of things the Spaniards did to the Taino — we wouldn't want anyone to repeat that abuse. Yes, Cassandra? [*emancipatory concepts one, two, six, seven, and nine*]
Cassandra
I thought about a way that we could work for equality and justice is that we could think about how we were treated and what kinds of rights and what kind of rules did we have to follow by and then we could speak about it and work it out with other people.

9   Multiple ways of knowing

Ways of knowing such as reason, personal and group experience, logic, intuition, the scientific method, authority, and empathic understanding and caring are positioned in heterarchal rather than hierarchal relation to each other in curriculum and pedagogy. This means that each way of knowing may 'lead' (in the sense of being the most effective way to know something in a particular context), and that no way of knowing is innately superior to others.

When Ms Goodwin was presenting indigenous knowledge regarding a Pre-Columbian African presence in the Americas and discussing it with students, Mr Baker asked her why we don't know this information. Why haven't we heard about it? Her response was, 'Geniuses know and that is what we are making here — geniuses! People in college learn about this, and some students in high school learn about it as well.' She used authority (based on her knowledge of the topic and her own person-hood) and empirical and experiencial knowledge about where this topic is taught and who learns it to confidently respond to a question that could have dysconsciously and unintentionally cast doubt on the content of the lesson or taken it off in the direction of 'proving' that Eurocentric content has omissions — an important point but not one that needed to be discussed at that time. This turning of possible doubt into engagement brought students' individual and collective attention to knowing something about themselves and their community. In this way, Ms Goodwin framed her African American students as potential geniuses and scholars — a pedagogical intervention that used *and* stimulated multiple ways of knowing.

Conclusion

Dramaturgy is a research practice that is congruent with emancipatory concepts found in multiculturality, culturally relevant teaching and learning, and Afrocentrism. It presents the multiple voices and perspectives of participants in heterarchal rela-tion to each other, and creates contexts within which specific uses of pedagogy can be identified and critiqued. This 'you are there' approach to data also carries an integrity with it because it exemplifies the connection between an intervention and the constructs that underlie it. Thus, dramaturgy allows constructs such as inclusion, indigenous representation, conscious and critical questioning, multiple epistemo-logies, and critical agency to come to life in an ethnographic account. Dramaturgy also allows readers access to enough information to develop their own interpreta-tions and meanings. My analysis of what occurred can inform readers but does not 'require' concurrence or engender indifference through the absence of enough data to allow readers to question my interpretations and make their own. While my author-ship privileges my interpretations, a dramaturgical form of ethnography more fully preserves the presence of others in the research process. By comparison, traditional ethnographies select and codify small snipets of conversation and snapshots of context to insert in authors' texts as support or verification for their essentializations of the re-cord(ing).

As a research practice, dramaturgy is filled with infinite and inferential strands of information and meaning; it has an aesthetic character that brings clarity to the quotidian and provides a valued place for each individual voice (Alexander, 1990; Geertz, 1990; Goffman, 1959). Standing within such strands it is possible to hear and retain multiple voices, to observe constraints and freedoms, and to see how context is interrelated with personal and social identities. The use of dramaturgy clarifies that ethnography has two 'presents' — the one of the actual events and the one that was re-corded. The later endures through writing and reading, the former in the bodies, minds, and hearts of the participants.[9]

Notes

1   The term 'Eurocentric' refers to a body of myths, symbols, ideas, theories, and practices that exclusively or predominantly value the cultural manifestations (e.g. philosophy, cosmology, history, politics, art, language, music, literature, technology, economics) and productions of people of European origin as superior and universal. As a worldview, Eurocentrism subordinates and often denigrates the cultural manifestations and productions of people from all other lands of origin as inferior (Keto, 1989; Swartz, 1992b). While comparatively few in number, the historical and cultural accounts and perspectives of people of European origin in the last five centuries that are *not* confounded by supremacy are not considered Eurocentric by this author. This is central to understanding the difference between that which is Euro-sourced or European-centered, and that which is Eurocentric.

2   'Standard' school knowledge refers to monocultural and monological curriculum, pedagogy, and other school practices that have historically privileged dominant cultures and groups (e.g. race, class, gender, nationality). 'Standard' school knowledge exists in all disciplines and predominantly reflects the history, culture, achievements, and productions of Europeans and their descendants who are white, economically advantaged, and male. Women, Indigenous and diasporic African, Native American, Latin American, and Asian cultures and groups are largely invisible in 'standard' knowledge or when present, are typically marginalized and misrepresented (Asante, 1991/1992, 1993; Joseph, 1988; Sleeter and Grant, 1991).

3   Following are brief descriptions of multiculturalism, culturally relevant teaching and learning, and Afrocentrism:

   • Multiculturalism is a term that reflects an education shaped by theory, pedagogical practices, instructional materials, and school policies and practices which work toward fuller participation and empowerment of all constituencies in the school environment. While many versions of multiculturalism have been identified (Olneck, 1990; Sleeter and Grant, 1988), an emancipatory practice of multiculturalism creates contexts wherein cognition, affect, and behavior are vehicles with the capacity to produce transformative narratives throughout the schooling experience. Such narratives are collaboratively constructed by students, teachers, administrators, parents, support staff, and the community, and require the collective and equitable representation of diverse cultures and race, gender, and class groups. Likewise, the knowledge base of schooling is multiply informed through the gathering and integrating of race-, class-, culture-, gender- and other-specific data bases that have historically been omitted or misrepresented (Goodwin and Swartz, 1993). Pedagogically, an education that is multicultural (in an emancipatory framework) is problem-posing and problem-solving in the Freirean sense (1970). It promotes high expectations and standards of scholarship by teaching students how to critically interrogate, imagine, and produce knowledge, not only to remember and restate it.

   • Culturally relevant educational philosophies (Ladson-Billings, 1992a and b, 1994) acknowledges students as members of diverse and overlapping groups and search to know, invite, and incorporate the special strengths and ways of knowing and being of each culture or group into the classroom and into instruction. Culturally relevant educational philosophies acknowledge systemic oppression and use content reflective of students' cultures as a way of creating meaning and understanding; foster humane and equitable classroom relations in emotionally safe atmospheres of warmth and caring, and view knowledge as continually created, recycled, and shared.

- Afrocentrism is a philosophy and movement that seeks to center African peoples and their ways of knowing, being, and doing as the subjects of indigenously constructed narratives rather than objects of other peoples narratives about them Asante, 1980, 1987, 1991). It is an ethically-framed world view built upon an *à priori* core that takes as given that humanity is embodied equitably in all people and that none are inherently superior (Keto, 1989; Nobles, 1986). In the case of schooling, putting such a philosophy into practice counteracts the distortions, omissions, and misrepresentations evidenced in school texts, curricula, and pedagogy. In this way, Afrocentrism is an example of a centrist philosophy and practice that uses indigenous knowledge as a necessary component of accurate scholarship and an antidote for dominant ideology and the limited knowledge base that it produces.

4 Emancipatory practices involve the use of multiple ways of knowing, behaving, and being. In schooling, such forms of curriculum, pedagogy, and other practices contest and refigure dominant patterns of knowledge formation, dissemination, and perpetuation by identifying them and demonstrating how to replace them with patterns that are multiperspectival and antithetical to privileging relations of power (Swartz, 1992a). Emancipatory practices center students in a process of teaching and learning that is based on problem-solving and problem-posing rather than only on the transmission and reproduction of information. Students are viewed as critical agents able to combine scholarship with personal and cultural knowledge of themselves and others that can liberate themselves from such dominant patterns and practices. Emancipatory practices seek equity and justice in schooling and the reconstruction of practices that limit the life chances of some students while privileging the life chances of others (Apple and Weis, 1983; Freire, 1970; Giroux, 1983, 1986, 1992; Lather, 1989).

5 Indigenous scholarship is produced through the philosophies, spiritual practices, values, beliefs, and productions of specific groups whose membership is constituted through complex and overlapping subjectiities (e.g. race, class, gender, nationality, language, religion). Groups' past and present knowledge bases survive and cohere because they reciprocally meet the needs of the communities that have shaped them through time (Goodwin, 1995). Indigenous knowledge bases stand on their own — that is they exist through lived and daily-made ontological, epistemological, and cosmological expressions in all disciplines and in popular culture. For example, Afrocentricity seeks to further uncover and build upon indigenous knowledge, which, in the case of schooling, can counteract the distortions, omissions, and misrepresentations evidenced in school texts, curricula, and pedagogy. In this way, centrist philosophies and approaches use indigeneity as an antidote for dominant ideology and the limited knowledge base that supports it. If youngsters are not well connected to the indigenous knowledge bases that represent who they are (e.g. African, Native American, Asian, womanist, Latin American), *which are multifacted not monolithic*, they are dislocated from their community(ies). Students' individual as well as communal identities and linkages are obscured without exposure to indigenous scholarship (Asante, 1993; James, 1993; Karenga, 1990, p. 29).

6 The term 'subjectivities' refers to various group identities such as race, class, gender, nationality, language, religion, regionality, age etc. These multiple, overlapping, and contingent locations or subject positions are a major force in shaping the identities of individuals and groups (Giroux, 1992; Hooks, 1989).

7   The terms hierarchy and heterarchy refer to power relations and leadership. Heterarchy combines a form of the Greek work *heteros* (different, other) and *arch* (leader) as compared to the term hierarchal which combines a form of the Greek word *hiero* (holy, sacred) and *arch* (leader) (Lincoln and Guba, 1985). In education, using the concept of heterarchy means that curricula and pedagogy are not based on an innate 'natural' ordering or pre-arranged superiority of ideas, beliefs, groups, methods, etc., but on a shifting order determined by multiple, overlapping, and contextualized factors. Ordering within systems is seen as made through human constructions and interests and therefore differing and changeable — not inevitably ruled or led by any one of them.

8   This list of nine emancipatory concepts is not an exhaustive list, but one drawn from a particular pedagogical context. In other words, other lessons or other reviewers might elicit some of the same but also some other concepts. These concepts became the basis for discussions, pedagogical critiques, and critiques of students' productions during the case study (Swartz, 1996b) from which examples were drawn for this article.

9   I wish to thank Susan Goodwin for her insightful assistance in developing my understanding of emancipatory teaching and learning, and for her artful modeling of these practices. I am also grateful to Molefi Asante and Gloria Ladson-Billings whose respective articulations of Afrocentrism and culturally relevant teaching and learning have been a guide in the development of my work.

References

ALEXANDER, J.C. (1990) 'Analytic debates: Understanding the relative autonomy of culture', in ALEXANDER, J.C. and SEIDMAN, S. (eds) *Culture and Society: Contemporary Debates*, New York: Cambridge University Press, pp. 1–27.

ANYON, J. (1981) 'Social class and school knowledge', *Curriculum Inquiry*, **11**, 1, pp. 3–42.

APPLE, M.W. and WEIS, L. (1983) 'Ideology and practice in schooling: A political and conceptual introduction', in APPLE, M. and WEIS, L. (eds) *Ideology and Practice in Schooling*, Philadelphia: Temple University Press, pp. 3–33.

ASANTE, M.K. (1980) *Afrocentricity*, Trenton, NJ: Africa World Press.

ASANTE, M.K. (1987) *The Afrocentric Idea*, Philadelphia: Temple University Press.

ASANTE, M.K. (1991) 'The Afrocentric idea in education', *Journal of Negro Education*, **60**, 2, pp. 170–80.

ASANTE, M.K. (1991/1992) 'Afrocentric curriculum', *Educational Leadership*, **49**, 4, pp. 28–31.

ASANTE, M.K. (1993) *Malcolm X As Cultural Hero and Other Afrocentric Essays*, Trenton, NJ: Africa World Press.

ASANTE, M.K. (1994) *Classica Africa*, Maywood, NJ: Asante Imprint Books and Peoples Publishing Group.

BANKS, J.A. (1992) 'African American scholarship and the evolution of multicultural education', *Journal of Negro Education*, **61**, 3, pp. 273–86.

BANKS, J. (1995) 'The historical reconstruction of knowledge about race: Implications for transformative teaching', *Educational Researcher*, **24**, 2, pp. 15–25.

CHRISTIAN, B.T. (1995) 'All of we are one: A conversation with Barbara T. Christian', *Raising Standards, Journal of the Rochester Teachers Association*, **3**, 1, pp. 21–31.

FOX KELLER, E. (1985) *Reflections on Gender and Science*, New Haven: Yale University Press.

FREIRE, P. (1970) *Pedagogy of the Oppressed*, New York: The Seabury Press.

GEERTZ, C. (1990) 'The Balinese cockfight as play', in ALEXANDER, J.C. and SEIDMAN, S. (eds) *Culture and Society, Contemporary Debates*, New York: Cambridge University Press, pp. 113–24.

GIROUX, H. (1983) *Theory and Resistance: A Pedagogy for the Opposition*, South Hadley, MA: Bergin and Garvey Press.

GIROUX, H.A. (1986) 'Radical pedagogy and the politics of student voice', *Interchange*, The Ontario Institute for Studies in Education, **17**, 1, pp. 48–67.

GIROUX, H.A. (1992) *Border Crossings, Cultural Workers and the Politics of Education*, New York: Routledge.

GOFFMAN, E. (1959) *The Presentation of Self in Everyday Life*, New York: Doubleday.

GOODWIN, S. (1995) 'From a conversation about emancipatory praxis with Susan Goodwin', 26 January, Rochester, New York.

GOODWIN, S. (1996) 'Teaching students of color', *Raising Standards, Journal of the Rochester Teachers Association*, **4**, 1, 23–35.

GOODWIN, S. and SWARTZ, E. (1993) 'Multiculturality: Liberating classroom pedagogy and practice', *Raising Standards, Journal of the Rochester Teachers Association*, **1**, 1, pp. 19–33.

GRANT, C.A. and SLEETER, C.E. (1986) *After the School Bell Rings*, Philadelphia: Falmer Press.

GRUMET, M. (1978) 'Curriculum as theater: Merely players', *Curriculum Inquiry*, **8**, 1, pp. 37–64.

HARRIS, M.D. (1992) 'Africentrism and curriculum: Concepts, issues, and prospects', *Journal of Negro Education*, **61**, 3, pp. 301–16.

HILLIARD, A.G. III (1986) 'Pedagogy in ancient Kemet', in KARENGA, M. and CARRUTHERS, J.A. (eds) *Kemet and the African Worldview, Research, Rescue, and Restoration*, Los Angeles: University of Sankore Press (2560 West 54th Street, Los Angeles, CA, 90043), pp. 130–48.

HOOKS, B. (1989) *Talking Back, Thinking Feminist, Thinking Black*, Boston: South End Press.

HOOKS, B. (1991) *Yearning, Race, Gender, and Cultural Politics*, Boston: South End Press.

HOOKS, B. (1992) *Black Looks, Race and Representation*, Boston, South End Press.

JAMES, J. (1993) 'African philosophy, theory, and "Living Thinkers"' in JAMES, J. and FARMER, R. (eds) *Spirit, Space, and Survival, African American Women in (White) Academe*, New York: Routledge, pp. 31–46.

JOSEPH, G.I. (1988) 'Black feminist pedagogy in capitalist white America', in COLE, M. (ed.) *Bowles and Gintis Revisited: Correspondence and Contradiction in Educational Theory*, New York: Falmer Press, pp. 176–86.

KARENGA, M. (1990) *Kaiwaida Theory*, Los Angeles: Kawaida Publications.

KETO, C.T. (1989) *The Africa-centered Perspective of History and Social Sciences in the Twenty-first Century*, Blackwood, NJ: K.A. Publications.

KING, J.E. (1991) 'Dysconscious racism: Ideology, identity, and the miseducation of teachers', *Journal of Negro Education*, **60**, 2, pp. 133–46.

LADSON-BILLINGS, G. (1992a) 'Culturally relevant teaching: The key to making multicultural education work', in GRANT, C.A. (ed.) *Research and Multicultural Education, from the Margin to the Mainstream*, London: Falmer Press, pp. 106–21.

LADSON-BILLINGS, G. (1992b) 'Liberating consequences of literacy: A case of culturally relevant instruction for African American students', *Journal of Negro Education*, **61**, 3, pp. 378–91.

LADSON-BILLINGS, G. (1994) *The Dreamkeepers, Successful Teachers of African American Children*, San Francisco: Jossey-Bass.

LAMPERT, M. (1990) 'When the problem is not the question and the solution is not the answer: Mathematical knowing and teaching', *American Educational Research Journal*, **27**, 1, pp. 29–63.

LATHER, P. (1989) 'Ideology and methodological attitude', *Journal of Curriculum Theorizing (JCT)*, **9**, 2, pp. 7–26.

LINCOLN, Y.S. and GUBA, E.G. (1985) *Naturalistic Inquiry*, Beverly Hills, CA: Sage Publications.

MCLAREN, P. (1986/1993) *Schooling As a Ritual Performance* (2nd edition), New York: Routledge.

MORRISON, T. (1992a) *Playing in the Dark, Whiteness and the Literary Imagination*, Cambridge, MA: Harvard University Press.

NIETO, S. (1992) *Affirming Diversity: The Sociopolitical Context of Multicultural Education*, New York: Longman Publishing Group.

NOBLES, W.W. (1986) 'Ancient Egyptian thought and the development of African (black) psychology', in KARENGA, M. and CARRUTHERS, J.H. (eds) *Kemet and the African Worldview*, Los Angeles: University of Sankore Press, pp. 100–18.

NODDINGS, N. (1991/1992, December–January) 'The gender issue', *Educational Leadership*, **49**, 4, pp. 65–70.

OLNECK, M.R. (1990 February) 'The recurring dream: Symbolism and ideology in intercultural and multicultural education', *American Journal of Education*, **98**, 2, pp. 147–74.

SHAKES, G.R. (1995) 'African American women's pathways to intellectual empowerment of female students of color', Unpublished dissertation, University of Rochester, Rochester, New York.

SLEETER, C.E. and GRANT, C.A. (1988) *Making Choices for Multicultural Education*, Columbus: Merril Publishing Company.

SLEETER, C.E. and GRANT, C.A. (1991) 'Race, class, gender, and disability in current textbooks', in APPLE, M. and CHRISTIAN-SMITH, L. (eds) *The Politics of the Textbook*, New York: Routledge, pp. 78–110.

SWARTZ, E. (1992a) 'Multicultural education: From a compensatory to a scholarly foundation', in GRANT, C. (ed.) *Research and Multicultural Education, from the Margins to the Mainstream*, London: Falmer Press, pp. 32–43.

SWARTZ, E. (1992b Summer) 'Emancipatory narratives: Rewriting the master script in the school curriculum', *The Journal of Negro Education*, **61**, 3, pp. 341–55.

SWARTZ, E. (1996a) 'Emancipatory pedagogy: A postcritical response to "standard" school knowledge', *Journal of Curriculum Studies*, **28**, 4, pp. 397–418.

SWARTZ, E. (1996b) 'A postcritical study of omnicentric praxis', Doctoral dissertation, University of Rochester, Rochester, New York.

TEDLA, E. (1995) *Sankofa, African Thought and Education*, New York: Peter Lang.

THOMPSON, K. and TETREAULT, M. (1986) 'Integrating women's history: The case of United States history high school textbooks', *History Teacher*, **19**, pp. 211–62.

TURNER, V.W. and TURNER, E. (1982) 'Performing ethnography', *Drama Review*, **26**, 2, pp. 33–50.

UNDERWOOD, P. (Turtle Woman Singing) (1991) *Three Strands in the Braid, a Guide for Enabling of Learning*, San Anselmo CA: A Tribe of Two Press.

WYNTER, S. (1990a) 'America as a "world": A black studies perspective and "cultural model" framework', Unpublished manuscript submitted to the California State Board of Education, 9 September.

WYNTER, S. (1990b) 'A cultural model critique of the textbook: America will be', Unpublished manuscript submitted to the California State Board or Education, 24 September.

Chapter 9

Romancing the Curriculum with Student Research: Recreating Kent State[1]

Shirley R. Steinberg

Education should be learning . . . education should be teaching. Learners and teachers should participate in both of these essentials to complete an 'act of knowledge' or knowing. As teacher/facilitators we walk a tightrope between setting agendas/lesson plans and attempting to cultivate empowered students. I believe that we are obligated as teachers to construct a curriculum, to produce an agenda and to guide/lead/teach our students. A democratic classroom is not one in which the teacher/professor sits at a table and invites students to just 'talk and share'. Far too many 'democratic' educators sit back and expect education to simply emerge, unattached to agenda or guidance. Not understanding authority, they confuse preparation and knowledge of subject with oppression. To convey knowledge, knowing that all knowledge is tentative and incomplete, is a necessary act to any critical pedagogy. As critical as I consider myself, as opposed to Ravitch/Bennett/Hirschian notions of essential knowledge as I may be, I find myself 'siding' with them on at least this issue: that some of the teaching that takes place in the name of democratic education is soft, fluffy and nonsensical. I am not embarrassed that I have an agenda and that I am a teacher. All this said, however, I believe that students should participate in their education and as educators, that we be prepared to change directions, listen to ideas and 'let' knowledge progress naturally. I believe improvisational drama to be an incredible pedagogical tool in which both students and teachers are able to allow knowledge to reveal itself.

Alfred North Whitehead contended that there are educational stages that should be anticipated and followed, consequently allowing a fullness of learning to take place. Suggested by Whitehead are stage one, 'Romance', stage two, 'Precision', and three, 'Generalization'. Determined in Whitehead's mandate for education is the admonition that all three stages need to be followed in order, thus completing a cycle of education. However, I believe that the Romance stage is a necessity throughout the entire learning process and allows the richest of learning experiences, rather than reducing the pedagogy to the next stage. With the use of drama and theater arts, we are able to capture the Romance stage, build upon it through an 'in-role' process, and build classrooms that are filled with an experiential magic of learning. By accommodating our students to 'become' within the environment of the curriculum, students are free to feel and learn with out the threatening and pedantic aspect of the Precision stage.

In a very personal approach to illustrating the successful use of drama in education, I will indulge in relating a remarkable experience in learning, one which remained in the Romance stage throughout the process.

Course: Social Studies, Grade 11/12; Topic: 1960s — Student Unrest, Civic Disobedience

How does one return to an era? Is there a way to allow students to become personally involved in historical knowledge? What are the most important curricular ideas I want them to understand? What decisions would the students have made if they had lived in the historical period? Can we ever, really, identify with the past? Does history and the past affect our lives, our futures?

These questions were the basis upon which to build a suitable framework for the learning experience. As I worked through the process, I kept these questions in mind. My goal was not to answer the questions, but to keep them in my sight for directions.

I chose the May, 1970 Kent State University killings for the basis of the experience. The majority of my students were born in 1970, and I had found that little or no mention of the deaths of four students was in the social studies curricular materials. I hoped that this incident would bring to life the moments, emotions, atmosphere and consciousness of the time and that the students would add the experience to their lives in both an intellectual and personal way.

My own preparation included research through magazines, films, and historical books on accounts of the killings. The best resource was the account as recorded by James Michener in *Kent State*. Michener's narrative was very human in relating the history preceding, during and after the deaths, his research on the personal lives of the students allowed me to design the appropriate outline for my own process. It was important, however, to keep in mind as a teacher-researcher, that I was attempting to engage in a learning experience, the outcome should not be predetermined in my 'lesson' planning. What the students would conclude would remain to be revealed after debriefing the experience.

I set up the drama studio as an environment, using minimal sets and props to add to the atmosphere. I set up a music and lighting system for the theatrics.

Using my research materials, I diagramed the events and the groups of people surrounding the area. I studied the 'stories' of each of the four dead students and wrote journal entries in their voices — entries that would document their 'thoughts' and actions throughout the experience. I wrote news bulletins that covered the three days that we would re-enact. (Looking back, I would have engaged the students in the writing of these 'scripts' as well, however, as a teacher/researcher, I needed to be intricately aware of the period of time and the mechanics of the experience). I phoned several students, asking them to take leadership roles, I told them who they would portray and asked them to dress appropriately the next day; when they came into the class, they were to come 'in-role'. The day was designated as 'Hippie Day' and the entire school was encouraging dressing-up for the day, so costuming was taken care of for the entire class.

The players that I contacted were:

- four victims (those killed at Kent State)
- one militia leader
- one Black Panther leader
- one radio announcer

These seven student/facilitators received a prepared dossier about who they 'were'. They would come to class early and look over their folder. In the room I placed signs for each 'area' a few wooden blocks, some silk flowers, some rifles and some army jackets. The middle of the room was clear, only a tall stool stood on a step with a soft light on it. In each corner of the room was a tall stool and a fixed spot light. These lights would serve as directoral devices for me — I would function as the invisible stage manager during the experience. The rest of the room was lighted low, the stereo was set to play songs from the era at a very soft level.

A town sign greeted the students as they walked in. The seven facilitators had already chosen where they would be: the four students destined to die had each claimed a stool in which to return to when cued, the news commentator was on the middle stool. The leader of the militia had built up a barricade and gotten very organized, the Black Panther leader had a sweat band his forehead and had created a soapbox-type of speaking stage. The music, Woodstock-genre was playing quietly. As students came in, the only thing that they knew for sure was that they had entered Kent, Ohio and it was 1970. The militia leader and Panther leader immediately started to recruit workers, as the Panther stood on the platform and discussed ideology and power, the militia leader went to individuals and explained that indeed, they had a patriotic duty. About 10 participants were not recruited by either group and started to make flower necklaces, sat on the ground and started to sing softly with the music.

I darkened the room, intuitively everyone paused; I turned the spot on the middle of the room, and the disc jockey welcomed the audience to the morning in Kent, Ohio. Along with her news brief, she mentioned that there were a number of students and protesters gathered in the town who were having a rally about the war; she also mentioned that townspeople were getting nervous. After the short broadcast she fell silent; I changed the lights and the room came back to life. I noticed that the participants continued their actions somewhat in light of the broadcast, that is, the militia started to get more organized, the flower children started making signs and planning demonstrations, and the Panthers started to preach that it wasn't their war, that black brothers and sisters needed to unite. The group interacted for about five minutes, I then changed the lights on to the corner spot where one of the four students had climbed on to the stool. This student read from his journal, who he was, what he was doing, why he was in school. The journal reading was about two minutes long. When he ceased reading, the lights were changed back. The room immediately began to breathe again.

Throughout the entire morning, the students interacted within the environment. My only participation was to dim and spot the lights. The 'spots' alternated on the disc jockey, who kept the group abreast of unfolding events, and each of the four students had two journal readings. As the lights faded from each spot, Kent campus came back to life.

The morning progressed and I noticed that the Panthers had moved to a far corner; they declared they would stay out of the situation. They discussed possible welfare programs and ideas for publicity in the future. Several Panthers were nervous with the militia movements and made it clear that if anything happened, they thought it would be blamed on them. Consequently, they stayed away. I noted that the students who had been singing and making flower necklaces had started to approach the militia (who had taken up arms and lined the parameter of the area); some of the girls put flowers in the gun barrels; a few altercations started between the 'flower children' and the soldiers.

When I would dim the lights, the disc jockey would give a news report (note that she had only the first report prepared, the rest of her broadcasts were written during her observations of what was going on in Kent during the day). Consequently, the newscasts served to move the action, and the action served to move the newscasts.

As I mentioned earlier, the four students who were to die gave short monologues based on journal entries. They, in essence, told their stories — why they were in Kent, where they were from, what they cared about, who they were. None of the students were protesters, several mentioned that they were quite oblivious to the public demonstrations. After the four students had told their stories, about 90 minutes had transpired; it just 'felt' like tension was mounting; there was a tightness and dread that started to be felt. I walked up to the newscaster and handed her a bulletin and changed the lights — she announced with panic that there was a break in the programming, that a news flash had just been handed to her. At that time, she read the bulletin that the militia had opened fire on the campus of Kent State University, that there were several wounded and unconfirmed deaths. The four students each got off of their stools and sat on the ground.

Naturally, I was not sure what would happen. The entire room was still, it seemed for a very long time. I went to the stereo and put on the song 'Ohio' by Crosby, Stills and Nash: 'tin soldiers and Nixon's coming . . . we're finally on our way . . .' We listened to the song. Everyone had taken seats on the floor; we were all very tired. After the right amount of time (I don't know how we knew), we started to talk. The students talked about themselves in role, why they did certain things, why they said certain things. We began 'debriefing' at a reunion of those who had been there those many years ago. Part of the debriefing follows:

> I really got angry when those girls started to put flowers in my gun. Why did you do that anyway?
> It just seemed natural. We put them there to make you think about peace and love, not war.

It wasn't our fault we were there, that was our job. We were there to protect the country.

What danger was a bunch of protesters? Why were you so frightened?

Don't you understand? It was our job. We didn't like what we were doing. I'm just glad that my group (Panthers) stayed out of the way.

Why is that?

You know, every time anything happens, they blame black people.

Who blames black people?

You know, them, the government.

How do you think I felt (victim)?

What do you mean?

How do you think I felt, getting gunned down because I was walking across the lawn. All I was doing was walking across the lawn, I was late to class. I didn't ask to die. I don't even know anything about the war, except that it's there.

Maybe that's the problem, a lot of us don't know what is going on in our country.

Oh, do you think we could have saved those kids?

I think that we need to know how to be heard, how to be citizens, and not get killed by mistake.

Naturally, the discussion flowed, we continued it the next day and the students insisted on writing and drawing and on more talking. It has been 10 years since our Kent State, students I meet remind me of the day and speak about it like it was last week. Can't history, literature, even science be taught in memorable ways? Ways in which the Romance is kept within education and research. Allowing students role play, with restrictions and conditions, yet providing them the safe space to improvise gives them a bottomless ocean of ideas, feelings and data. Teaching with precision; with prediction invites linear attitudes and convergent thinking. Instead of precisely teaching skills and factoids we are able to integrate education into a whole experience. To isolate skills and facts insults our students and keeps us from professionalism. Whitehead did not give enough credit to the Romance stage. We should expect Romance to stretch throughout the learning process, if we continually strive to facilitate a process to occur, and to consider 'an experience' instead of 'a lesson', we remain within Romance as our active stage.

I saw one of my militia men a year ago; he recalled the day in May we created and remarked: 'I was there.'

Note

1   This essay is dedicated to Kari Matchett, the flower child who plugged the rifle with a rose.

Chapter 10

Creating North

Lana Krievis

Conundrum

Forty percent of a remedial English class for deaf students at a community college answered north on a question. The oddity is the airplane was flying from east to west. This reminds me of a New York joke: a tourist stopped and asked the operator of a newsstand which way was north. The man replied, 'We got up town, down town, and cross town. We don't got no north.'

There was no north in the question either. Yet, the deaf students had a north. They were wrong, right? East and west isn't north. What is north? We all know that north is Canada. North is cold. North is snow. North is wintry. What if you lived in New Zealand? Is north Canada? Is north cold, snow, and wintry? No, that is south. In fact, on a globe, at what point does south become north or north become south? Does anyone living in California actually know which side of Africa is west?

Contemplations

Dyslexic map making aside, there are known absolutes (and I say this with more than a tad bit of cynicism) that are obviously touchable and measurable. For instance, 'chair'. What is a chair? A chair has four legs, a seat, and a back. Does that make a one-legged man a disabled chair? A bed — something you sleep on. So, what does it become when you sit on it. Who sleeps in a flower bed or for that matter sits on a rose bed. 'Do you sell alligator shoes?' 'I don't know madam. What size is your alligator?'

A tiny kernel of corn is fed to the pigs in Germany, popped in America, and used to sweeten puddings in Indonesia. Would an Indonesian's description, expectations, and use of corn be wrong on a German test?

Who decided that rabbits were animals? If a test asks you what a rabbit is, you had better put animal, if not a mammal. If you answer, little Billy's pet, Grandpa's garden scourge, or last night's dinner you are wrong. If you are deaf and answer big teeth, long ears you will be accused of not being able to think in the abstract.

Polkinghorne states, 'Much of the philosophical confusion about the realm of meaning has been related to the attempt to identify it as a substance' (1998, p. 4). As long as attributes rule meaning there will be confusion.

Deaf people of various ages were asked to identify the following:

- What is a TV? Response: I watch.
- What is a book shelf? Response: I put books.
- What is a phone? Response: I talk.
- What is a chair? Response: I sit.
- What is a desk? Response: I write.
- What is a book? Response: I read.

To deaf people, people who are extremely visual — things, or nouns, are not primarily visual things. Nouns are not even primarily substances. In American Sign Language most nouns are not separated from their action: sit and chair; plane and fly; food and eat all maintain a common hand shape and spatial placement. One identifies the other.

Vygotsky rejectied the idea that meaning making could be separated from activity. However, in our post-Fordist world meaning invariably produces commodity. Meaning must (invariably) create 'Other', something separate from ourselves (and, other also is a consumable commodity subject to the market). Abstract thinking is produced (and once again the production metaphor is also tied to a symbolic sort of capital). Function as definition is viewed with alarm by deaf educators. As an interpreter I was warned that certain religious concepts or certain scientific ideas would be very hard to interpret because 'deaf people are so literal'. As an interpreter I realized it may not have had as much to do with the literal as it did with particular political priorities. As a teacher for deaf students with severely limited English and American Sign Language I have been offered sympathy several times, 'Don't you get frustrated having to be so concrete all the time?' 'Deaf people can't do analogies, much less metaphors.'

Deaf people who are not fluent in English do have problems with American analogies and metaphors. But, that has nothing to do with understanding concepts. My mentor (Dr Karen Anijar) was once told by her favorite professor to stay out of Herman's Circle. Hermeneutic understanding of linguistic data requires a process of analogy. But who decides what anchors the analogy? Pigs are to food what gasoline is to fuel. Who got to decide that pigs are food? (certainly not Hassidic Jews) Somehow analogies, and metaphors, which are socially constructed categories, are treated as though they are an activity of the brain.

Function or activity, which are authentic brain processes, have become filled with body fluids. Bodily fluids have become so swollen that the brain doth runneth over. Functional definitions aren't scientific. They are too personal, too open to point of view, too subjective, too unmeasurable, indeed they are inherently ideological. In deaf education nouns are never narratives.

A swarm of fish?
A herd of fish?
A pack of fish?
A school?

A swarm of bees?
A flock of bees?
I'll never learn the rule.

A herd of cows?
A school of cows?
A bunch of cows?
A pack?

A pack of wolves?
A flock of wolves?
I'll never get the knack.
            (L. and J. Hymes)

The Know — Don't Know of Deafness

Deaf students have a sign for 'know' and a negated inflection for 'don't know'. If you aren't experienced, you might mistake it to mean simply 'I know or I don't know'. However, to sign 'know' means 'I have experienced this.' It doesn't necessarily mean I can pass a test on it, or even explain it. It means that, like the Greeks, deaf people have a word for experiential knowing. English doesn't. The negated meaning is intensified if the chin is slightly dropped and a deep frown appears between the eyebrows (an inflection upon the hand — shape and movement). It doesn't mean I can't explain, it means 'I cannot act upon this information. It doesn't fit in with anything I have ever done.' And if the signer is very adamant the meaning also includes 'I don't think it will ever be important to my life, so forget the whole thing.'

Bakhtin says 'we operate out of a point of view and shape values into form' (Morson, 1990, p. 10). We know only our view, or one point of view. Without a true dialogue of interaction with others we can know only partially. We can't see the backs of our heads. Even in dialogue we use language to fit our particular partiality whether it is the functional forms of sign or the so called abstractions of English. Adjustments are made for better understanding, change is accepted, language becomes, is constantly becoming. Educators of the deaf expect language to fit only their partiality, if not, it isn't language. Not, '*my* language', *but non*-language. Since, as the teacher 'I hold the power' it is definitely a wrong answer on a test. Without even reversing the situation, I ask: do English speaking people know everything there is to know about north? What do we know about animals with big teeth and long ears? Is there more to life than a category named animal?

Anijar continually has contended that all things in life are in process and in flux (1996). Knowing itself, is both now and future. When north only points one way we have become blinded by our own enlightenment — a vulgar scientism. Is it even north anymore, or is it just a positivitisic, quantifiable rubric? Definitely! A quantifiable north, divorced from function and experience, is no longer part of the life in process or as process. It is therefore no longer to know. It has become known.

Known is of the past, not the present and definitely not of the future, therefore it becomes frozen in its partiality, incomplete, understood only in part.

What happens to us when north only points one way, when north only exists in one dimension of understanding. To paraphrase Bakhtin we become fossilized corpses; like sea shells thrown onto the sand unable to move from our static state to become, to experience, to know.

If we live the American dream, which is often a nightmare: is anyone's right to fossilize, to name the conditions of another, to speak before even listening to the other? Educators are not paleontologists. We are however, notorious proselytizers. The truth has been made known to me, it has been revealed to me! I'm your teacher and there is only one known answer. You will accept my known or you will be damned. You will be damned for all of eternity. So praise the lord and pass the collection plate, I need my paycheck on the thirtieth.

The known, however is partial; it is never complete. Known is like an iceberg: the tip of an iceberg. When deaf children maintain their distance and dutifully parrot merely size, shape, and color, they also become frozen in a cryogenic state of stasis in their immobile partiality.

If the deaf children have not been dry docked or dry iced in their ambition to know, if they reach out and try to touch the full iceberg, they will be Titantic-sized: torn asunder, set into a tempestuous sea without a raft. In no less a dramatic way than the sinking of the Titanic, the student impaled, and immobilized, eventually is disabled, destroyed: a series of minuses rather than pluses or possibilities,

> What is a chair? 'I sit.'
> Where is the plane? 'north.'

From a missionary perspective, (much like any missionary position), the world is black and white, it is either or. The deaf students have answered incorrectly; there is only one sanctioned way to do things. There can only be one north. We declare deaf students have no language, (the heathens, the deviants). We blame the victims, but not our own perceptions. It is much easier to say deaf children cannot learn.

Frankenchrist

In the 1980s a punk rock group, The Dead Kennedys, wrote a social protest song called 'Frankenchrist'. It protested the brutalizing and killing of others for the sake of greed and colonization. Can we place deaf education in such a grim light?

'In the silent sounds of Aleph are all the sounds of the universe, that seemingly esoteric Jewish saying has tremendous contemporary purchase value in terms of post — modernism; clearly the axiom is far more accepting and inclusive than paradigmatic prejudices held onto so tightly by practitioners.

There is a deaf industry. Like any other industry, someone benefits, someone always benefits. However, the deaf students do not benefit by being labeled as language-less and unable to learn.

'(Language) is a distinct piece of the biological makeup of our brains. Language is a complex, specialized skill, which develops in the child: spontaneously, without conscious effort or formal instruction, is deployed without awareness of its underlying logic, is qualitatively the same in every individual, and is distinct from more general abilities to process information or behave intelligently. For these reasons some cognitive scientists have described language as a psychological faculty, a mental organ, a neural system, and a computational module. I prefer the admittedly quaint term "instinct."' (Pinker, 1994, p. 18) The only way *not* to have a language is to be brain dead.

The creation story in *Genesis* posits this notion politically. The first act of a human being was to name. Naming is power.

HOW COME
When I was born I was black.
When I grew up I was black.
When I'm sick I'm black.
When I go out into the sun I'm black.
When I die I'll be black.
But you:
When you were born you were pink.
When you grow up you are white.
When you get sick you are green.
When you go out in the sun you are red.
When you go out in the cold you are blue.
When you die you turn purple.
And you call me colored? (Unknown)

Naming creates norms and deviations. Naming includes or excludes. Naming tells me who I am and who you are in ways far beyond words like Mary and Pete. To take away the power to name is to take away the power to experience one's own life.

When a deaf child comes to school with a 'home-sign' for mother, that is, a gesture created by the child to represent or name his mother, we (deaf educators) immediately say one of two things.

1   No, that is not mother. Mother is this particular shaping of your mouth and tongue.
2   No, that is not mother. Mother is this particular shaping and movement of your hand.

Mother is no longer in the child's experience. Mother has become something else. Mother has become someone else, and someone else's. Robbed of the concept of motherhood. The child's understanding of mother comes under the rubric of somebody else's world. Talk about domination! Mother is no longer the child's to know. Mother has become a cultural definition separate from experiential knowing.

Language is world interaction because people are interactors. Language shapes the world as directly as the opposing thumb or a bulldozer. But when deaf children come to school they are only allowed to use the dominant language — which they often don't know. Teachers place deaf students in tombs of ignorance, that are socially constructed, thereby denying deaf students interaction, and denying access to knowledge.

Native Americans who went to government schools during the 1920s and 1930s tell of terrible acts of suppression and oppression. Much of the victimization occurred while robbing the students of their native language. The children were beaten, locked up and endured other violent acts of punishment if they spoke anything but English. To rob someone of their language robs them of their ability to name the world.

Deaf adults who went to state schools between 1900 and 1970 tell of teachers tying their hands to the chair if they tried to sign or use them to communicate.

Such things aren't done to deaf children today because it is against the law. It is considered a form of corporal punishment. However, although things seem superficially to have changed, there has not been an epistemological change, and there certainly has not been an ontological change. Not binding the deaf child's hands has nothing to do with an ideological shift, or, any form of humane-ness. Deaf students are chained and shackled by a system that says they cannot know.

Whatever the educators of that not so pastoral past time thought of sign language, there is no doubt in my mind that it was a form of language. Sign language was such a successful form of language they were afraid it would interfere with the children's desire to learn English. Today, in our retro-nostalgic essentialist mode educators merely feel deaf children have no language! At least while the deaf students of the past had their hands tied, they had language!

Not to long ago another teacher and I were watching a group of deaf high school students discussing the prom. The prom was the following week and the girls were comparing dresses, and talking about where to buy shoes. They were using what I call *lingua schoola* (my naming of the language) or school sign. It is a language that is visual and spatial and it was clearly understood by the students. Alas, it is not American Sign Language, and unquestionably not English.

The teacher turned to me and said, 'It is a shame they don't have a language, they would be able to learn English so much easier if they did.'

A student in a Deaf/Hard of Hearing teacher credentialing program told me that it is extremely hard for deaf children to learn English after the age of 12 because they never had a first language.

To be completely rhetorical: what then is the definition of first language? American Sign Language. A visual/spatial language developed in a local region, or interacted into being by the deaf students in a specific school district is not a language. Communication is not considered language. Communication with rule driven order is not language. Communication is only language if it fits a quantifiable criteria. Since children know neither ASL or English they are languageless. In Papua-New Guinea over 400 unrelated languages are spoken; socio-linguists and anthropologists come from all over the *developed* world (and note that developed is italicized because it is a sardonic descriptor). Just because only a few people speak a language, does it make that language so invalid that it is not a language at all?

The invalid language creates and sustains invalids whose experiences are completely invalidated.

The Bicultural/Bilingual movement in deaf education asserts children who never learned ASL have had their mental processes deformed in some way and are incapable of learning English (Strong, 1990). Does this mean that deaf children are mutants? Are deaf children some form of science fiction monster who do not even have the capacity to communicate telepathically?

By deaf standards deaf children have no language if they don't know American Sign Language. By hearing standards deaf children have no language if they don't know English. A double helix, and politicized paradox, indeed! This is not tying someone's hand to a chair, this is annihilation.

To Speak or not Speak: That Is the Determinant of Humanity

Vygotsky's Socialization, Bakhtin's 'Other', even Heidigger's 'Word' speak of to know as some form of interaction. Experience is the primary form of socialization, other, and word in a deaf child's life. These experiences are usually: '*do this, put here, go there*'. Often these experiences are disconnected from dialogue, from negotiation, from exchange. Only part of experience is visible to the deaf child. Yet the child does not live without meaning. People are always constructing meaning from lived experiences. How is this possible? It is possible because the deaf child is human.

From Aristotle's Enlightenment to Hermeneutics to narratives — from Descartes' thoughts to Heidigger's nothing all humanity knows. Newtonian physics or Bakhtin's completion of and by other, we know. A deaf person knows.

I refuse to justify the prejudices of Otherness, or the absurdities of colonialism and imperialism by proving that deaf people know. Deaf people are human, that should be enough. Deaf people know the same way all humans know. Do deaf people know the same thing as hearing people? No — no-one knows the same thing as someone else, we just share the same paths of knowing, and by sharing text we can enrich each other's knowing — Knowing not known. Known becomes fractured and partialized. Known becomes proselytized. Knowing as continual now and continual future allows the creation and adjustment of meaning. Knowing is experiencing.

So, why did that plane fly north? Because in American Sign Language the sign for north and the sign for up use the same movement and spatial placement with only a very small variation in hand shape. Please fly up; up and north are the same, so planes fly north. On the other hand, I still think north is Canada.

Students do construct significant knowledge; too bad we are hearing and not looking.

References

ANIJAR, K. (1996) 'Bakhtin and the dance of the dialogical', *Impulse*, Spring, pp. 56–87.
MORSON, G.S. and EMERSON, C. (1990) *Mikhail Bakhtin: Creation of a Prosaics*, Standford, California: Standford University Press.

NEWMAN, F. and HOLZMAN, L. (1993) *Lev Vygotsky: Revolutionary Scientist*, New York: Routledge.

PINKER, S. (1994) *The Language Instinct: How the Mind Creates Language*, New York: W. Morrow and Co.

POLKINGHORNE, D.E. (1988) *Narrative Knowing and the Human Sciences*, Albany, New York: State University of New York Press.

STRONG, M. (ed.) (1990) *Language Learning and Deafness*, New York: Cambridge University Press.

Chapter 11

Engaging Students as Researchers: Researching and Teaching Thanksgiving in the Elementary Classroom

Leila Villaverde and Joe L. Kincheloe

The Enigma of Thanksgiving

Thanksgiving is one of many enigmatic celebrations in the North American pantheon of holidays. A large part myth and historical erasure, Thanksgiving celebrations and school lessons paint a picture of American Indian–English settler relations that is quite misleading. Such a depiction is important because Thanksgiving serves the central cultural role of providing a national origin myth. From the traditional morality play of the settler-Indian interaction, students gain an ideological understanding of America as specially blessed by God, America forged by civilizing both the savages and the wilderness in which they resided, America as the representation of order in the sea of indigenous chaos — an ethnocentric vision of nation and self. The complexity and importance of the holiday are revealed when such ideological understandings intersect with the portraits of the Plymouth settlement provided by historians of seventeenth-century Massachusetts.

In these chronicles we find a group of settlers giving thanks to God for the smallpox plague spread by pre-Plymouth European explorers that devastated the Native populations of the region. The Pilgrims are often seen as grave robbers who relied on Indian generosity and food stores to survive the early years of the settlement. The English settlers are also viewed as violent neighbors who within a half century after the Plymouth landing had killed a large percentage of the Indians living in their proximity. As to Thanksgiving as a holiday, we find that even though Abraham Lincoln proclaimed Thanksgiving a national holiday in 1863, the association of Pilgrims, Indians, and a grand feast with the holiday didn't emerge until the end of the nineteenth century. Indeed, school curriculum with the morality play between settler–Native replete with Squanto and the planting of corn is for the most part a twentieth century phenomenon.

When such historical images are contrasted with mainstream elementary education's curriculum of turkey bulletin boards, handouts with Pilgrims in their starched black and white suits extending outstretched hands to the near-naked Indians, descriptions of the divinely-inspired piety of the Christian settlers, and the moral foundations of America's settlement, elementary educators find themselves faced with some profoundly troubling decisions concerning how they should teach Thanksgiving. As methods teachers we wanted our elementary social studies teacher education students to appreciate the moral and pedagogical dilemmas caused by the collision of the mainstream school's expectations for the teaching of Thanksgiving with their sophisticated historiographical understandings of the foibles of the traditional story. In this problematic context we asked the students to conduct research on seventeenth century Indian–settler relations as well as on curriculums taught in mainstream schools. Grounded on the basis of their research and speculation, students devised Thanksgiving units for various elementary grade levels that indicated their awareness of the complexities involved in such curriculum making.

Research in the Critical Methods Class:
Questions of Purpose and Context

Research is crucial for the success of any pedagogical model, particularly when the focus is on the critical empowerment of students. When students are engaged to take an active role in the learning process they are empowered to shape their experiences, what they search for, interpret, understand, and apply. Not only do methods students as researchers become critically aware of what is included and excluded in and out of traditional curricula, but they are forced to continually expand their fund of knowledge as one question leads to the next in any line of research. The excerpts in this chapter are taken out of the interdisciplinary Thanksgiving units designed by our students. The class was taught by Joe Kincheloe, Shirley Steinberg, and Leila Villaverde and revolved around questions raised by a critical approach to social studies education.

We introduced the class by focusing on issues of what social studies education is and what it could be. Social studies in elementary schools have been abused, misused, misunderstood, hated and ignored. When researchers examine the teaching of social studies in elementary education they find few bright spots. Good teachers do great things in some schools, but too few elementary teachers have a sense of purpose in relation to social studies education. In this class we attempted to acquaint the students with the problems of social studies, and what elementary teachers can do to overcome them in their professional lives. To begin this process, we wanted our students to search their consciousness and their own educational history to understand what they already knew about social studies. Then we asked the questions, What are the social studies? What are methods? How can teaching and methods be critically and significantly taught? What do you expect from a social studies 'methods' class? We worked together in the class as teachers/students/researchers to explore in the spirit of the Frankfurt School what social studies *can* be.

As we discussed cognition, social studies and elementary education, we demonstrated different methods within the classroom. We covered integrated education in regards to using other content areas within social studies to enhance and broaden our curriculum. As a class we explored new ideas on higher orders of teacher thinking and how we might share these abilities with our students. We tied these new forms of thinking into social studies teaching methods that are connected to the fine arts (art, drama, and music). In addition to learning to think in new and exciting ways, we learned some very specific and practical teaching methods that could be applied directly to the students' future elementary social studies classes. As methods teachers we engaged students in the analysis of social studies in terms of the larger society, in terms of race, class, gender, power, sexuality, religion, economics, etc. Constantly acting as researchers, we asked questions about traditional methods (our own student histories) and what we will keep or improve upon.

In their units students were asked to draw upon their research, use and/or expand on the approaches we discussed in class, and make reference to their understanding of the purposes of social studies as they created an interdisciplinary two-week Thanksgiving curriculum. They were given the flexibility to create any type of situation for their classrooms — thus, some students included famous speakers or planned for a variety of extravagant field trips. What follows are excerpts from the units created by three excellent students: Elizabeth McNeil, Melissa Shine, and Kristin L. Persichini. Although these were many excellent units, we found these particularly interesting given their use of a research-grounded interdisciplinary, post-modern, epistemological, socially conscious approach towards teaching about Thanksgiving in elementary school. All three units relied primarily on giving the students every opportunity to be researchers, taking advantage of every resource possible including an emphasis on the internet. This chapter provides a conceptual and practical framework for a methods course that empowers teacher education students as researchers creating the experience necessary for successful and confident application of these concepts in their own classrooms.

Elizabeth McNeil's Thanksgiving Unit

McNeil begins her unit with a quote from Michael Dorris's 'Why I am Not Thankful for Thanksgiving':

> Considering that virtually none of the standard fare surrounding Thanksgiving contains an ounce of authenticity, historical accuracy, or cross-cultural perception, why is it so apparently ingrained? Is it necessary to the American psyche to perpetually exploit and debase its victims in order to justify its history?

She then states:

> Until recently, I had this notion in my head that I wanted to create a Thanksgiving unit that would include none of the stereotypical aspects of the holiday. I did not even want to mention the word Pilgrim in the unit. I considered it a challenge to go beyond the norms of what we believe Thanksgiving to be, and to introduce new definitions for the word 'Thanksgiving'.
>
> I began with the subject of dance. Dance has always been a way to express a myriad of feelings, from anger and hate, to love, and finally, to thanksgiving. I

wanted to concentrate on how various cultures use dance to give thanks; in this way, I would be reinventing the word 'Thanksgiving' for the imaginary class for whom I was designing this unit.

Then, after reading the endless amount of information available on Thanksgiving, I decided that I would be doing a disservice to my imaginary class if I did not try to problematize the subject with them. I still wanted to integrate dance into the unit, but I wanted it to be a part of what the holiday called Thanksgiving was and is in the United States.

There is a consciousness evident in this passage that demonstrates a concerted effort to challenge and analyze the standard in order to mediate between the traditional curriculum and one that would empower the students and better prepare them for society. Her unit is designed for ten days of work, integrating basic curriculum subjects with various subjects within the arts and technology.

McNeil designates Day One: 'Tradition, deconstructing the Thanksgiving holiday and discussing the word tradition'. She asks the students to create a Thanksgiving page in their class webpage addressing the multifaceted topics in their units with the only requirement of starting the webpage with the word tradition. She states:

I will open the unit with the class by brainstorming with the kids what the word tradition means to them. I will ask them if their families or friends have any special traditions that they would like to share with the group. After discussing traditions within the family, we will talk about the above definition, which I will have posted on the board. We will spend quite some time discussing what each definition means, and whether people are active or passive in the definition. I will ask them if they notice any faults in the definition, and why. Following the discussion, the class will compose together a new definition of the word tradition, which would address all the problems, such as the gender biases, in the antiquated Webster's version. . . .

After lunch, the kids will go to art class which will be taught by our guest lecturer, Annie Liebowitz. After a discussion of the specifics of her photography, the artist will talk about different methods of capturing light and shadow in photographs. A science lesson will ensue, as the kids ask the artist how film works. The kids will turn again, to the Internet, to find information on film. . . . Ms Liebowitz gives the students the assignment to create a photographic essay on traditions they see every day. The essay is to be completed using the newly created definition of the word tradition. . . . They also have been assigned to go to the library and find information on photography and science behind film developing.

The first day began with one word, tradition. From that one word, our amazing class branched out to learn creative writing, computer, science, and art skills. We explored different cultures through our traditional lunches and gained appreciation for the art of photography.

She stresses research of the unknown and familiar, provides experientials, and caters to the differences within her classroom. She also respects the natural flow of research and learning in revolving the day's lessons around where the research leads.

Everyday McNeil begins the day with a discussion of the student's photo-graphic essays monitoring their progress and answering any questions. Day Two: 'Thanks, but no thanks!' addresses stereotypical Thanksgiving feasts, events, and books that represent Thanksgiving erroneously. She shows films depicting the feasts.

> Especially offensive is the 'Brady Bunch' portrayal of the first feast, using a Brady-made movie to capture the event. The kids will watch that footage and then discuss what they have seen. I will ask them what they know about the holiday, and if they think that the event happened as it was portrayed on television.

She places a quote from James W. Loewen's *Lies My Teacher Told Me* on the overhead projector which the students discuss. Instead of imposing a topic on the students, discussions are facilitated so that the students are part of the deconstruction and construction of knowledge.

> We will talk about the implications of placing stereotypical images in books and in media and representing them as the norm. We will then go to the library to locate books that perpetuate the stereotypes of Pilgrims in black and Indians wearing war paint and carrying tomahawks. . . . I will pose to the class the question: 'What is the truth about Thanksgiving?' Has this tradition been handed down to us inactive receptors of knowledge as *Webster's* definition indicates? We will again turn to the Internet for help. The Center for World Indigenous Studies has an excellent website. . . .

The students were assigned to research specific aspects that the webpage included so that at the end of the day they would come together to present what they found. They also had the option of presenting their information in a variety of ways — a multimedia production, book, song, etc. — as long as it would help in the creation of the unit home page. Overall McNeil encouraged the students to use a variety of resources, to question, compare, contrast, and discuss.

Day Three: 'Irreconcilable differences?' highlights an excerpt from the 1970 speech on the 350th anniversary of the Pilgrim's arrival. As always the day began discussing the photographic essays. But the focus of the day is on the diseases that Indigenous people often contracted from European settlers.

> First we will examine the disease from the perspective of a traditional sixth grade history book. We will then compare the depiction of the diseases to those indicated in *Lies My Teacher Told Me*. . . . The kids will be asked to write a reflective journal assuming the role of the person who spoke at that 1970 ceremony. They will be encouraged to write about their life as a Wampanoag or about the day that they were to give the speech. Was that person nervous? Did that person have the help of another to write that speech? What circumstances brought that person there to give that speech?. . . . The kids will be free to find a quite place to compose their pieces.

Creating a space to imagine another's consciousness is crucial to demystifying biases and racist behaviors. Exploring other experiences through research and intellectual as well as emotional knowledge is also very important to fostering a well-rounded student.

> The kids who have finished their stories early will begin a large mathematics assignment which will encompass the rest of the unit. Because the class agreed that books and the media are influential in how people see the native American people of this country, they will begin a 'detective mission'. They will become introduced to statistics by analyzing the books in their library. They will have to look up all the dealing with Native American issues and devise a way to interpret that information on their website. They may do graphs, charts, etc., but it must be clear what the ratio of stereotypical books is compared to more appropriate books. . . . This statistical analysis will be completed over the course of the next two weeks.

Day Four: 'Detectives aren't just for television'; 'Statistics aren't just for college kids' deconstructs the meaning of 'detective' and the implications of what the students find in the library.

> If the kids are being detectives by hunting down stereotypical books, then does that make the library an accomplice to the crime? Furthermore, does that make the authors punishable by law? The children will discuss courses of action to take in the school in order to relay the message to the other students that some of the books in their school are problematic.

The students spend the rest of the day in the library researching and exploring other books that stereotype people. A highlight of this day involves the emphasis on action oriented research utilizing the knowledge students have learned to raise others' awareness in regards to how and why knowledge is constructed.

Day Five and Six: 'Letters with a mission' provides the final steps for the students to apply what they have learned through their detective assignments.

> Many of the children will start to have concerns about the quality of books in their library. The kids will begin letter-writing campaigns to the libraries in their school district and to the people responsible for purchasing the books. Included in the letters will be the students' research findings on the materials promoting negative stereotypes in the school libraries. Also included in the letter will be a list of recommended books by and for Native American. . . . The letters will be . . . mailed to the appropriate locations by day six. The children will also call their local news media to explain what they have been doing to increase awareness of stereotypical books in schools.

Elizabeth provides a good example here of how to use math within the classroom so that the numbers do not become sterile, but useful, a means to a socially productive end. Continuing to work on the photographic essays, the students experiment with different settings, as they photograph traditions outside of their families.

Day Seven: 'Return to day three' goes back to working on the reflective journal the students began on day three. The day continues as follows:

Today we will be talking about the Native American commitment to nature and how we can work to encourage ecologically sound practices. . . . The kids will talk about their own ecological practices and those of their families. . . . We will make a book about the possible dangers imposed upon us if we do not begin to recycle. . . . We will discuss the work we have done throughput the past few days which has led us to the place where we are at the moment.

The children will spend the rest of the afternoon working on their webpage. They must maintain it by adding any new material to it or answering questions posed by outside sources. While working on their pages, some of the children may start receiving responses to the letters they wrote regarding the book debate. The kids will probably receive a lot of 'thank yous', but not a lot of action. Perhaps another sixth grade class somewhere in the country could respond to our page by asking questions about our findings. This will instill in my students a sense of accomplishment for all their hard work. It is possible that news will travel and people will start questioning Disney's *Pochahantas* book and movie.

Day Eight: 'Shall we dance?' looks at dance for its international and cultural significance. McNeil plays traditional Wampanoag music and asks the students for their reactions. She then induces them to dance to the music, perhaps even closing their eyes if they feel comfortable in order to feel the music.

From there, I will brainstorm with the kids some other times people dance to give thanks. In Europe at Oktoberfest, for example, . . . We will spend a good part of the morning studying different dances intended to give thanks. . . . The children will spend the rest of the morning writing short narratives a child their age who lived during the time of an ancient harvest celebration. They can write about Asian, Native American, European, and African cultures among many others as long as they have some historical background included in the narratives. The kids will rehearse these narratives as if they were soliloquies and be ready to present them on day 10 of the unit.

The students research their characters and read more books that will help them in their soliloquies. During the dance lessons, the students examine the kinesthetic effects of dancing.

Day Nine: 'Photographic essay day with Annie Liebowitz' culminates the students' experience as photographers. During the morning they develop the film and in the afternoon they display their essays for their families, explaining what they meant to them. Traditional food representing the students' culture is a part of the afternoon events. Realistically, the students would need extra days for the film to dry, a contact sheet to be printed, and the specific shots to be selected, printed, and dried. Also, they would need some time to organize the sequence of the essay and decide whether or not to include text.

Day Ten: 'The Final day':

On the last day of our Thanksgiving unit, the kids will reflect on the cognitive restructuring that they had to go through in order to re-interpret the holiday in a new light. They will rehearse their soliloquies in the morning and then perform them in the afternoon for their families.

McNeil's unit comes to a close with a variety of experiences, resources, and de-mystifying practices designed for elementary students. Using her abilities as a re-searcher, Elizabeth is empowered to lay out a set of compelling activities for her students. Aware of the importance of research as a pedagogical act, she is able to tie research, interpretation, and knowledge production to the Thanksgiving activities.

Melissa Shine's Thanksgiving Unit

Shine's unit begins with a description of the school and classroom for which it is designed. Her classroom is a third grade full of ethnic and religious diversity, students from stable and abusive families, and some children with varied physical and developmental disorders. In her school Melissa has made it a priority to include aides to work along side with the teacher. She states, 'This allows the teacher to present challenging lessons to all of the students and still ensure that all of the students are learning and benefiting.' Her unit is divided into eight parts that deal with the historical construction of the time period from which Thanksgiving was supposedly born.

Part 1: 'Planning the voyage' (Day 1, part of 2) introduces the students to the story of the Pilgrims and strangers who boarded the Mayflower to come to the new world. For the next two weeks, the students would be acting the parts of both the newcomers and the Wampanoag Indians.

> The first activity that we will do will be making journals to record our events in the following days. The students will be encouraged to write and draw how they feel, what everything looks like and the events that are happening around them. The students can write these journals from a newcomer or a Wampanoag Indian's point of view. They can also choose to be a man, woman or child and write from that perspective as well. The students will write in the journals everyday, and the first day's activity will be to write about why they are traveling on the Mayflower.

From this activity the students plan and map the boat trip, study the wind currents, calculate the mileage and supplies needed. The students will also rewrite the Mayflower Compact and design the Mayflower to be an appropriate vessel. Shine uses *If You Sailed on the Mayflower* to read aloud to the children throughout the unit.

Part 2: 'The New World' (second part of Day 2, Day 3) paves the arrival of the newcomers from setting up their village to building their homes. Math skills are used to lay out the village so that all the families have an equal share. The students are divided into three groups that read *The First Thanksgiving Feast, Samuel Eaton's Day*, and *The Pilgrims of Plimoth*. The students will then present the information to the rest of their peers, comparing and contrasting the stories in order to design their own village from all they have read and heard.

Part 3: 'Pilgrim life' (Day 4) discusses the vestments and customs of the new-comers considering the temperature in order to later design appropriate clothing.

The teacher and students will then discuss the roles of the men, women, and children in each group. The journal entry for today will have the students explain what their role as a man, woman or child is in the village and how they compare to the roles that each of these groups hold in today's society.

The class also discusses nutrition and caring for the crops the newcomers cultivated on the plantation. The students experiment with planting seeds and monitoring the effects of water, sunlight, and fertilizer on the plants' growth. Shine carefully weaves a variety of subjects into the day's lesson to maximize the students' learning and create a more holistic approach to teaching.

Part 4: 'Indian life' (Days 5 and 6) concentrates on the dress, customs, and culture of the Wampanoag Indians so that the students can design clothing.

The students will be asked to draw a picture of what these Indians looked like. Since there is the stereotypical view that most Indians had headdresses and mohawks, many students will draw pictures emphasizing these looks. The teacher will show the student show the Wampanoag Indians actually dressed so that the students can become aware of the fact that what they are sometimes told or think is not the truth in all cases.

The students are also asked to observe and discuss the phases of the moon and draw what the moon looks like in their journal every night. This is designed to initiate the student with reading and discussing the significance of nature for the Native American culture.

The students will . . . read and discuss *Lightning Inside You*, . . . 'How Glooskap made human beings' which is found in How *Glooskap Outwits the Ice Giants*. The students would then record in their journal a story in which they think of a way the Great Spirits and nature can collaborate and teach a lesson.

The students also learn some Algonkian language as well as the history behind the meeting between Squanto and Captain Miles Standish. The students will prepare a re-enactment of this meeting.

The journal entry for this section will have the students record how they, as Wampanoag Indians, would feel about the newcomers, and how the newcomers would feel about the Wampanoag Indians. . . . The students will also learn about the autumnal Thanksgiving feasts that the Indians had each year and will realize that they celebrated these feasts long before their Thanksgiving with the newcomers. They will find out that this Thanksgiving feast was actually the Wampanoag's fifth of the year.

At this point the students invite each other to the Thanksgiving festivities. Throughout this lesson, the students have had the opportunity to expand their frames of reference by adopting another's position or consciousness as a simulation of Thanksgiving and its history.

Part 5: 'Preparing for the feast' (Day 7), the students plan for the event as newcomers deciding how much food needs to be prepared, what ingredients are needed and how much time is needed to cook.

> The students will spend half of the day in the library researching books and the internet to find authentic Thanksgiving recipes to serve at their feast, such as corn soup, succotash, white fish, red meat, fowl, berries, beans, squash, pumpkins and sweet potatoes. . . . They will also be able to use their research to find games that the children of this time period played, and they can also invent games that could have been played using the available resources of the land back then.

As the students prepare everything, Shine asks another class to join in hopes to reproduce the story as closely as possible by having more guests come than expected and then solving the dilemma presented by the need to stretch and divide the food.

Part 6: 'The first Thanksgiving' (Day 8), at the outset the students must tend to the insufficient food.

> 'Squanto', one of the children in the other class, will instruct some of his tribe members to go hunt and get more food for the feast. These students will leave and return with the food they had prepared.
>
> Before eating, 'Squanto' will say the Thanksgiving Prayer from the Iroquois People. Both classes will eat their meals and will participate in activities that happened during the first Thanksgiving. The students from the other class will have previously learned how to make corn husk dolls. They will then partner off with someone from my class and will teach them the story of the corn husk dolls and . . . teach them how to make one. By having the other class tell the story out loud, the students will be able to see how the Indians usually passed on their stories orally and not in written language. Each partner group will discuss what the moral of the story was and then ask another group to tell their version of the story. Most likely, the stories will be somewhat different and the students will be able to see how oral stories can become distorted if they are continually passed down. The teacher will then explain that to prevent this from happening, the Indians often had storytellers that were really good at telling their own stories, but also at telling the traditional stories accurately.
>
> The students will read both versions of *The First Thanksgiving* . . . and the teacher will finish *If You Sailed on the Mayflower* . . . then *The Thanksgiving Story* . . . and ask the students how it was different from what they had learned in the past few days. . . . At the end of the day (the students will be informed that the First Thanksgiving actually lasted three days), 'Captain Standish' and 'Squanto' will decide to write a peace treaty between the Wampanoag Indians and the newcomers. Both classes will collaborate and write in the treaty what they feel are important issues.

The students are empowered in the continuous application of what they research and learn. History is not left untouched or regarded as sacrosanct, it is understood, deconstructed, and revamped from a socially conscious agenda.

Part 7: 'The Thanksgiving celebrations since then' (Day 9) compares and contrasts how Thanksgiving celebrations have changed throughout the decades.

They will discuss the foods and customs that their family celebrates, as well as the information that they learned this year and how it differed from years in the past. The students will read the 'Thanksgiving Day' chapter of *Celebration* which describes how Thanksgiving became a national holiday and how it has been celebrated through the years.

In this same part of the unit students monitor the progress of their plants and write a letter to a person in the school for whom they are thankful.

As the final discussion, the teacher will read 'Lin's first Thanksgiving' aloud. The story explains how a young girl from Vietnam interprets Thanksgiving by comparing it to her leaving Vietnam because of the new political power. The students and teacher will discuss Lin's story and the story of other immigrants and why they choose to move to America.

The class will end the day by discussing that some people do not celebrate Thanksgiving simply because they have no family or money to do so. As a pre-arranged class trip, the students will then spend the rest of the afternoon working in a soup kitchen for the homeless. Their homework for the night will require them to reflect in their journals about the people that they met there and how they felt about it.

The students' learning is expanded cross-culturally through the above lesson and internalized in the reflective writing captured in the journal. Providing these kinds of experiences for elementary students fosters an experiential research opportunity that allows for the paradigms of inquiry to be transformed by what is being studied or experienced. In this way it transcends the mechanical delivery of 'proper methods' from methods professor to teacher education student.

Part 8: 'Indian life now and human rights' (Day 10):

Today's class will wrap up the Thanksgiving unit, but will also provide a lead in to a discrimination and human rights unit. . . . The students are shown a copy of the treaty signed by the newcomers and the Wampanoag Indians, as well as the one the students wrote in class. . . . The Pilgrims did not think that the Wampanoag Indians were equals because they found their religion and beliefs to be inferior. Even though they had endured religious persecution, they continued the cycle by inflicting oppression on others. The teacher will then talk about King Philip's War and how the two groups ended up killing each other with the death toll much higher on the Indian side.

Shine's students read and respond to the 1970 speech from the Thanksgiving ceremonials held annually at Plymouth rock. They also analyze how different groups are treated unfairly and study actions that can be taken to oppose such injustice.

Today will also include a discussion of what Indian life is like now. We will talk about how Indians were forced onto reservations and the attitudes and stereotypes that people have about Indians. The students will reflect in their journals about how they feel about these issues and how they would feel if someone treated them like this.

Shine's unit provides a good flow and progression of information and experiences as she finishes the unit with relevant race relations in contemporary society. Ending with yet another goal, another pursuit, is the backbone of any research oriented pedagogical model that empowers students to make learning a life long endeavor in and outside of the institution of school. Like McNeil, her consciousness of the role of research in pedagogy empowers her students to think and act in exciting ways.

Kristin L. Persichini's Thanksgiving Unit

Persichini's unit is structured completely different, partitioned by themes flexibly overlapping during the two week period. Her unit is designed for a middle-class fourth grade with children from diverse backgrounds. She provides a rationale for her unit:

> Our world is constantly changing, and therefore, I believe that our teaching strategies should also be changing in order to accommodate our learners.
>
> I have reached this conclusion only through many nights of struggling with right and wrong, traditional and non-traditional, accepted and perhaps a bit controversial teaching styles. However, after reflecting on my own learning experiences, I have finally realized why nothing in the area of history ever made sense or even interested me in all my years of school. Unfortunately, a movement of 'information feeding' educators have created numerous generations of people who do not know anything about our country's history. The problems occur due to the obvious gap between the information being 'taught' and the lives of those learning it. The material needs to be meaningful, and in order for this to happen the children have to be involved in the research of these facts. Simply, teachers should present crucial issues and children should actively research the issue as problematic situations which directly or indirectly affect their lives.
>
> Knowing this, I have constructed a unit on Thanksgiving entitled, 'You're invited' . . . invited to a unified world composed of many differences. In this unit, I have asked the children, using the history of Thanksgiving as their focus problem, to investigate differences which are included in our world. . . .
>
> The children will begin each day of this two week unit by expressing their feelings in a journal which will allow them to consistently reflect on their progress in beliefs. . . . They will be allowed to work on these activities as they wish throughout the unit as long as they complete them all by Thursday of the second week. At this time, the children will come together and discuss each activity as a group. These discussions will allow the students to discover new ideas from one another. These collaboration days can include anything from poetry readings, commercial reviews, and drama skits to food samples, sports activities, and song rounds. . . . The end of Friday will be dedicated to a 'Thanksgiving feast' which recognizes a wide variety of cultural celebrations that occur throughout the year. In actuality, we will be giving thanks to our own individual family traditions and creating our own idea of a Thanksgiving celebration.

The above situates her unit and her particular agenda for her students demonstrating an acceptance for difference and an encouragement towards the students finding their own voice throughout the research and learning process. She has also made it a point to include the parents as much as possible for their cooperation and input. The students will look at mainstream Thanksgiving stories and then other stories that have been marginalized by the western paradigm. Through a variety of experiences, the students will critically look at the knowledge that is presented to them as unquestionable. Her activities are described under different subject areas; only a few will be highlighted.

Language Arts: The students will write about what they already know about Thanksgiving, including family traditions, historical knowledge, and personal concerns.

> After completing a written description of what Thanksgiving is to you, interact with a partner on the Internet and in the library to research another point of view pertaining to the history of Thanksgiving as we know it.

The students will also read *The True Story of the Three Little Pigs* by Jon Scieska, discuss it and compare the different versions of the same story in light of their research.

Science: Through the use of science, the students become active participants in their learning process, learning to utilize a variety of resources available to them.

> Locate a local farmer and interview him or her about agriculture within your community. Survey what crops are grown and then analyze their usefulness to your community as opposed to other areas. You may want to consider the effects of weather on the various crops.

Social Studies: This sections expands the student's imagination and cross-cultural awareness.

> Pose an 'I Wonder' question that you can research using any and all resources accessible to you. Please feel free to work with others that wonder the same thing you do. For example, if you wondered what type of activities the Amish participated in for fun, you may contract a person from this culture, surf the Internet, or read informational literature pertaining to Amish culture. Prepare an oral presentation of this newly gained knowledge for the gathering at the end of the unit.

Mathematics: The first assignment deals with entering the results from tomato experiments they were previously working on into Microsoft Excel in their computers. Two other assignments follow:

> Get a partner and go to the media room. While there, watch 15 minutes of television. During this time, one of you keep track of how many times reference was made to male stereotypes such as associating males with roughness or other stereotypical assumptions. The partner needs to keep track of references of female

stereotypes such as a mother in the kitchen. After recording the results, discuss why these stereotypes are continually portrayed and where we are most likely to encounter them. Then, use your discussion to decide why such stereotypes as face painting and savage behavior are associated with Indians.

Design the ideal playground in your neighborhood. Be sure to specify the calculated area, or length times width, which this will take from your neighborhood. How do you think the people living in the house where the playground was just built felt when they lost their home so that children had a place to play? Now, look at a map of the land which the Indians once occupied. Mark what portion was originally taken from them. Be sure to specify the calculated area of this land using the proper scale from the map. How do you think the Indians felt when the Pilgrims showed up only to take their already cultivated land, as one story claims?

Health: Here the students will look at the stereotypical Thanksgiving dinner menu and analyze the nutritional value of the foods. They will also investigate the causes for the deaths in the 'Trail of Tears' while identifying the unhealthy conditions which led to the deaths. Then Persichini poses:

Your best friend just admitted to you that he/she has been starving him/herself because of the extra weight put on over the summer. Does this 'difference' seem like a problem? Explain. Should we treat those starving themselves differently because of their eating habits?

Physical Education: The students are instructed to:

Surf the Internet to find a site that discusses various dances common to the Indian culture. Watch the video footage and attempt to learn the dance in a sequence of short, simple steps. Collaborate ideas with others to come to a consensus of what role dance played in the Indian culture.

Again, here we see the students exposed to the Internet so that they can have a plethora of information at their fingertips.

Music: The arts in general are given much attention in Persichini's unit as basic subjects offering a variety of experiences.

Work in groups to establish an overall opinion of the benefits which result from a diversified community. Take these ideas and incorporate them into a song of any style that tells your story. Experiment with home-made musical instruments to enhance the performance.

Also, above improvisation is encouraged which is pivotal for fostering creativity.

Discuss with others why music is or is not important in your life. Look at another culture's view of music and observe how music affects their lives. How do the differences between music in cultures affect our society? You may want to look at some issues including group interaction, home environment with or without music, and the communication skills of various groups.

Art: Through visual representation and imagery, Kristin focuses her lessons on identifying, deconstructing, and displacing dubious representations assigned to various groups.

> Often, Indians are stereotyped to wear head dresses and face paint. However, they are people just like you and me. They dress in clothing and do not make it a habit to paint their skin on a daily basis. Identify another stereotype found within a culture of interest to you. With the intent to put an end to such stereotypes, create a portrait of a member from this culture which illustrates the invalidity of the ideas currently held.
>
> Videotape a commercial which tells me how differences affect your lives and what the society looks like which makes you feel that 'You are invited.' Please be open with your ideas and share the rationale to your beliefs. After this is completed, attempt to create a commercial that depicts the way the Indians felt when differences entered their society. Why were the reactions conflicting between your ideas and the Indian's ideas?

Drama: The lessons and activities planned for this section recognize the need for fourth graders to kinesthetically express themselves as well as emphasizing other ways of knowing.

> Create a skit which portrays the story of Thanksgiving that you created in this two week period. Feel free to be creative with language, costumes, personalities, and roles. 'Different' interpretations of this holiday are welcome. Make it a goal to give us an inside view of your Thanksgiving celebration.
>
> Play charades with a group of peers that depict the typical stereotypes involving gender, culture, race, attitude, and socio-economic status. After using stereotypes, take interesting facts that you have learned within this unit that disprove these assumptions and attempt to act them out.
>
> Finally, during the last day of the unit, we will all contribute our own traditional family gatherings to an 'Around the world' dinner feast. By doing this, we will be able to rewrite our own stories of the Thanksgiving feast. Hopefully, this culminating activity will provide a sense of being 'invited' for all of the members of this learning experience.

It is Persichini's belief that students would experience a substantial amount of success given the flexibility and freedom permeating the unit. She states, 'Overall, I hope that this learning experience will open up the children's minds to many views of stories and also encourage them to problematize traditional stories which have previously been taken for granted. Persichini also offers the following websites for further research:

> http://www.night.net/thanksgiving/lesson-plan.html 'Teaching About Thanksgiving'

> http://media3.com/plymouth/thanksgiving.html 'The Truth About the Pilgrims and Thanksgiving'

http://www.census.gov/ftp/pub/edu/diversity/llele.html
  'Celebrating Our Nation's Diversity'

http://www.census.gov/ftp/pub/edu/diversity/divtext.html
  'Our Diverse Nation'

gopher://ericir.syr.edu:70/0R0-14688-/Lesson/Subject/LanguageArts/
  ceclang.37 'Spiro Mounds'

gopher://ericir.syr.edu:70/0R0-1765-/Lesson/NewLesson/SocialStudies/
  diversity 'Diversity of Cultures in America'

gopher://ericir.syr.edu:70/0R0–5087-/Lesson/Subject/SocialStudies/cecsst.82
  'Native American Interdisciplinary Educational Unit'

http:www.eduplace.com/ss/act/wonder.html 'What's the Wonder?'

http://www.eduplace.com/ss/act/celtime.html 'A Celebration Timeline'

http://raven.ccukans.edu/kansite/ww_one/comment/Cmrts/Cmrt3.html
  'Portraying the Indian'

http://www.minnetonka.k12mn.us/support/science/lesson45/thanks.html
  'Thanksgiving Unit'

http://www.eduplace.com/ss/act/fabric.html 'The Fabrics of Our Lives'

http://pc65.frontier.osrhe.edu/students/plumleyo/cloth.html
  'Women's Southern Cloth'

http://pc65.frontier.osrhe.edu/students/plumleyo/straight.html
  'Men's Southern Straight Dance'

http://one-web.org/oneida/lacrosse.html 'Lacrosse: An Iroquois Tradition'

http://www.si.edu/organiza/museums/amerind/edu/eduschol.html
  'School Programs'

http://www.si.edu/organiza/museums/amerind/exhibit/index.html
  'Exhibitions'

Conclusion: The Power of Student Research

In order to summarize the three units we have delineated in this chapter, we will list the strengths and highlights that all three units share that make them such powerful pedagogical documents. The list contains the components to successful student researcher frameworks that are applicable to any subject or grade level. The list is as follows:

1 research expertise
2 deconstruct/question/compare/contrast
3 utilization of multiple resources
4 experientials/multiple, varied experiences
5 expanding knowledge (traditional)/focusing on other ways of knowing
6 exploring other's consciousness
7 interdisciplinary focus
8 consciousness of students' needs
9 studying bias, stereotypes, culture, and tradition
10 emphasizing cross-cultural definitions
11 journaling — a respect for the need of private self-expression resulting in heightened learning, reflection, analytic skills, and empowerment
12 inviting speakers, family members, and other classes
13 focusing on multifaceted, kinesthetic, emotional, intellectual, and artistic expression and development
14 encouraging respect for and demystification of difference

McNeil's, Shine's, and Persichini's Thanksgiving units model the use of research in elementary education. These three young women were teacher education student researchers conceptualizing, writing about, and creating conditions for their students to become researchers. These teacher education students experienced and practiced the research and pedagogical skills they will apply in their classrooms. They are schools who use in their scholarship to produce young scholars. They and many of their fellow classmates whom we are unable to mention here prove that teachers who are interpreters and knowledge producers are better equipped to become inspirational teachers. Particularly impressive in their curricular plans is their savvy about the controversial nature of Thanksgiving as a scholarly topic and the politicized nature of schooling. In all three units the students were able to use research as a means of defusing the volatility of their lessons. None of them can be accused of politicization, as they allow their students as researchers to find differing perspectives on the ideological meaning of Thanksgiving as part of their inquiry process.

One of the central tenets of any critical pedagogy — whether it be in graduate school, college, secondary, or in this case, elementary education — involves the ability to conduct research. Critical teachers provide students with the skills and space to do it, interpret it, use it, and continuously change it within different contexts. As much as student abilities allow, critical teachers acquaint students with secondary research skills in libraries, book and magazine outlets, and the Internet. In the same way they acquaint students with primary research methods including historical, ethnographic, semiotic, textual, and other processes of producing original knowledge. We argue that such methods can be taught to all students, even young elementary students. The ability to perform research provides students with a cognitive skill immeasurably important in all phases of life. It grants them a historicity and a contextual appreciation of learning that no other skill can furnish. As a result students (and their teachers) experience the slippery empowerment that many pedagogies only reference in the abstract. They are empowered by what they can do and what they know — doors are opened in the process to new ways of seeing that expand the cognitive envelop and move human beings to new levels of consciousness.

Acknowledgments

Many thanks to Penn State Education Students Elizabeth McNeil, Melissa Shine and Kristin L. Persichini.

Chapter 12

Social Studies Teaching and Learning: A Descriptive Analysis of Concept Mapping

Nancy Fichtman Dana

In recent years, there has been a move to reconceptualize teacher education from a set of technical skills prospective teachers must master and subsequently demonstrate during field experiences to more reflective and critical examination of one's own teaching practices (Angell, 1991; Carter, 1992; Dana and Tippins, 1993; Kennedy, 1988). Therefore, many teacher educators are presently structuring programs and classes in order to create opportunities for prospective teachers to reflect on their own experiences as students and teachers as well as their own beliefs about teaching and learning (Tabachnich and Zeichner, 1991).

One challenge facing educators of prospective social studies teachers is to design new and innovative approaches to traditional 'methods' classes. One example of alternative teacher education pedagogy in the social studies is described by Adler (1991). Adler discusses the use of imaginative literature in an elementary education social studies methods class as a way to 'provide preservice teachers with alternative perspectives toward human history and social interaction' (p. 79). Adler reflects on the challenge facing teacher educators:

> the pedagogical problem presented to the teacher educator is that of finding the stimuli which will open students to asking questions, to taking new perspectives, to examining alternatives . . . The problem of teacher education is . . . how can we emancipate students from mindlessness; how can we free them for the difficult task of making choices. (Adler, 1991, p. 79)

Faced with the pedagogical problem described by Adler, many teacher educators have joined Adler in the search for pedagogical approaches that will foster critical reflection on the part of prospective teachers (Tabachnich and Zeichner, 1991). One promising strategy teacher educators may employ to help prospective teachers practice thinking about teaching social studies is concept mapping (Novak and Gowin, 1984). Concept maps are defined as 'a visual representation of knowledge; a picture of conceptual relationships; a pulling together of thoughts' (Antonacci, 1991, p. 174). Concept maps are constructed by selecting and writing major concepts and ideas in a circle or oval, and then joining related concepts with lines and connecting verbs that explain the relationships between concepts (Tippins and Dana, 1992). Although Angell (1991) suggests that 'because social studies . . . invites so many differing interpretations and is often vaguely understood by preservice teachers, . . . mapping may be critical to understanding the kinds of experience and beliefs preservice teachers bring to a methods course', there exists little research that addresses how prospective teachers experience the process of sense-making through concept mapping. Past research has focused on conceptions of social studies developed during the course of student teaching (Adler, 1982) and during the duration of a methods course (Wilson and Readence, 1993). Prospective elementary school teachers can make sense of teaching social studies through conceptual mapping, creating a pedagogical tool which teacher educators may employ in order to foster reflection.

Methods

To examine how prospective teachers make sense of the social studies through concept mapping, I incorporated the technique of pre- and post-course concept mapping into three sections of an elementary school social studies methods course that I taught at two universities over a period of three consecutive semesters from 1990 through 1992. Pre- and post-methods course concept mapping was incorporated into the three credit hour methods course in the following way. On the first day of class, I introduced concept mapping as a way that teachers can assess student prior knowledge before beginning or planning a unit. I asked students to think about their own experiences with elementary school social studies and create a concept map that represents their thinking about elementary school social studies. Individuals discussed their concept maps in small groups which was followed by whole class discussion of common themes that were evident across all maps. Concept maps were collected. Three weeks prior to the end of the methods course, I asked students to create a post-course concept map for their final project for the course. Directions read:

> Based on your readings (textbook, reserve readings at Curriculum Resource Center, and other), class sessions (instruction and discussion with your peers), notes you've taken during class, classmates' presentations, reflections you've written this semester, and assignments you've completed this semester, concept map your learning and your conception of elementary school social studies. Begin with elementary school social studies or social studies in the elementary school as your main concept. Keep a brief dated log that documents your thinking as you complete this assignment.

Following the initial assignment a portion of the next class period was devoted to discussion of concept map evaluation. The notion of a holistic scoring rubric was introduced to the prospective teachers and, collectively, the class developed a holistic scoring rubric to distinguish the quality of student concept maps. An example of the scoring rubric appears in Figure 12.1.

Students shared their final concept maps with class members at the last class session. Following the sharing session, I handed out students' original maps

Figure 12.1   Concept map scoring rubric

Level 4 A level 4 concept map is exciting (and perhaps even inspiring!) to examine. A level 4 concept map accurately conveys to the instructor an original but viable understanding of what social studies is, what information is known concerning fundamental aspects of teaching social studies, and the ways in which the individual would like to organize and present social studies to his/her students in the future. The map reflects its creator's growth and personal philosophy of teaching. The map contains concepts that emanate from a variety of sources including SSED 430W class sessions, textbook and other readings, unit preparation, special topic reports, and personal thoughts and experiences. The map should read in such a way that the viewer can easily tell the difference between major and more minor points and can easily follow the connections made. Connections that are made must be necessary and must be made with care — there must be evident reason for making any connections. There is evidence that the concept map was well planned. The map *may* (but does not have to) be presented in a creative form, and the format that is selected must be compatible with and make sense in light of the general understanding of social studies evidenced in the layout and choice of content. Map represents considerable effort, learning, growth, and reflection.

Level 3 A level 3 concept map is satisfactory, but lacks the creativity and evidence of personal growth and reflection apparent in a level 4 concept map. There is evidence that the student has spent quality time working on the project, but more personal growth and reflection is needed to come to a richer understanding of what it means to teach and learn social studies in the elementary school. The map contains concepts that emanate from a variety of sources including SSED 430W class sessions, textbook and other readings, unit preparation, special topic reports, and personal thoughts and experiences. As with a level 4 concept map, the viewer should be able to distinguish between major and more minor ideas as well as follow and comprehend all connections. The map may be presented in a creative format, but there is a lack of connection between the format and the basic ideas put forth by the map's creator. Map represents considerable effort.

Level 2 A level 2 concept map demonstrates an understanding of materials presented throughout the semester but is limited in number of concepts presented or is too great in number of concepts presented and therefore the connections made between these concepts are superficial and difficult to follow. The map is dominated mainly by concepts emanating from one or two sources only (class sessions or the text) and the map creator mainly relies on a pre-established organization of ideas for presenting the concept map (for example, the map is organized based on the course syllabus or table of contents of the text). The map may be presented in a creative format, but there is a lack of connection between the format and the basic ideas put forth by the map's creator. Portions of the map may not represent a personal, grounded understanding of teaching social studies in the elementary school. It is clear that more personal growth and reflection is needed to come to a richer understanding of teaching social studies.

Level 1 A level 1 concept map shows a lack of preparation, planning, and depth. Major concepts may be lacking, and/or there is no apparent underlying theme or rationale for connections made between concepts. It is clear that the student has put little or no effort into the concept map creation.

constructed on the first day of the semester, and asked students to add a final entry to their log reacting to the original concept map in relation to the final map.

Mapping as an Act of Student Research

The foundation for the study of the process of concept mapping just described is laid by the recent efforts in educational research to listen to the voices of teachers. Many educational researchers are joining with teachers to study and document their lives in the context of the classroom situation. Hence, action research, defined as 'the application of tools and methods of social science to immediate, practical problems with the goals of contributing to theory and knowledge in the field of education and improving practice in schools' (Oja and Shulyan, 1989, p. 1) has gained popularity.

Ironically, as teacher educators/researchers form partnerships with teachers to engage in research on their teaching practices, few teacher educators research their own practices. When teacher educators/researchers research their own practices, a number of benefits are possible including the documentation of the real world of teacher educators, a literature that is sparse. Such documentation may lead to insights and understandings into the various approaches to the education of teachers and, hence, yield meaningful improvement in teacher education. Additionally, if teacher educators research their own teaching practices, an opportunity to model reflection and action research for prospective teachers emerges.

In this chapter I hope to provide social studies teacher educators with insights into the ways concept maps may be a viable tool to use to assess student thinking about elementary school social studies. The following questions guide my goals:

1 How do pre-service teachers make sense of teaching elementary school social studies?
2 How do pre-service teachers experience the sense making process of constructing a concept map to organize and represent their thinking about elementary school social studies?

The Constructivist Educator

The methods employed in observing the implimention of concept mapping were interpretive (Erickson, 1986), in that they involved the collection and interpretation of qualitative data through document analysis. A constructivist epistemology (Bruner, 1986) was embodied into the collection and interpretation of data. Constructivists view learning as an interpretive process in which individuals engage in unique constructions of knowledge as they make sense of their experiences (Bentley, 1993; Fleury, 1993).

Kincheloe (1993) in *Toward a Critical Politics of Teacher Thinking*, provides an overview of constructivism as well as implications of constructivism for schooling and teacher education. For constructivists, 'no truly objective way of seeing exists. Nothing exists before consciousness shapes it into something we can perceive' (pp. 107–8). The following vignette simplifies constructivism and what constructivism means for the teacher and teaching:

> An environmentalist, a real estate developer, an artist, a hunter, and a bird-watcher are walking through wetlands. Each of them sees and responds to the wetlands in different ways. To the environmentalist, it is a source of life; to the real estate developer, it is land to be cleared so beachfront condominiums can be constructed; the artist sees it as something to paint; to the hunter, the wetlands are a cover for game; the bird-watcher sees a natural setting to explore. Thus the backgrounds and expectations of the observers shape their perceptions. In the same way, consider

how a classroom is perceived by a class clown, a traditionally good student, a burnt-out teacher, a standardized test maker, a bureaucratic supervisor, a disgruntled parent, or a nostalgic alumnus. The way our psychosocial disposition shapes how the world is perceived holds extremely important implications for teaching. Each of our students brings a unique disposition into the classroom. Indeed, each teacher carries a unique disposition with her or him. (Kincheloe, 1993, p. 108)

Hence, particular attention in this study and in my teaching was given to the knowledge social studies prospective teachers carry with them into the methods class, prospective teachers' notions of where knowledge exists, and the sense making process prospective teachers engage in as they construct their conception of elementary school social studies through the process of concept mapping.

As I read and sorted the results of the use of concept mapping for inclusion in this chapter, to a certain extent, the decisions I made depended upon my own subjectivities and biases as a social studies teacher educator interested in constructivism as a way of knowing and thinking about the complex process of learning to teach. Two techniques I used to enhance the quality of this analysis and ensure the trustworthiness of the study include source triangulation and the reporting of negative cases.

Source triangulation is defined as 'checking out the consistency of different sources within the same method' (Patton, 1990, p. 464). I collected data from three separate classes of prospective teachers at two different universities at three separate points in time, and compared the sources against each other to look for consistency of information derived from prospective teachers at different times and in different places. Source triangulation:

will seldom lead to a single, totally consistent picture . . . The point is to study and understand when and why there are differences . . . At the same time consistency in overall patterns of data from different sources and reasonable explanations for differences in data from divergent sources contribute significantly to the overall credibility of findings. (Patton, 1990, pp. 467–8)

The results reports the patterns that were found consistently. In addition, I report and explain negative cases, defined as cases that did not fit the pattern. By considering cases that do not fit the patterns, understanding of the patterns, themselves, may be increased and the credibility of a study is enhanced (Patton, 1990). A final read of the organized information/results (sorted into categories) lead to the following patterns:

Results

Pattern 1: Reflecting on Conceptions of Social Studies Through the Process of Concept Mapping

Four pre-course concept maps were selected to portray the dominant pattern that emerged from an analysis of the 92 maps used in this study. A computer reproduction of the students' maps appear in Figures 12.2 through 12.5.

Figure 12.2   Concept mapping, example I

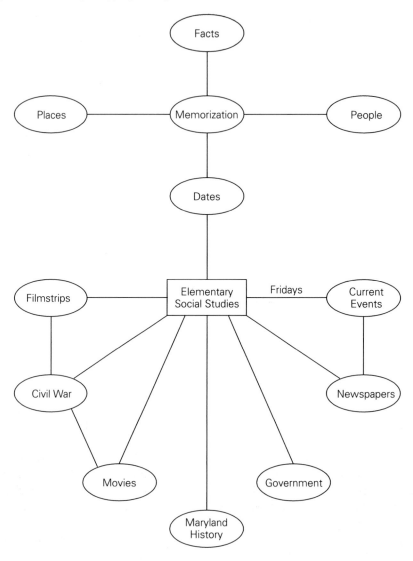

The most striking pattern that emerged across all maps was the strong association prospective teachers made between social studies and meaningless memorization. This analysis confirms Adler's assertions that 'to many students in an elementary teacher education program, social studies is boring and lifeless. The images they too often hold are those of memorizing lists of names and dates for tests' (Adler, 1982, p. 79). This view of social studies can be interpreted as being grounded in an objectivist epistemology, as knowledge exists 'outside of the individual' and the individual acquires knowledge through the memorization of 'the facts' that exist 'out there'. For most pre-service teachers in the study, 'the facts' of social studies

Figure 12.3   Concept mapping, example 2

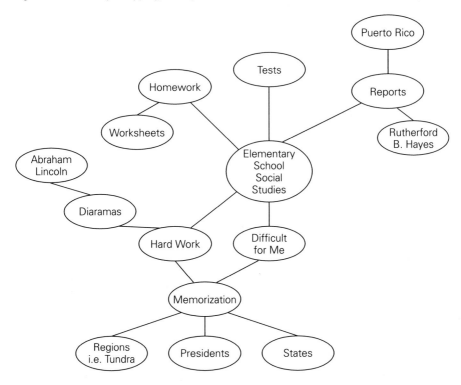

include memorization of dates, people, and places, as indicated in the concept map reproduced in Figure 12.2. The concept map reproduced in Figure 12.3 is also indicative of memorization related to presidents, states, and regions. In addition to the memorization of 'names, dates, and places', the concept map in Figure 12.4 also portrays an objectivist view of knowledge. Knowledge is seen as existing in a textbook through the connection made between 'elementary school social studies', 'teachers' and 'teach from the book' and 'follow unit'. This same map indicates that students are to 'follow along with the teacher'. The student, therefore, is not active in the construction of knowledge.

The creators of these concept maps, as well as majority of pre-service teachers engaging in the creation of the pre-course concept map, indicated that the view of social studies grounded in an objectivist epistemology was unpleasant and meaningless. For example, a direct connection is made between elementary school social studies and 'difficult for me' and 'memorization' in Figure 12.3. Perhaps Figure 12.5 best illustrates meaninglessness through the connections made between 'elementary school social studies', 'American History', and 'Had to memorize the 50 states and their capitals — only remembered them long enough for the test', and 'Elementary school social studies', 'Field trips', and 'Since I live 30 minutes from Gettysburg we had many field trips to the battlefields — after a while we didn't even want to hear about G-burg.'

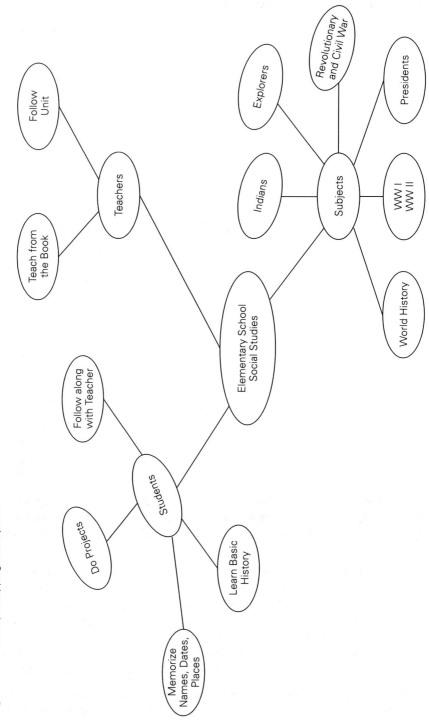

Figure 12.4 Concept mapping, example 3

Figure 12.5   Concept mapping, example 4

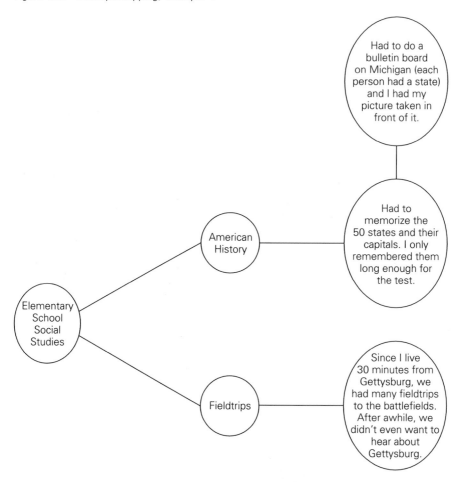

The view of social studies that pre-service teachers bring with them to their college study of learning to teach is not surprising as studies completed during the time period when most pre-service elementary school teachers were in elementary school report the following:

- Almost all elementary school teachers use one or more text books;
- Sixty percent of the time allocated for social studies instruction in the elementary school is spent using printed materials such as the text;
- Teachers employ lecture and discussion as their main instructional strategy when teaching social studies; and
- Teachers expect students to learn 'the facts' (see, for example, Shaver, Davis and Helburn, 1979 and Superka, Hawke and Morrissett, 1980).

This is a view, however, that many teacher educators have desired to change (Wilson, Konopak and Readence, 1994). The construction of pre-course concept maps helped pre-service teachers explore their conceptions of the teaching and learning of social studies. Therefore, pre-course concept mapping may offer the teacher educator a tool to help prospective teachers articulate their images of social studies. Once images exist as a visual representation in the concept map, teacher educators can lead students in the questioning of the image throughout the course. From an analysis of the maps constructed in this study, in order to change the image of social studies as 'memorization of names, dates, and facts', teacher educators may wish to develop pedagogical strategies that help students question their conceptions of where knowledge exists. As will be demonstrated in the next section of this paper, concept mapping itself holds promise for being one of these strategies.

Pattern 2: Questioning Where Knowledge Exists Through the Process of Concept Mapping

Data in this section support that final course concept mapping engages prospective teachers in the process of constructing personal knowledge regarding the teaching of elementary school social studies, as they reflect on their experiences in light of what they have read and learned throughout the semester. During the construction of maps, prospective teachers are forced to reflect on their beliefs regarding knowledge as they pass through four stages during map construction: 1 comfort, 2 trepidation and frustration, 3 resolution, and 4 elation and pride.

Stage 1: Comfort

When the prospective teachers first received the instructions to concept map 'elementary school social studies' for their course final assessment, they were asked to immediately enter a reflection in their log to describe their reaction to the project that was ahead of them. Overall, the prospective teachers' logs indicated that they felt quite comfortable with the assignment. For a few prospective teachers, that comfort was generated by being given the opportunity to personally make sense of what they had learned throughout the semester. For example, one student wrote:

> It appears as though the process for this project can be done by reflecting on the past semester. The end product will provide a thorough analysis of my thoughts about elementary school social studies. This project will allow me to organize my thoughts, plans, and goals as I prepare to teach.

For a few students, like the one cited above, comfort was experienced because they had already begun to move from viewing knowledge as existing outside the individual to viewing knowledge as constructed by individuals as they make sense of their experiences. These students often made reference to 'where knowledge exists' in their initial journal entries:

> Today we received our final exam assignment and I feel very relieved that it is not a traditional exam in the sense that it is asking us to draw answers from a

'pre-determined pool of knowledge' that we have no use for in the future . . . We have learned useful information that can be made meaningful to us in the future. We all experienced the same class, but took different things from it that we can apply to future teaching. Everyone's personal experiences were different.

One student even articulated the paradigm shift through an analogy to the movie she watched during the time period in which she was constructing her final map:

> As I started my concept map, I was thinking of how much education has changed or is changing. I believe this change is needed . . . I was flicking thought the TV channels and I stopped at AMC (American Movie Classics). I love old movies so I decided to wait and see what was coming on. Well the presenter, who introduces movies came on and gave a synopsis about 'An Apartment for Peggy'. It was about the GI Bill and the soldiers going to college. I rationalized that I should watch it considering it did have to deal with education . . . The relevance it has to my log is the one scene where Peggy's husband is talking of quitting college so he could work in order to provide her with a better life. Peggy asks him to give her a quarter. He does. She holds it in front of his face and asks him what he sees. He responds by saying 'a quarter'. She pulls it farther and farther away and keeps asking the same question, while he replies with the same answer. She keeps doing this till she reaches the other end of the room. She then gives him back the quarter and says, 'If a quarter is all you saw, then just think about how much you are missing.' I believe that education when I was little tried to only have one focus on the coin (which stands for facts) . . . Now education has finally met Peggy and is looking beyond the quarter now. We came from 'just the facts, ma'm' generation. We did not have any control over our learning because it was defined for us. Knowledge was given to us in an objective approach. We, as students, were sounding boards or 'satellites' that took in information and then sent it back. We were taught stereotypes about 'Indians', holidays, families, etc. Basically, we were taught to see the world in an unrealistic, sheltered way. Everything controversial was hushed, avoided and not talked about. They kept us wondering. There was no relevance or connection to the outside world in what we were taught. Why did we need to know . . . because we were told 'you will need it later on'.

These students' logs indicated that they were comfortable with the assignment because they viewed it as a way they could make personal sense out of elementary school social studies. These students, representing negative cases in this analysis, progressed through concept map construction with ease in comparison to the majority of their peers.

The majority of prospective teachers also experienced the initial stage of comfort, but their logs reflected no critical thought about the reflective nature of the assignment or the epistemological implications of the assignment. Instead, comfort arose from a sense of relief that this was not a traditional test and therefore, would not require studying, would not be time consuming and subsequently would be 'easy'. The following excerpts from logs illustrate this experience of relief and comfort:

> I am relieved! I expected this final project to be a very time-consuming, research-oriented assignment. I anticipated that the task would require extensive time periods.

> When I first learned of this project, I thought it would be so simple. Ideas crossed my mind and I thought in no time, I will be finished. I was very wrong.

Other students acknowledged that it would take time to complete, but expressed relief that it was not the traditional test:

> I was really worried when I first thought about this final project because I did not know what to expect. Now that I see what it is, I am still worried but relieved that it is not a multiple choice test, a 20 page research paper or something else like that. It will still require a lot of work, but this should be fun.

> I am pleased (that our final) is a concept map rather than a multiple choice test. We would have just had to memorize facts if it was a test.

These students' sense of comfort grew from a relief that the project was something different than the normal mode of assessment they had previously experienced as meaningless. However, they stopped short of reflecting on the epistemological meaning of the assignment they were about to complete. For these students, comfort was quickly replaced by trepidation and frustration.

Stage 2: Trepidation and Frustration

As students began to work more on their final concept maps, fear and panic replaced the feelings of comfort initially expressed. This trepidation was borne out of a realization that because constructing a concept map was quite different from the traditional forms of assessment students were used to, they did not know the 'rules of the game'. In traditional assessment such as the multiple choice test so many students made reference to, there exists one right answer. Students began to imagine that there was one right way to construct a concept map, but did not have a clue as to what the 'right way' could be. In this stage, students understood concept mapping as representing the 'right way' to think about elementary school social studies, and that 'right way' existed somewhere outside of themselves. For many students, that 'somewhere' was inside the instructor's head:

> I now think this final is confusing. What are we exactly supposed to do? From the looks of it we are to make sort of a semantic web or map of what we have learned this semester. I hope Dr Dana explains this final more clearly or shows us examples of what she wants. Are we supposed to fit everything on one piece of paper?

> I am kind of confused now . . . I'm not sure what you are looking for in a good concept map.

> What does Dr Dana want me to do? What is expected in a concept map? What am I to be writing in this log?

In this stage, students did not believe or trust in themselves as viable constructors of knowledge regarding the teaching of elementary school social studies. Rather, they feared that in their organization of knowledge about the teaching of social studies they might 'leave something out'. This caused a great deal of frustration as students reviewed their notes, the textbook, and other sources:

> I am frustrated! I have reviewed my notes — lots of material — including hand-outs and copies of the reserve material and text. How do I relate all this material? Very frustrating.

> Man, I really had no idea what I was in for in thinking about what social studies is . . . I am very frustrated about what I will do and how I will do it. Every time I start thinking about doing it I start getting brain overload and say 'Oh! what am I doing?!'

> My brain is beginning to ache from thinking so much.

> So I've just looked over all of my notes, reflection papers, and book, and now I am thoroughly confused, or maybe scared. I don't even know how I feel! There seems to be so much information here. I don't think I'll ever be able to make it fit in a logical, organized manner. It's just that I'm the kind of person who panics about stuff like this. I mean, what do I include — all of it?

For some students, this fear and frustration led them to do a 180 degree turn from their initial comments about the ease of the task because it was not a multiple choice or essay exam:

> I wish this *was* an essay exam! . . . I guess this is mainly about what I learned and what I got from the course, but I'm so afraid of leaving some crucial aspect out.

Trepidation that there was one right way to construct a concept map led to a fear about how the concept map would be graded, despite class discussions of the evaluation of concept maps and the creation of a holistic scoring rubric (Figure 12.1):

> Everyone is worried about this project. I wonder what kind of grade I will receive.
> I feel confused and I'm not really sure about how I will do this.

For these students, being able to regurgitate the 'right answers' that existed in a text or in the teacher's head was equated with the external reward of a good grade. In this stage, students had not yet realized that the answer to what elementary school social studies was and how it would play out in their classrooms as they began to teach did not exist outside of themselves. In order to construct a final concept map, students would have to make sense of their experiences over the course of the semester and construct a visual representation of what was inside their own heads. Once students made this realization, they progressed to a stage of resolution.

Stage 3: Resolution

This stage is characterized by the students' realization that their personal construction of elementary school social studies is viable. One student wrote:

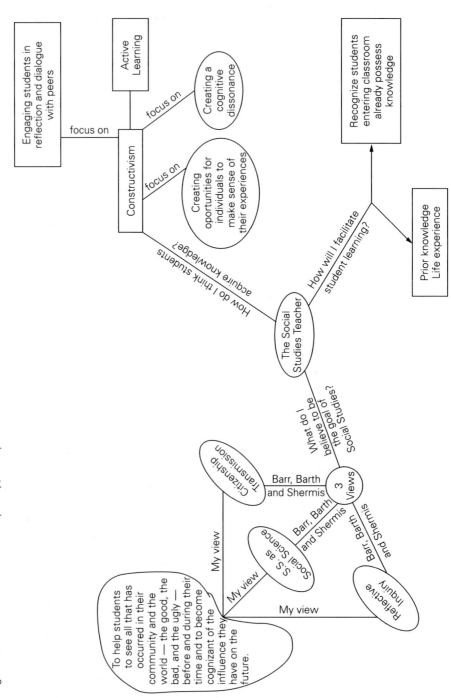

Figure 12.6 Portion of a final concept map, example 1

> I think one of the greatest things I realize is that this concept map is *my opinion.* Boy, does that seem to make a world of difference. I feel a little bit better about it this way. I am able to include what I feel social studies education in the elementary school is. I don't have to worry about having everything, too little or too much. It is surely what I think it is. What a novel idea! This could actually be fun — (Well — *no*!) [Weak moment] I guess I just need to do some brainstorming.

As students began to trust themselves and their personal constructions of what it means to teach and learn social studies in the elementary school, many articulated experiencing a sense of power.

> I like the idea that this final project is based on my opinion, because it gives me the power to include what I see as necessary and important.

> I am on the final steps of conglomerating my map. I feel confident with the progress I have made with it. It is a great accomplishment to see all these ideas that were and still are up in your head. This feels like power, It is so powerful to know that you have this knowledge and can use it to your benefit. This is what education is all about. Making a reinforcement, a bond, to what you know and what you have just learned. I find myself constantly questioning what I 'know', why I know it, how I know it, and try to make sense of it.

Hence the realization that there is no such thing as one correct concept map representing what it means to teach elementary school social studies and that a concept map was a way for each student to personally make sense of what they were thinking empowered prospective teachers. This realization also helped prospective teachers reflect on the nature of social studies, knowledge, and how one knows what they know as illustrated in Figure 12.6.

Figure 12.6 represents a portion of a final concept map that was reconstructed by computer from a map that was approximately 7–1/2 feet long. It was logistically impossible to include complete representations of the final concept maps constructed by students in this article due to their size, detail, and complexity. The map that appears in Figure 12.6 consisted largely of connections that represented personal questions the student pondered during map construction. In addition to the three questions that appear in Figure 12.6 that indicate the student's reflection on the nature of social studies and knowledge, other connections included 'What is social studies?', 'What is the role of social studies?', 'What is the teacher's role?', and 'What are important components in my classroom?'

According to final concept maps and logs, prospective teachers' reflections on the questions of what is knowledge and where does it exist transferred to how these prospective teachers would teach social studies. For example, in Figure 12.6, a connection is made between constructivism and active learning. Every final concept map and log contained some connection or mention of active learning. One example appears in Figure 12.7, a representation of a portion of another final concept map.

This student connected active learning to some of the pedagogical strategies discussed in class, connecting these strategies to a theme that occurred in many of

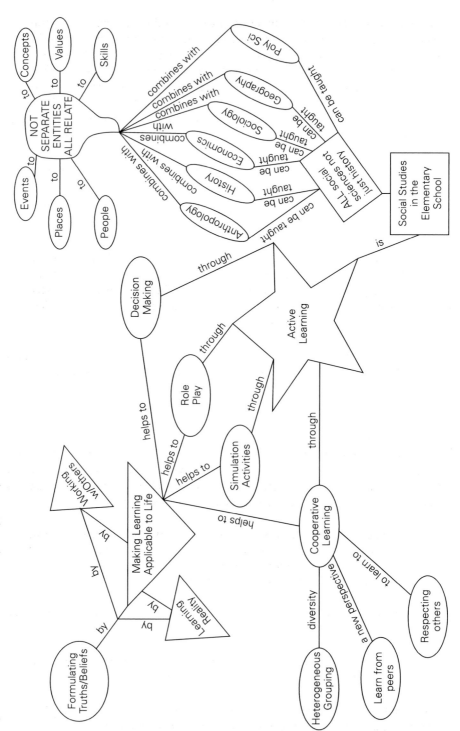

Figure 12.7 Portion of a final concept map, example 2

the connections she made in the entire map — making learning meaningful and 'applicable to life'. This departs dramatically from the original concept maps' focus on memorization of history and geography 'facts' from texts. This departure is also evident in a second connection made by this student, where she indicates that social studies is not just history, but all social sciences with an emphasis on how they relate to each other and to people, places, events, concepts, values, and skills.

Additional examples of prospective teachers' reflection of knowledge transferring to how students will teach social studies were evident in log entries:

> Now I am finally seeing a beginning to what I feel my concept map will resemble:

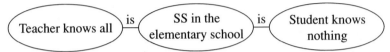

> Joke! Just to see if you're paying attention. Yet this is a wonderful example to demonstrate what I don't feel social studies education is. I strongly believe in teacher and students working together to help and teach each other. Paulo Freire calls them 'critical co-investigators', which I feel explains the relationship precisely.

Prospective teachers' empowerment to construct their own image of elementary school social studies was followed by feelings of elation once their project was completed.

Stage 4: Elation and Pride

As students completed their maps, they reported a shift in the way they thought about the process of learning. Unpleasant conceptions of learning characterized by the memorization and regurgitation of facts were replaced with positive thoughts about the learning experienced through conceptual mapping:

> Holy guacamole! I am very engaged in this project. There is flow occurring. Challenging. Not in a state of anxiousness. Optimal arousal. Research papers and tests always put me in that negative state of learning — anxiousness. I feel good about the process of learning I am experiencing now.

As prospective teachers completed their maps, their journal entries were filled with reflections of elation:

> About 3 am. God, it's beautiful. Flawed, but I don't think seriously or irreversibly . . . I can't stop looking at it. It's as if I've given birth.

As indicated by the 'birth analogy' above, feelings of elation were coupled with feelings of accomplishment and pride in their personal creations:

I am finally finished with my concept map . . . I did not include all that we discussed, read, and learned this past semester in class . . . I did this concept map for me, so that I could leave this class with an idea of how to approach teaching social studies education in the classroom — and I am very happy with the map I created from my reflections.

For many students, this feeling of pride initiated a rejection of the academic game they had played during most of their lives as students, the same game that characterized their memories of elementary school social studies — memorization of 'facts', tests, and grades. Students were empowered to construct maps that made the teaching of social studies meaningful to themselves, rather than searching for the 'one correct' construction that would earn them a good grade:

I've completed my map . . . It's the best activity, I think, that we did all year. The project was left up to me. I was able to do anything I wanted and I think my map is really good and even if I would get a lower grade than expected I still liked the feeling I got while doing it.

The experience of constructing concept maps helped prospective teachers think critically about what it means to teach and learn social studies in the elementary school. Critical reflection was furthered as students compared their initial concept maps with their final concept maps:

Looking back at what I thought of social studies at the beginning of the semester shows me how much I learned and have grown. I knew I learned a lot this semester and changed my opinions because of it, but I never realized the extent of changing I'd done till I looked at the two concept maps. Looking back on this I feel wonderful because I've grown and changed in positive ways. Doing this project has helped me to think critically about how I want to teach social studies and what I want to teach!

In addition, the comparison of the initial and final map created a feeling of confidence and advocacy with the teaching of social studies:

Wow! What a difference. I am astounded at all that I have learned and studied and discussed through this semester. I was so narrow minded in January — it is amazing how much you can grow over 15 weeks. I really feel that I now have a solid base of applicable information that I will be able to use and refer to when I teach social studies in the classroom. I am so amazed as I look at this first concept map I drew — I wonder how or if I would have ever 'taught' anything of importance in my classroom social studies class. Thank goodness I did this map. I really feel comfortable now in teaching social studies.

Telling me how to teach social studies would not have left much of an impression on me. Allowing me to figure out how to teach social studies through this final has made this course the most rewarding course I've ever taken. I'm grateful for that, but more importantly, I've acquired a much more exciting attitude toward teaching social studies in the elementary school. It is a subject I will not slight.

Implications for Social Studies Teacher Education

Pre- and post-course concept mapping appears to be a viable tool to help prospective teachers reflect on their experiences and conceptions of the teaching and learning of elementary school social studies. In this study, pre-course concept maps provided an opportunity for prospective teachers to articulate their memories and pre-course understandings of elementary school social studies. This, in itself, may be a valuable activity. Certainly, teacher educators can use pre-course concept mapping as a way to evoke existing images of social studies and to subsequently lead prospective teachers in consideration of alternative possibilities to those images.

The analysis of pre-course concept maps in this study indicated that the image that dominates most prospective teachers' images of social studies is grounded in the belief that knowledge is objective and exists outside the individual, obtained through the memorization of names, dates, and facts. For those prospective teachers, social studies was a quest to memorize that knowledge. Therefore, teacher educators who find that their methods students have similar images of social studies, may wish to incorporate into methods course discussions focused on the nature of knowledge. Raising questions such as what is social studies knowledge, how do we know what we know, and where does knowledge of social studies exist can be one way prospective teachers begin to examine alternatives to their preconceptions about teaching and learning social studies. The construction of final course concept maps can also aid prospective teachers in the examination of alternative notions of where knowledge of social studies exists as they progress through four stages during final map construction.

The stages prospective teachers in this study experienced during final map construction included: 1 Comfort, 2 Trepidation and Frustration, 3 Resolution, and 4 Elation and Pride. As prospective teachers began to think about constructing an image of elementary school social studies through concept mapping, they left initial thoughts of the simplicity of map construction behind when furious searches through their textbook, their notes, and the instructor's head for the 'correct way to construct a map' ended in frustration. Out of frustration was born the realization that although they may consider their textbook and notes as well as other valuable sources such as ideas that their peers and social studies teachers are willing to share, ultimately they must turn inward rather than outward in the search for knowledge about what it means to teach and learn elementary school social studies. Hence, for the prospective teachers in this study, the process of final course concept mapping itself led to their questioning the nature of knowledge and where it exists. If social studies teacher educators incorporate final map construction into their methods courses, however, they must realize that the construction of concept maps may evoke emotions of fear and frustration as prospective teachers struggle with conceptions of knowledge as existing outside of themselves as occurred in this study. Therefore, social studies teacher educators may need to create a supportive and non-threatening learning environment so that prospective teachers may pass through the stages of trepidation and frustration to achieve resolution, elation, and pride in their understanding of what it means to teach elementary school social studies.

It is in the stages of resolution, and elation and pride that prospective teachers may realize that knowledge about the teaching and learning of elementary school social studies exists inside their own heads as they reflect on and make sense of their experiences. The prospective teachers in this study described this realization as empowering, and were proud of their final concept maps.

Final course concept mapping can provide an opportunity for prospective teachers to articulate visions of social studies and social studies instruction, and allow teacher educators to gain valuable insights into the sense making process of prospective teachers. The results of this study serve to offer thick description and analysis of the way in which concept mapping was incorporated into three social studies methods classes in order to provide an opportunity for teacher educators to assess the value of as well as the ways in which they may make concept mapping a part of their instruction. As social studies teacher educators use concept mapping in different ways, with different students, in different contexts, additional studies are called for to further assess the promise, possibility, and problems that concept mapping hold for social studies teacher education.

References

ADLER, S. (1982) 'Elementary school social studies: Student teacher perspectives' (Doctoral dissertation, University of Wisconsin, 1982), *Dissertation Abstracts International*, **43**, 3199A.

ADLER, S. (1991) 'Forming a critical pedagogy in the social studies methods class: The use of imaginative literature', in TABACHNICH, B.R. and ZEICHNER, K. (eds) *Issues and Practices in Inquiry-oriented Teacher Education*, London: Falmer Press, pp. 77–90.

ANGELL, A.V. (1991, November) 'Social studies methods, student teaching, and the restructuring of preservice teachers' beliefs: Two case studies', Paper presented at the annual meeting of the College and University Faculty assembly of the National Council for the Social Studies, Washington, DC.

ANTONACCI, P.A. (1991) 'Students search for meaning in the text through semantic mapping', *Social Education*, **55**, 3, pp. 174–94.

BENTLEY, M.L. (1993, November) 'Constructivism and the new reform paradigm', Paper presented at the annual meeting of the National Council for the Social Studies, Nashville, TN.

BRUNER, J. (1986) *Actual Minds, Possible Worlds*, Cambridge, MA: Harvard University Press.

CARTER, K. (1992) 'Creating cases for the development of teacher knowledge', in RUSSELL, T. and MUNBY, H. (eds) *Teachers and Teaching: From Classroom to Reflection*, London: Falmer Press, pp. 109–23.

DANA, N.F. (1994) 'Building partnerships to effect educational change: School culture and the finding of teacher voice', in O'HAIR, M.J. and ODELL, S.J. (eds) *Partnerships in Education: Teacher Education Yearbook II*, New York: Harcourt Brace College Publishers.

DANA, N.F. (1995) 'Action research, school change, and the silencing of teacher voice', *Action in Teacher Education*, **16**, 4, pp. 59–70.

DANA, N.F. and TIPPINS, D.J. (1993) 'Analyzing social studies teaching in the elementary school: Metaphors lead the way', *Social Science Record*, **30**, 1, pp. 57–67.

ERICKSON, F. (1986) 'Qualitative methods in research on teaching', in WITTROCK, M. (ed.) *Handbook of Research on Teaching* (3rd edition), New York: Macmillan, pp. 3–36.

FETTERMAN, D.M. (1989) *Ethnography Step by Step*, California: Sage Publications.

FLEURY, S.C. (1993, November) 'Trivial constructivism and the politics of social knowledge', Paper presented at the annual meeting of the National Council for the Social Studies, Nashville, TN.

GLASER, B.G. and STRAUSS, A.L. (1967) *The Discovery of Grounded Theory: Strategies for Qualitative Research*, New York: Aldine Publishing Company.

KENNEDY, M. (1988) 'Establishing professional schools for teachers', in LEVINE, M. (ed.) *Professional Practice Schools: Building a Model*, Washington, D.C.: American Federation of Teachers.

KINCHELOE, J.L. (1993) *Toward a Critical Politics of Teacher Thinking: Mapping the Postmodern*, Westport, CT: Bergin and Garvey..

NOVAK, J.D. and GOWIN, D. (1984) *Learning How to Learn*, Cambridge, England: Cambridge University Press.

OJA, S.N. and SHULYAN, L. (1989) *Collaborative Action Research: A Developmental Approach*, New York: Falmer Press.

PATTON, M.Q. (1990) *Qualitative Evaluation and Research Methods*, Newbury Park, CA: Sage Publications.

SHAVER, J., DAVIS, O.L., Jr. and HELBURN, S.W. (1979) 'The status of social studies education: Impressions from three NSF studies', *Social Education*, 43, pp. 150–3.

SUPERKA, D., HAWKE, S. and MORRISSETT, I. (1980) 'The current and future status of the social studies', *Social Education*, **44**, pp. 362–9.

TABACHNICH, B.R. and ZEICHNER, K. (1991) *Issues and Practices in Inquiry-oriented Teacher Education*, New York: Falmer Press.

TIPPINS, D.J. and DANA, N.F. (1992) 'Culturally relevant alternative assessment', *Science Scope*, **15**, 6, pp. 50–3.

WILSON, E.K., KONOPAK, B.C. and READENCE, J.E. (1994) 'Preservice teachers in secondary social studies: Examining conceptions and practices', *Theory and Research in Social Education*, **22**, 3, pp. 364–79.

WILSON, E.K. and READENCE, J.E. (1993) 'Preservice elementary teachers' perspectives and practice of social studies: The influence of methods instruction and the cooperating teacher', *Journal of Research and Development in Education*, **26**, 1, pp. 222–31.

Chapter 13

Getting Beyond the Limits in Social Studies: Reconceptualizing the Methods Class

---

Joe L. Kincheloe

Let us turn our attention to the social studies methods class. What is typically taught in social studies methods classes? The answer to such a question depends totally upon the professor in question. Under the title of social studies methods students experience courses ranging from simplistic, rote-based exercises to sophisticated thinking adventures in the discipline. While scores of sophisticated, creative teachers introduce elementary and secondary teacher education students to the world of social studies teaching, our explorations have found far too many professors who offer a non-conceptual, technical view of social studies teaching uninformed by a content knowledge of the social sciences.

These non-conceptual classes are consistently marked by an absence of analytical questions about the nature of the social studies curriculum or the discourse of the social sciences. Questions concerning the origins of practices, the implicit assumptions underlying certain language used in the discipline, the connections between social studies teaching and larger socio-political issues, and the general purposes of social studies methods classes often dictate the *topics* covered in these non-conceptual classes. While many of the textbooks may attempt to provide a conceptual context for the topics they cover, this context is often overlooked by the non-conceptual methods professor.

There is a tendency for these non-conceptual classes to assume a rather common format. The subject matter of some of the methods textbooks probably contributes to this uniformity. In every social studies methods textbook we surveyed the following topics were examined with varying degrees of sophistication: lesson planning, behavioral objectives, evaluation, values, social studies materials, current events, and alternative strategies/inquiry. In every methods class we labeled as non-conceptual these same topics were emphasized. We are not arguing that such topics are not valid — not at all. Given an analytical content-rich context such topics can be developed conceptually and quite productively. Our attempt is to simply describe what often occurs in the non-conceptual methods class in an attempt to get some of that which passes as social studies methods teaching out of such an unproductive rut.

An examination of the teaching of each of the seven common topics is in order.

1 Lesson planning

The non-conceptual social studies methods professors and the methods texts almost always delineate the types of plans used in the schools — unit plans, short-range plans focused on a central topic, and daily plans. Components of a lesson plan are then listed. Though they may vary from author to author and teacher to teacher, the format is generally the same — title for lesson, statement of objectives, introduction, sequence of learning activities, evaluation, and a list of materials to be used. Tests in non-conceptual class often ask students to list these components of a lesson plan.

Of course, lesson planning is an extremely important skill. The salient question becomes: How do you best teach such skills? We argue that teaching the skills in contextual isolation, as do the non-conceptual professors and some of the methods texts, does not work. If one of the most important goals of a methods class is to teach prospective social studies teachers to think analytically about the discipline, then such a fragmented approach fails. Lesson planning should be learned in the context of putting a real class together. *Substance* of planning should take precedence over *form*, as prospective teachers grapple with the problem of determining what is significant about a body of information as it relates to a certain age group.

Little attention is granted to the ways in which larger educational purpose and dominant forces of power may influence or determine the types of lesson plans utilized or the content of the plans. Such non-conceptual methods teaching fails to engage the student in the magic of the discipline of social studies, for it strips methodology from the subject matter of social studies. The reasons individuals are attracted to history, geography, political science, sociology, anthropology, or economics is buried under a preoccupation with lesson plan format.

2 Behavioral objectives

In the non-conceptual methods classes lesson planning is often followed by a study of behavioral objectives. The key element in the examination involves precision of the statement of objectives. Such clarity, it is argued, will lead to purposeful and meaningful activities in the classroom. Great effort is delegated to the task of teaching prospective teachers the proper language of behavioral objective writing. Methods students often are asked at this point to memorize infinitives such as to name, to locate, to choose, to provide examples — these are the 'correct' verbals; infinitives such as to understand, to believe, to enjoy, to appreciate are to be avoided.

Again, the concrete concern with format is overemphasized. The non-conceptual methods teacher typically misses an excellent opportunity at this point to explore the culture of the classroom. What are the objectives of an exciting social studies class? What happens when learning outcomes are specified in a behavioral manner? Is conceptualization compatible with such a specific format? What are the assumptions that underlie social studies classes taught in American schools today? Is there an ideological impulse that directs the nature of social studies teaching?

3 Evaluation

The study of evaluation in the non-conceptual methods class often degenerates into a listing of testing methods. An idea common to most methods classrooms involves the recognition that a variety of testing procedures should be used by the teacher. After pencil and paper tests (both objective and subjective), evaluation strategies such as group discussion, observation, checklists, teacher–student conferences, anecdotal records, work samples, and student attitude scales are commonly mentioned. It is extremely important to understand that such evaluation techniques exist — but more understanding is needed.

Prospective social studies teachers need to understand the biases and assumptions underlying the use of the various evaluation strategies. Certain evaluation strategies are specifically tied to certain perspectives on the goals and purposes of social studies. John Jarolimek in his popular text, *Social Studies in Elementary Education*, does a good job of addressing the biases of standardized minimum competency tests used in the social studies. Such tests, he contends, do not encourage a balanced assessment of student skills, knowledge, or abilities. Their use often results in factually based social studies teaching by intimidated instructors who cover themselves by directly teaching the test.

Discussions based on the type of information that Jarolimek presents rarely find their way into the non-conceptual methods class. In the race to provide students with so-called 'practical' skills, the analysis of the origins, epistemologies, and larger meanings of such evaluative practices as minimum competency testing is sacrificed. The social and political contexts that give birth to such educational strategies are neglected. It is this type of understanding that builds the analytical ability necessary to the professionalization of social studies teachers. Without it social studies teachers are mere technicians condemned to a work life marked by an attempt to survive day to day.

4 Values

The teaching of values in the social studies is undoubtedly one of the most complex and ambiguous aspects of the discipline. For this very reason the subject is often ignored in the non-conceptual classroom. Because of its complexity and ambiguity the teaching of values reflects the spirit and essence of the social studies better than most any other topic. Accordingly, an analysis of values teaching should occupy central position in social studies methods.

The topics that can be examined under the values umbrella are numerous. The debate over moral reasoning by Kohlberg and his detractors, authoritarian values versus relative values as illustrated by New Right textbook and curriculum controversies, and teaching personal values via values clarification and all of the accompanying argument this topic has elicited are just a few values-related social studies topics. How can a social studies methods class ignore an examination of democratic values and an accompanying reading of Dewey on the nature of democracy and the role of social studies education in a democratic society? The non-conceptual methods class seems to ignore the fact that value choices determine what goes on in a social studies class. Values are real — either consciously or unconsciously they shape what social studies teachers do. Instructors need to understand the role of tacit values in so-called objective materials so students can understand the insidious way power works.

5   Social studies materials

In the non-conceptual social studies methods classes we have observed the study of materials usually involve a survey of the different categories of materials available. Some professors brought examples of materials to the classroom, setting up displays of filmstrips or supplemental paperback texts. The purpose of the lessons on materials involved merely exposing prospective teachers to the materials — analysis was neglected. Evaluative statements typically involve indications of personal preference for one book or filmstrip packet over another.

Most non-conceptual classrooms cover the following materials: textbooks, encyclopedias, supplementary books and references, pictures, films, filmstrips, slides, overhead projectors, maps, auditory aids, TV, bulletin boards, and computers. Classroom discussions of such materials offer an excellent opportunity to explore some basic questions about social studies. While most non-conceptual professors make the points that knowledge of a variety of materials is helpful because not all children learn in the same way and that students remember better when more than one sensory system is involved in the learning process, the discussion usually stops there.

Analysis of these materials can help social studies teachers understand the social forces that have shaped social studies. If research indicates that most elementary and secondary social studies teachers rely heavily on the textbook, then textbook content certainly determines much of what goes on in social studies classrooms around the country. We can thus determine what is often taught in social studies via textbook content decisions? On what basis are textbook content decisions made? The attempt to answer such questions opens a new world for the prospective social studies teacher. Literature such as Frances Fitzgerald's *America Revised* provides great insight into the process by which social studies texts are produced. Methods students soon learn form Fitzgerald that marketing considerations, pressure from special interest groups and political power groups exert very important influences on textbook writers. Armed with such information social studies teachers approach materials with a greater degree of sophistication.

Television in the non-conceptual methods class is often viewed only in the context of its direct use in the classroom. TV discussions revolve around what shows may be valuable for social studies classes or how VCRs may open new vistas for classroom TV use. Rarely are the learning effects of TV examined. What an excellent opportunity for a study of how TV often shapes the way teachers and students approach social studies. The medium helps shape our view of the world, current events, what it means to be informed politically, the nature of our modern political system, our study habits, and our attention spans. The analysis of materials in the social studies can be exciting and can grant a unique vantage point for discovering new ideas and insights about the subject.

6   Current events

As with other topics, the non-conceptual approach to teaching about current events in the social studies involves the listing of various means of transmitting subject matter. Such classes minimize the effort to examine the role current events play in achieving the goals of the social studies. The study of current events in the non-conceptual methods classes typically revolves around the use of newspaper, student publications (including classroom newspapers), listings of information sources, current events days, and news bulletin boards. Of course, all of these vehicles for current events can be used with great effectiveness. The point here is that awareness of the existence of such vehicles and how to set them up in the classroom is merely a first step. Social studies teachers need to understand how to relate current events knowledge to other aspects of the social studies curriculum.

A critical social studies teacher must be ready to connect current events to any phase of a social studies program. Current events can become an ever-present laboratory of information that can be used to illustrate any social studies concept. Current events can be a living part of the curriculum — not an isolated curricular fragment that is addressed on Friday afternoons from 1:15–1:30. Teachers must possess an ethic which moves them to be well informed. Indeed, they must be familiar with the publications of various ideological perspectives, so that they are ready to set up situations where students can compare and contrast differing viewpoints on current events.

Given these understandings a news-bulletin board or a student newspaper becomes something special. Students no longer pick stories at random but select topics which evoke debate. Such news stories tend to be the ones with long range significance and as such are well suited to facilitate the development of a critical world view. Few topics present a better opportunity to facilitate analytical thinking than do current events.

7   Alternative strategies: inquiry

One of the most important means of developing analytical thinking among prospective social studies teachers and their future students involves an understanding of inquiry methodology — students and teachers as researchers. In our non-conceptual methods class the examination of inquiry often receives little attention. One of the reasons for such neglect involves the fact that social studies students in both the elementary and even secondary education programs have little opportunity in their teacher education courses or their liberal arts classes to study research methodology. Probably the shortest route to teaching a prospective teacher how to administer an inquiry-based social studies program is to provide a basic familiarity with research. For this reason we feel that it is important for social studies teachers to engage in first-hand social science research. Social studies methods classes present a great occasion for valuable and exciting experiences. They offer professors and students alike the opportunity to learn how to teach social studies while becoming involved in the workings of their local communities. In its unique position as a course of study that brings together a variety of disciplines, social studies methods grants the opportunity not only to prepare social studies teachers with creative teaching strategies but to integrate social science knowledge for the society's most important cultural workers — its teachers.

Many social studies methods texts point out that inquiry-based teaching rests on the assumption that social studies is not concerned only with the accumulation of knowledge but with both the accumulation and the application of knowledge.

Such a concept is a good starting place for an analysis of inquiry methodology. Once this concept is discussed attention can be directed to specific examples of how inquiry-generated knowledge can be applied. Social studies knowledge is thus connected to the lived world in such a way that students understand its meaning in their own lives. Unfortunately, the non-conceptual methods class fails to take advantage of this opportunity.

Instead of attacking the infinite possibilities offered by an analysis of the application of social studies knowledge, the non-conceptual methods professor often turns his or her attention to a brief look at 'thinking development' and 'finding information'. Inquiry is valuable as an alternative strategy, the argument goes, because it fosters thinking. Thinking, the argument continues, must be liked at as a process which is divided into subskills. Of course such information is correct and valuable, but actual practice in inquiry with concurrent attention to the types of thinking utilized in the process would be more valuable for the prospective teachers. Typically, the examination of thinking subskills amounts to little more that a role listing. The approach to 'finding information' rarely transcends a listing of social studies information sources.

Social studies methods teaching must get beyond the non-conceptual approach. It is such as approach which gives methods classes a bad name. Few courses in the university have a better opportunity to foster analytical thinking than does the teacher education methods class. To examine the various purposes analysts have devised for social studies, while at the same time taking the subject matter of the social science and searching for a concrete and practical strategy of classroom implementation is a sophisticated task. Throughout the ages good teachers have done it routinely.

Exploring Water: A Case Study in Social Studies Methods

One successful implementation of a primary research-based critical social studies methods class involved an exploration of the infamous water problems of Shreveport, Louisiana. The class convened in the fall term of 1982, immediately after a summer marked by a rash of water problems in this north-west Louisiana city. A mayoral election was being held during the period and citizen dissatisfaction has pushed water to the front of both candidates' agendas. As the class considered what problem to attack, water could not be ignored. The class consisted of 10 students — none of whom had ever engaged in a research project of any magnitude, but who all planned to teach elementary social studies. As the project began they were unsure of themselves and frightened by the prospect of the research.

Indeed, the research background of most students was weak. Many confided that they had never before had to undertake a research project of any magnitude. This revelation illustrated a broader problem among elementary and even many secondary social studies teachers: the inability to conduct research. It is no wonder that inquiry methodology has often not worked in the public schools — too many teachers do not have the research skills necessary to make it work. Students in an inquiry project are lost, if they do not have a teacher who can give directions on where to go for further information on a topic. Before social studies classes can escape the rote memorization, textbook-oriented strategies that have paralyzed young minds for so long, sophisticated teacher research skills are a necessity.

At the beginning of the project the students were hesitant to jump into the research. Being so inexperienced with primary research, they didn't know quite where to begin. This realization of research deficiency when combined with the fact that they would soon be in the schools teaching social studies seemed to awaken them to the need for better preparation of social studies teachers. Understanding their own backgrounds in light of the goals of social studies personalized the insufficient preparation in social science methodology that most elementary teachers possess. Some of the students had no understanding of what exactly sociology and anthropology, for example, were designed to study. Political science, some thought, was an alien discipline that had something to do with politics and politicians. Such a lack of understanding had little to do with the failure of colleges of education alone. Such realities indicate problems in all branches of the educational establishment. Once alerted to such considerations the students' outlook toward the project become quite positive and their commitment to an improvement in the quality of social studies teaching was unqualified.

The students had rarely thought of the relationship between social studies skills and everyday life, nor had they considered the application of social studies skills to real problems in their community or nation. The project enabled them to see social studies as a living entity, something that served to explain real events and that could be applied to real problems. Coming into the class, these students were no more or no less informed about social studies than students in other social studies classes taught over the years. For all the talent that exists among social studies/ social science teachers in public schools, colleges of education and colleges of liberal arts, student awareness of the potentialities of social studies is very low. The problems are apparent, college level social studies methods teachers must initiate a campaign of awareness. Social studies methods teachers must induce teachers to think in terms of the applicability of social studies concerns and insights. They must illustrate the need for those concerns and insights in contemporary society.

The city of Shreveport had been having trouble with the taste of its water for years. The city government and the water department had been deluged with complaints for a long time and a sometimes bitter debate over solutions to the problem had affected city planners in administration and after administration. Numerous studies had been commissioned but because of competing political interests progress toward any solution had reached an impasse. The summer before the class met in the fall has been a particularly bad time for the water department and complaints had risen to a near record level. So, when the class began its research, city water was a hot political potato fresh on everyone's mind.

The water problem found its origin in the fact that the source of Shreveport's water, Cross Lake, was an aging body of water plagued by all the problems which accompany lake maturity. As a lake ages organic matter collects on its bottom and in periods of low water the algae growth which coincides with the organic matter causes aesthetic problems of taste and color. Add to this the development of homesites within the Cross Lake watershed accompanied by homeowners' use of phosphate fertilizers that eventually run off into the lake and the problem is magnified. Not only do the phosphates 'fertilize' the yards but they stimulate organic growth in the lake as well. The summer is a particularly bad time for an aging lake because of increased nutrient concentrations, warm water temperatures and long periods of unobstructed sunlight, all of which promote algae growth.

Some water officials argued that the Environmental Protection Agency's decision to discontinue the use of chlorine in water purification contributed to the city's water problem. The EPA ruling forced water departments to substitute the weaker chemical, chloramean, for chlorine. The addition of chlorine to water was found to produce chloroform, one of the trihalomethanes that have proved to be a human carcinogen. The uses of the less potent chloramean did not limit algae growth as effectively as did chlorine and as a result the taste and odor problems were accentuated. The debate over the use of chlorine continues in Shreveport and around the country. Public concern over Shreveport water has also continued since the class project, as new city administrations continue to fund studies of the problem.

The term opened at a running pace, as an attempt was made to provide the students a background in the goals and major issues of elementary social studies. The students examined different perspectives on the goals of elementary social studies and during the third week of the term completed a comparative content analysis of a couple of elementary textbook series in light of specific elementary social studies goals. Before students could tackle a project with its emphasis on skill development and its variety of objectives, they needed to gain an understanding of traditional social studies goals. Also, students were informed about more traditional ways of teaching elementary social studies methods courses in order to provide a context in which they could better understand the logic behind the primary research project as a means of teaching social studies methods.

A key point in the course involved the choosing of the topic and the formulation of a plan for dividing the study into components. As students chose one of the subtopics, they conducted preliminary research for the purpose of producing a tentative outline for the inspection of the teacher. This division of the project components was important on a number of levels. In the first place it was a necessary step in the completion of a successful project. Unless the topic was viewed from a number of perspectives there would be no way that any holistic sense of the problem could be gained. If the various perspectives did not complement one another while avoiding redundancy, project success was highly unlikely. Secondly, the division of the topic was based on the disciplinary breakdown of the social sciences (political science, sociology, history, anthropology, etc . . .), and it was through the different perspectives granted by the various social sciences that students could learn the problem solving value of the social studies. In other words this division of responsibility had to be performed effectively if the students were to understand the value of the method. Thirdly, the teacher had to be aware of the *process* of dividing the project into manageable parts for this would probably be the only time that the prospective teachers would see such a method of division before they attempted to implement it in their own classrooms. Thus, each step had to be fully explained so that the students understood the logic behind the procedure.

The project forced the students to confront the question: How does a group go about studying a city's water problems from the perspective of the social sciences? Using the natural divisions of the social sciences to get started, the problem was examined from historical, economic, and political vantage points, as well as from a comparative perspective borrowed from anthropology. In addition to these basic divisions one student served as a synthesizer, attempting to present an overview of the role water plays in our lives while introducing the readers of the final report and the audience at the public forum to the scope of the study and the contributions of the specific student participants. Other reports involved a special look at all the problems associated with Shreveport water, a study of environmental aspects of the water problem, and two papers on practical alternatives to the present system. The table of contents of the students' final report read as follows:

<table>
<tr><td>I</td><td>An Introduction to Water</td></tr>
<tr><td>II</td><td>History of Shreveport Water, 1839–1917</td></tr>
<tr><td>III</td><td>History of Shreveport Water, 1917–1982</td></tr>
<tr><td>IV</td><td>An Overview of Shreveport Water Problems</td></tr>
<tr><td>V</td><td>Political Aspects of Shreveport Water</td></tr>
<tr><td>VI</td><td>Shreveport's Water Source: A Comparative Study</td></tr>
<tr><td>VII</td><td>Shreveport Water: Economic Considerations</td></tr>
<tr><td>VIII</td><td>Shreveport Water: Environmental Considerations</td></tr>
<tr><td>IX</td><td>Alternatives to Shreveport's Existing Water Supply: Part 1</td></tr>
<tr><td>X</td><td>Alternatives to Shreveport's Existing Water Supply: Part 2</td></tr>
</table>

After the topics were agreed upon and each student chose his or her part, the research began in earnest. The students quickly found that the director of the water department and his staff were especially helpful. Not only did the water department officials welcome a parade of students to their offices, but they came to the university and worked with students who felt uncomfortable with the technical aspects of the topic because of weak or non-existent backgrounds in chemistry. All told, water department personnel donated hours of their time to the edification of the social studies students, consistently maintaining the attitude that such services were merely a part of their job. Also, invaluable was the help of specific members of the university community. One chemistry professor who was also a leader in the region's environmental awareness movement spoke to the class on numerous occasions and granted interviews to students who had further questions. The students were impressed by the fact that there were so many people in the community including water department staff members, university professors, and local political leaders, who were willing to help them. It was a realization that would not be lost, as they acquired teaching positions in the public schools.

The students' first meeting with the water department staff was interesting on a number of levels. Not only did the students realize how interesting and controversial the topic was, but they came to understand how technical some aspects of it could be. They realized that a better understanding of chemistry was a necessity and set out to sophisticate their understanding of the discipline. This was one of their more impressive accomplishments — their success in acquainting themselves with the basic physical scientific knowledge so as to make sense of the water controversy. Once such understandings were gained students could talk comfortably about trihalomethanes and their production in the chlorination process.

As the project proceeded the students kept diaries in which they examined the nature of their research, their frustrations and successes, and how the process could be related to the teaching of elementary social studies. Some students displayed a sophisticated insight into the connection between the project in a college setting and its use in an elementary context. Some students needed the point explained that there was not a *direct* transfer between a college social studies project and an elementary project. The idea of primary source orientation, a flexible problem-centered curriculum, an emphasis on skills improvement and not factual acquisition, the need for teacher research abilities, the view of social studies as a pragmatic tool for investigation, the liberation of students and teachers from a textbook-oriented program were all concepts that students were encouraged to address in their diaries, along with personal feelings, observations, and suggestions to the teacher for future improvement of the class.

After a couple of months of research the students presented oral reports to the class on their findings. They were questioned by the professor about inconsistencies and their attention was directed to further research where it was needed. The oral reports were very valuable in the respect that students had an opportunity to question one another — not in a competitive way but in an attempt to reconcile contradictory findings and induce one another to ask new questions of their material. Of course, the project was designed to culminate in a public forum with the students presenting information and facilitating a public discussion of the issues. Newspaper and TV reporters were invited along with individuals who had played some role in the students' search for information. The forum added an element of excitement and offered an overt reminder of the connection between the project and the world outside of the classroom.

The students turned in their research papers to the professor two weeks before the forum. At this point mechanical errors were corrected, a few sentences were added or deleted, and students were asked to check any questionable assertions. The papers were returned with corrections and the students rewrote a final draft. These were re-submitted, copied, collated, and bound into a volume to be distributed at the forum. Many students found this part of the process to be valuable in that they had to present a 'perfect' copy for public distribution. They had never been involved in this final step where a professor had actually rewritten parts of their final draft.

The forum was well attended. Members of the university community, the visual and print media, environmental groups, water department, as well as students and politicians were present. Students presented a brief overview of their research, and a set of agreed upon recommendations were issued after the individual presentations. The floor was then opened for discussion and the students and the audience exchanged questions and considered the major issues involved. Local TV and radio stations ran features on the event on their news programs. Local newspapers printed pieces on the forum and one newspaper followed up with a front page feature on the project and the unique method it presented for educating social studies teachers. The project was certainly a success in introducing students to alternative methods of teaching elementary social studies, improving their primary source research skills, connecting the social studies classroom with actual social problems, improving student writing, speaking, and organizing skills, alerting students to resources in the community and ways of incorporating them into education, and providing students with an opportunity to work with a group in a problem solving activity.

The project was also a success in informing the community of the sophisticated capabilities of prospective elementary teachers, the creative potential of teacher education, the value of social studies in the public schools, and the possibilities provided by education which transcends mere rote memorization. In other words, the students were not just learning to teach social studies but were actually serving as ambassadors for education in a larger community that often looked at them and others like them with condescension. This multidimensional role was one that they could not lose after their association with the class had ended. Teachers must wear many hats as educators with classroom teaching a primary but not solitary concern. If social studies education is to improve, critical social studies teachers must display the possibilities of the subject to the communities in which they teach. The water project provided teachers with good practice for such a goal.

Chapter 14

Action Experiments: Are Students Learning Physical Science?

Penny J. Gilmer and Paulette Alli

Rationale

There is a great national need to improve science education in the United States, as evidenced by how American students are not prepared for the workplace in our increasingly technological age. The recent Third International Mathematics and Science Study (TIMSS) report indicates that eighth grade students in the United States are ranked in the middle of eighth graders from 41 countries in the study (Peak, 1996; Schmidt et al., 1997), while fourth grade students in the United States rank second of 26 participating countries, only behind Korea (NSTA, 1997). These results suggest that we need to continue our efforts at improving science education countrywide, if we are to achieve number one status in the world by the year 2000, a goal set by then President Bush of the United States of America (National Education Goals Panel, 1991).

Objectives

An important approach to reaching this goal is to teach science to teachers, both practicing teachers and prospective teachers who are still in training. There is an amplification effect, when one teaches teachers, as each teacher will interact with 30–150 students per day, depending on whether they are teaching in elementary schools, middle schools, or high schools. It is critical to teach science in an active way that is consistent with how people learn, if we are to have an impact on the teaching and learning of our K-12 students.

This paper set describes action experiments that are utilized to teach graduate level physical science to practicing elementary school teachers.[1] The idea behind these action experiments is to get the teachers in the graduate level class to be students, asking questions, gathering data, making inferences, and building understandings about the natural world. If teachers experience learning in this way they can encourage their students to do likewise. Hereafter in this study, the practicing teachers will be called teacher-students, because they are both teachers of children and graduate students in their physical science classroom.

Action experiments are experiments in which the participants must act or 'move to action'. The teachers must become active learners of science. I organized the teacher-students into cooperative groups, and asked them to select action experiments from a series of possible experiments suggested to them. The experiments call upon their experiences from living in the physical world. To learn the concepts of physical science, fancy equipment is not needed. Most experiments utilized supplies that are readily available in their homes. By using materials with which they are familiar, teachers will start to see physical science all around them. It will empower them to use such everyday supplies to teach science to the children in their elementary school classrooms.

This paper examines the discourse among teacher-students and between the instructor and the teacher-students, for improving the learning of physical science. This discourse occurs in the classroom, on the worldwide web, through field experiences, and in their writing.

Theoretical underpinnings

The teacher-students work in collaborative groups (Johnson et al., 1991), to learn the science content, using the language and discourse of science (Lemke, 1995). There are no lectures given, so the teacher-students must construct their understandings based on their prior knowledge and their experiences in the physical science classroom, in their reading of the textbook (Hewitt et al., 1994), with their web-based learning, and during their field experiences. Constructivism is the primary theoretical underpinning (Glasersfeld, 1989; Tobin, et al., 1990; Marzano, 1992; Tobin, 1993; Tobin and Tippins, 1993; Brooks and Brooks, 1993; Appleton, 1997).

Methods

Data sources include audiotapes and videotapes from the physical science class, dialog journal postings on the web, postings of action experiments on the web, and visits to teacher-student classrooms. I utilized fourth generation evaluation methods in this research study (Guba and Lincoln, 1989).

Electricity, magnetism, sound, light, and chemistry were some of the topics included in this course. Simple experiments are selected from several books of basic experiments in physical science (e.g. Churchill et al., 1997; Challoner, 1995; Feldman, 1995). For instance, for the unit on sound, experiments from Churchill et al. (1997) included 'Noisy paper', 'The screamer', The tapping finger', 'The listening yardstick', 'The strange vibrating bowl', 'Can you tune a fork?', 'Tuning a glass', 'Tune more glasses', and 'Seeing sound waves'. After being alerted to the materials that would be needed in the experiments by the instructor on the website, teacher-students brought their own equipment from home to the class. This encouraged teacher-students to take ownership to their experiments and ideas. For instance, in the unit on sound a group of four teacher-students each brought country-type musical instruments (e.g. wash tub with string attached to make a stringed instrument) to class, and played a song. After singing and playing a song about our class, they showed how to create different pitches on different types of 'instruments'.

Each day after performing action experiments the cooperative groups shared their learning with the instructor and the other groups in the class. Each group reported orally on their understandings and learning in the experiments of their choice. Everyone had a chance to contribute to the dialogue and learning. Sometimes debates about interpretations of data occurred.

There was a five-week field experience after the first three weeks of intensive classroom experience. This was followed by one additional week of intensive classes, in addition to a teacher-as-researcher week-long conference in the evenings. During the field experience each teacher-student wrote their favorite action experiment on the website for all teacher-students to read. The website postings served as a reminder of what we had done in class and what we learned. This serves as a device to get the teacher-students to use the language of science (Lemke, 1995) to describe their favorite experiment, and to reflect on the experiments that their fellow teacher-students have chosen to share with the others. All teacher-students needed to utilize the language of science and share their understandings of the physical world. Most of the teacher-students taught summer school during this field experience, so they had opportunities to test their new understandings and ways to teach physical science with the children in their classrooms. One of the advantages of teaching a group of teacher-students is that you get feedback very quickly on the quality of the learning, on what worked and what did not, in the physical science course designed for the elementary school teachers.

Some teacher-students created experiments that went beyond the ones offered to them. One teacher-student demonstrated the Doppler shift in which the frequency of sound is shifted through the motion of the object making the sound or the receiver of the sound. A number of physical science concepts (i.e. especially frequency and motion) must be understood to explain the Doppler shift. First, a teacher-student learns that sound is a longitudinal wave with compressions and rarefactions with an amplitude and a frequency. The teacher-students observe that a wave of compression (i.e. the vibration) moves from one end to the other end of the slinky when a lateral impulse is given to one end of the slinky while the other end is held stationary.

Findings

Teacher-students with experience in elementary school teaching, in general, had little background in the topic of sound, except for a few who have played musical instruments. The instructor encouraged the teacher-students to select several experiments to do, utilizing their textbook and their prior knowledge to see if they could make sense of sound.

Some teacher-students tried an experiment at home, and then brought the materials from home into the classroom to share with their collaborative group. For example, one student, Sabrina (a pseudonym), decided to research sound, and learn about the Doppler effect, by recording for herself what a horn sounds like when it approaches a stationary tape recorder and as it moves away from the tape recorder. Therefore, she did the experiment on her own, and brought the tape recording to class. It was an impressive recording. Sabrina learned science content by preparing this tape, trying to make sense of her data, and sharing her results with the other teacher-students in the class. By Sabrina using the language of science, the instructor could help her with some misconceptions.

The instructor could tell that even the teaching assistant, Bruno (a pseudonym), did not have a full understanding of all the concepts on sound and asked him to prepare a similar tape and explain the concept of the Doppler effect to the second section of graduate level physical science class. The instructor did not help Bruno when he collected the data, as he tried to make sense of the recording. Below is a transcript from class. There are many misconceptions, embedded within his dialogue:

Bruno

So, think about, so think about the slinky, and think about you're standing here in the middle of the slinky. OK. Now. And, and it *sounds* . . . OK? So what's going to hit you, first? I mean, just, just, just say, you're going to get hit by two things. What are you going to get hit by? Compression and then a, and then?

Teacher-students [in unison]

A rarefaction . . .

Bruno

OK. So then you're going to be hit by a compression and a rarefraction [sic]. All right, so, when you are hit by a compression and you're hit by a rarefraction [sic], all right, and you listen to sound. It's very easy, I want to do it, I want to tell you so bad, but I know the concept I want to tell you, but I want you to construct it in your mind.

Bruno [continuing]

OK, now, say, when I started honking the horn, and it was *real* loud, and then it goes down, and then it, as it passes me, it goes back up. OK, all right, so think about the wave, think about the whole wave. All right, now, think about I'm in the middle of a wave. OK, when it's loud, do a lot of waves hit me? As opposed to when the sound, when it's, it's down, the pitch is low?

Teacher-student

Yeah.

Bruno

Which way would a lot of waves hit me?

Teacher-student

When it's up. When it's a compression.

Bruno

Well, when will a lot of waves . . . I'm talking about waves now, and the number of waves?

Teacher-student

When it's a compression.

Bruno

OK, so, well, how is it going to sound? Here I am, standing, louder, or . . .

Teacher-student

Louder than before.

Bruno

OK, at first, it's going to be louder, and after a while it's going to go . . . ?

Teacher-students [in unison]

Lower.

Bruno

It's going to go lower. Are you saying lower is a higher frequency or a lower frequency? Define higher and lower frequency. Is lower a higher frequency?

Teacher-student

If the pitch increases, it's higher.

Bruno

OK.

Teacher-student

If the pitch decreases, it's lower. Is that what you are looking for?

Bruno

OK, Let's talk about pitch. Let's go to pitch. OK, let's talk about pitch. All right now.

Transcribing this lesson was an important way for the instructor to see how confused individuals can be on the basic concepts. When Bruno was explaining the experiment in class, he confused even the instructor. When Bruno said, 'When I started honking the horn, and it was *real* loud, and then it goes down, and then it, as it passes me, it goes back up', he confused the concepts of amplitude and frequency of sound. Bruno also mispronounced the word, rarefaction, using 'rarefraction' instead.

It was not clear why Bruno suggested that the teacher-students imagine that they were traveling along the sound wave. What insight is gained by the construction that the teacher-students imagine they are in the middle of the wave on the slinky? The molecules in the medium only oscillate as the wave passes through the medium. Sound is the transmission of the vibration. Perhaps Bruno was trying to understand what happens to the sound in order for the pitch to be different for the receiver. With the Doppler effect the vibration itself remains the same, it is that either the vibrating object or the receiver of the sound is moving, which changes the frequency at which the vibrations are received.

Bruno was trying to use a constructivist epistemology in letting the teacher-students construct their own knowledge, as evidenced by his saying, 'It's very easy, I want to do it, I want to tell you so bad, but I know the concept I want to tell you, but I want you to construct it in your mind.' However, Bruno did not have a clear idea of what sound was, so he could not answer the teacher-students' questions. In fact, he confused the teacher-students. However, this generated dissonance in the teacher-students' minds which they wanted to clear, thereby motivating them to think about sound more deeply.

Bruno also experienced dissonance as his ideas on sound were not consistent with those of other students. During the field experience, Bruno did come to understand some aspect of the frequency of sound waves and the Doppler effect by suggesting an experiment that teacher-students could use in their classroom.

Here is a teaching tip on the Doppler effect. Model frequency with a student slowly rolling golf balls, or other similar balls, down a long chalk tray at regular intervals, with the balls representing wave crests. Have a second student stand at the other end of the chalk tray, collect and count the balls, measuring the time to calculate frequency. To demonstrate the Doppler effect, have the receiving student walk toward the sending student counting the number of balls collected in the same time period. Collecting the balls while walking away will produce fewer balls in the time period, representing a lowered frequency. Your class is now ready to discuss the Doppler effect. (Gordon, 1991)

Bruno's construction conveys the idea of the change in frequency when the receiver of the ball approaches or recedes from the person who is rolling the ball towards the receiver. One problem with this construction, however, is that with sound there is no mass being transmitted, it is only the vibration that is moving.

Another teacher-student, Paulette, whom the instructor had visited in her elementary school classroom during the academic year between the first two summers of the program, asked a question on the Doppler effect in the dialogue journal on the web:

Do you know if the Doppler effect can be heard if the sound source is stationary, but the listener is moving? For example: If a car drives by a non-moving car that is blowing its horn, will the moving car hear the Doppler effect? I had problem figuring that out. I know I can hear the Doppler effect if the sound source is in motion.

A teacher-student in Paulette's dialogue group wrote back the following entry, in response to Paulette's question on the Doppler effect:

As for the Doppler effect, I believe, that the car has to be moving because, according to our physical science book (Hewitt et al., 1994), the Doppler effect is a change in frequency of wave motion resulting from motion of the sender or receiver. I think the key words are 'motion of the sender or receiver'. On page 263 in the same book, it describes the bug moving in the water so I believe something has to be moving in order for it to happen. However, I could be wrong . . . let me know!!!

It was obvious that the Doppler effect was still not understood by the teacher-students. Therefore, after reading these dialogue journal entries, the instructor wrote back in the dialogue journal and suggested to Paulette that she try to do an action experiment herself, as we did in class. Penny, the instructor, wrote:

You asked an interesting question about the Doppler effect — whether you get the Doppler effect if the sound is stationary and the listener is moving. I was glad to see the discussion between you two [of you in the dialogue journal] on this. It is a simple experiment, so you might want to try to do it. You get a portable tape recorder and drive past a friend who is sitting stationary in the car blowing the horn steadily. You drive past the stationary car (with its horn blowing) and record what you hear. It would be a good experiment to include in your field experience for me. You could save the recording for your students.

Paulette conducted her field experience about sound. She was a researcher, and utilized the world wide web, her textbook, and the dialogue journal to discuss her ideas on our website. She chose her field experience to answer a question she had in her mind, based on what she did not understand in class. Paulette wanted to extend her knowledge:

> My reason for selecting this experiment on sound is . . . I couldn't visualize the Doppler effect after we discussed it in class. Before conducting this experiment, I thought it would seem sensible to assume the sound of a passing car would remain monotonous and not change pitch since the sound itself had no pitch variations.

Paulette found an experiment on the Doppler effect from one described on the website for the Exploratorium Museum in San Francisco (<http://www.exploratorium.edu>). However, she innovated and modified an experiment that she found on the world wide web and so that she could use materials that she had available. Paulette wrote the following in her field experience paper:

> I wanted to keep the experiments simple, so I decided to use things that were accessible around my house. The items I used were: a small battery-operated alarm clock, a strong string (about two yards), and masking tape. I assembled the instrument by using the masking tape to tape one end of the string around the alarm clock. I wrapped both the string and tape around the clock tightly. I made sure not to tape the alarm clock buttons. I rotated the alarm hand until it buzzed. I then had a buzzer. I held the opposite end of the string and used my other hand to extend and hold some of it for leverage.
>
> I twirled the buzzer around my head. I noticed how the pitch changed as the buzzer approached and moved away from me. When the oscillator (i.e. the buzzer) moved toward me, it, in effect, caught up slightly with its sound waves. With each successive pulse of the buzzer, the sound source was a little closer to me. The waves were being squeezed together, and more of them reached my ear each second than if the buzzer was standing still. Therefore, the pitch of the buzzer sounded higher. As the buzzer moved away from me, fewer waves reached my ear each second, so the resulting pitch sounded lower. The frequency of the buzzer itself did not change in either case. For my ears to detect the Doppler effect, the buzzer had to be moving toward or away from me at a minimum speed of about 15–20 miles per hour. As the buzzer moved faster, the effect became more pronounced. The pitch of sound increased when the buzzer moved toward me and decreased when it moved away. After this experiment, I had a better understanding of the Doppler effect. By twirling the buzzer, I could hear the 'neeeeeoowwm' sound.

Paulette really had her mind on her experiment, as she innovated and tested her ideas. These ideas became clear to her through experimentation. The experiments raised new questions in her mind. She reflected further (Schon, 1983) in her field experience paper:

I wanted to take the experiment a step further and hypothesized if there would be a Doppler effect if the buzzer was stationary and I was in motion. I tried doing this by putting the buzzer in the middle of the floor and running around it as fast as I could I am not a runner. I assume if I were to run around the buzzer at the same speed as I twirled it — about 20 miles per hour, I would hear the 'neeeeeoowwm' sound. At barely four miles per hour, I did not hear the Doppler effect. I also tried running closer and farther away from the buzzer, to see if that would make a difference (but it didn't).

I also experimented moving my head while I slowly twirled the buzzer. I thought I would not hear the Doppler effect, but I did. No matter how slowly I twirled the buzzer, my head moved slower than my rotating arm. This proves that the Doppler effect can result even with two moving objects. For example: When a car, blowing its horn, passes a slower moving car — the slower car will hear the Doppler effect. These experiments helped me realize that the Doppler effect is a result of a change in frequency due to the motion of the source or receiver.

A Perspective of Student Learning

To understand how a teacher-student comes to know and to learn science, it is best to listen to what Paulette reflects on her experience after the course is finished:

I gained knowledgeable insights on how students learn, both as a teacher and as a student. I recognized that students learning about their surroundings naturally and enthusiastically, and with proper techniques, can be utilized for effective teaching. Research supported the conclusion that to improve teaching we must first understand how students learn.

Richardson, as cited by Collins and Spiegel (1995), stated that 'research is conducted by practitioners to help them understand their contexts, practices and, in the case of teachers, their students. The outcome of the inquiry may be a change in practice or it may be an enhanced understanding' (p. 118). Collins and Spiegel (1995) further state, 'Whether it is termed action research, classroom research, or practical inquiry, the genre formalizes an aspect of teaching that expert teachers have known about and employed for a long time. They observe situations in their classrooms that are less than optimal, they identify the problem, they think about what and how to change, they make the change, and they evaluate the impact of the change on the situation and begin again' (p. 118).

In the past two years, I have examined how students learn, and how they process science skills. Research and experience reveal that, in many cases, traditional science classroom instruction led to less science understanding than I anticipated. 'When the teacher alone assumes the role of information giver, students may misinterpret the teacher's explanation, ignore the teacher or decide that "school" science does not make sense in "real life"' (Rutherford and Ahlgren as cited in *Science for All Students*, p. 36, 1997). Students often hold beliefs that are at odds with commonly accepted scientific thought. These misconceptions must be identified and confronted, before effective learning can take place (Florida Department of Education, 1993, p. 41).

The ideal learning environment, to benefit the students, should involve co-operative learning, concept and process learning, hands-on experiences, and self-assessment techniques. The ability to self-assess understanding is an essential tool for self-directed learning. Students need the opportunity to evaluate and reflect on their own scientific understanding and ability. Before they can do this, they need to understand the goals for learning science. Through self-reflection, students clarify ideas of what they are supposed to learn. They begin to internalize the expectation that they can learn science (National Research Council, 1996).

Considerable information has been accumulated on the way students learn. As a student, I have explored the concept, skill, or behavior with hands-on or minds-on experiences. I also elaborated and evaluated my understanding of these ideas by applying them to other situations. Additionally, I discussed and compared ideas with other students, while evaluating my own understanding.

In physical science class, my assignments were to read the textbook chapters, answer the questions at the end of each chapter, and select two activities to demonstrate in class, relating to the immediate lessons. These activities were done in class with preselected groups of four students. At the end of the term, I conducted a field experiment — a reflective thinking of what I read in the text, and of what I discussed and observed in group demonstrations. Reflective thinking helped me to store information in long-term memory, and assimilate what I learned. One of the advantages of reflection was that it helped to connect the concepts, and made ideas more meaningful.

Learning had a greater impact when it was combined with hands-on activities. By doing the hands-on activities, I was able to demonstrate what I read and how I understood it. I had a language to communicate what I understood, by reading the textbook.

Students learn best when they are allowed to construct their own understanding of concepts over time, and by active engagement in the learning process. If students engage in exploratory investigations and are allowed to construct meaning out of their findings, they can propose tentative explanations and solutions, and relate concepts to their own lives. That is how meaningful learning will take place.

In our groups, we selected activities we found interesting and/or which made us curious. We explained our ideas through demonstrations of the activities to the other students in class. The activities were simple and the materials were easy to obtain. As a group, we figured out concepts by thinking it through, and experimenting with what worked and what didn't work. We experimented and predicted what would happen when changes were made. We asked questions for clarification, and hypothesized how activities can be extended. The class members observed, as we discussed differences between the predictions and observations. We learned from each other by observing group activities done in class.

As we experimented, we referred to the textbook constantly, to make connections to related ideas. This allowed us to use the language necessary to communicate our findings or understandings between the group members, and to the class. The more we experimented, the better the text's terminology could be understood.

As a co-learner, I listened carefully to other students' explanations and questions. I justified my explanations and sometimes transferred an explanation to other situations in order to fully grasp a meaning. To understand a concept, I would ask myself questions that probed into how and why I thought of something. This helped to reveal how I was thinking, as I tried to restructure erroneous or incomplete ideas.

To understand science concepts, I predicted, observed, and explained my findings in conducting my action experiments. These strategies helped to support correct predictions, and helped to challenge incorrect ones.

After a concept or an idea was discussed in class, I reflected and evaluated my understanding of it. In this way, I selected to either assess my understanding or to direct my learning. For example, for my field experience, I experimented with the Doppler effect (the 'neeeeeoowwm' sound we hear from a passing car) because I could not visualize the Doppler effect after we discussed it in class. Before re-searching the topic by conducting the experiment, I assumed the sound of a pass-ing car would remain monotonous and not change pitch since the sound itself had no pitch variations. I corrected my assumption after I researched it in the field. After the experiment, I realized that the Doppler effect was a result of a change in frequency due to the motion of a source or receiver. Through this example, it was obvious how learning was sustained with the application of hands-on activity, and by using reflective and self-assessment procedures.

As Paulette returns to her elementary school classroom, she plans to utilize action experiments in her classroom. She will do this in the context of action research (Collins and Spiegel, 1995), using fourth generation evaluation (Guba and Lincoln, 1989), this is all part of a graduate program PROMASE (PROgram in Mathematics And Science Education), funded by the National Science Foundation (NSF) through the Miami Urban Systemic Initiative (USI).

In the physical science course, she also read and critiqued the recently published collection of action research experiences of elementary school teachers (Gilmer and McDonald, 1977) from the NSF-funded Science For Early Adolescence Teachers (Science FEAT) Program (Spiegel et al., 1995). As Paulette develops a theory of how children learn, she analyzes and describes her learning and her students' learning using a constructivist model (Glasersfeld, 1989; Tobin et al., 1990; Marzano, 1992; Tobin and Tippins, 1993; Brooks and Brooks, 1993; Appleton, 1997). Utilizing con-structivism is a powerful way for all of us to learn.

We want to encourage all our students to learn. We need to remember that students must start with their current conceptions and build (and reconstruct) on them. As they realize that they can think analytically, a part of the world that may have been closed off to them opens up. Analytical thinking is challenging and stimu-lating. As Bruno tried to make sense of his data on the Doppler shift in his presenta-tion to the class, he was obviously confused in his conceptions of frequency and amplitude, although he said that it was easy. I believe that he sensed that everything did not make sense probably during, and definitely after, his presentation to the class, especially when the students asked him questions and introduced conceptions that did not fit with his. After Bruno had a chance to reflect on his class presentation, he shared with the students on the course's web site how he realized he could do an experiment with his students to teach the frequency of a wave and the Doppler shift. In Bruno's suggested experiment as the student walks toward the rolling balls while catching them, he catches the balls more frequently than if he had stayed still (i.e. analogous to the blue shift). When he catches the balls while walking away from the rolling balls, he catches the balls less frequently than if he had remained stationery (i.e. analogous to the red shift). Therefore, Bruno shared his understanding on frequency with the other co-learners in the classroom.

I suspect that Bruno will never forget the Doppler effect and his understandings of frequency because he faced his misconceptions and figured out what makes sense and how he can test for it. He still needs to understand how to differentiate frequency and amplitude, but that will be another lesson. I suspect now that he understands frequency, amplitude will be much easier.

Conclusions

These results suggest that teacher-students can learn physical science when they utilize multiple opportunities to learn, including action experiments, textbook reading, dialogue both in class and on the world wide web, field experiences, and opportunities to innovate, utilizing everyday materials. Time will tell if the teacher-students incorporate a constructivist model for teaching physical science in their own elementary school classrooms, and if their students learn science when we teach science in this manner.

We need to help our students face that dissonance, that uncomfortable feeling, when everything does not make sense. We want our students to learn that if they conduct more action experiments, think deeply, using the language of science and confronting their misconceptions, they can learn to think analytically about physical science. Students will gain confidence in themselves, as evidenced in Paulette's statements, as they experience this. The teacher-students will want to share their way of thinking with their students. It opens up a new way of seeing the world.

Note

1   I acknowledge the help and vision of Ms Elizabeth Williams for co-authoring the selection of the experiments in the curriculum that I used in the physical science course for elementary teachers. In addition, I thank Professor Kenneth Tobin for critically reviewing the manuscript for me.

References

APPLETON, K. (1997) 'Analysis and description of students' learning during science classes using a constructivist-based model', *Journal of Research in Science Teaching*, **34**, pp. 303–18.

BROOKS, J.G. and BROOKS, M. (1993) *In Search of Understanding: The Case for Constructivist Classrooms*, Alexandria, VA: Association for Supervision and Curriculum Development.

CHALLONER, J. (1995) *The Visual Dictionary of Physics*, London, England: Dorling Kindersley Limited.

CHURCHILL, E.R., LOESCHNIG, L.V. and MANDELL, M. (1997) *365 Simple Science Experiments with Every Day Materials*, New York, NY: Sterling Publishing Company.

COLLINS, A. and SPIEGEL, S.A. (1995) 'So you want to do action research?', *Action Research: Perspectives from Teachers' Classrooms*, SPIEGEL, S.A., COLLINS, A. and LAPPERT, J. (eds) Tallahassee, FL: South Eastern Regional Vision for Education (SERVE).

EXPLORATORIUM MUSEUM (1996) *Exploratorium Snackbook: Sound*, San Francisco, CA, <http://www.exploratorium.edu/>.

FELDMAN, J.R. (1995) *Science Surprises. Ready-to-use Experiments and Activities for Young Learners*, Paramus, NJ: Center for Applied Research in Education.

FLORIDA DEPARTMENT OF EDUCATION (1993) *Science for All Students: The Florida Pre-K-12 Science Curriculum Framework: A Guide for Curriculum Planners*, Tallahassee, FL.

GILMER, P.J. and MCDONALD, J.B. (1997) 'Setting the scene for action research', *Science in the Elementary School Classroom: Portraits of Action Research*, MCDONALD, J.B. and GILMER P.J. (eds) Tallahassee, FL: South Eastern Regional Vision for Education (SERVE), pp. 1–7.

GLASERSFELD, E. (1989) 'Cognition, construction of knowledge, and teaching', *Synthese*, **80**, 1, pp. 121–40.

GUBA, E. and LINCOLN, Y. (1989) *Fourth Generation Evaluation*, Newbury Park, CA: Sage.

HEWITT, P.G., SUCHOCKI, J. and HEWITT, L.A. (1994) *Conceptual Physical Science*, Harper Collins College Publishers.

JOHNSON, D.W., JOHNSON, R.T. and SMITH, K.A. (1991) *Cooperative Learning: Increasing College Faculty Instructional Productivity*, ASHE-ERIC Higher Education Report No. 4, Washington, DC: The George Washington University, School of Education and Human Development.

LEMKE, J.L. (1995) *Textual Politics: Discourse and Social Dynamics*, London: Taylor and Francis.

MARZANO, R.J. (1992) *A Different Kind of Classroom: Teaching with Dimension of Learning*, Alexandria, VA: Association for Supervision and Curriculum Development.

NATIONAL EDUCATION GOALS PANEL (1991) *Executive Summary: The National Education Goals Report: Building a Nation of Learners*, Washington, DC: US Government Printing Office.

NATIONAL RESEARCH COUNCIL (1996) *National Science Education Standards*, Washington, DC: National Academy Press.

NSTA *REPORTS!* (1997) US students show outstanding scores in fourth-grade TIMSS study, American fourth graders rank second in science internationally, **9**, 1, pp. 1, 26–7.

PEAK, L. (1996) *Pursuing Excellence: A Study of US Eighth Grade Mathematics and Science Teaching, Learning, Curriculum, and Achievement in International Context* (Executive Summary and Conclusion), Washington, DC: US Department of Education.

SCHMIDT, W.H., MCKNIGHT, C.C. and RAIZEN, S.A. (1997) *A Splintered Vision: An Investigation of US Science and Mathematics Education*, Dordrecht, Netherlands: Kluwer Academic Publishers.

SCHON, D.A. (1983) *The Reflective Practitioner*, New York, NY: Basic Books.

SHAPIRO, B.L. (1994) *What Children Bring to Light*, New York, NY: Teachers College, Columbia University.

SPIEGEL, S.A., COLLINS, A. and GILMER, P.J. (1995) 'Science For Early Adolescence Teachers (Science FEAT): A program for research and learning', *Science Teacher Education*, **6**, pp. 165–74.

TOBIN, K. (ed.) (1993) *The Practice of Constructivism in Science Education*, Hillsdale, NJ: Lawrence Erlbaum Associates.

TOBIN, K., KAHLE, J.B. and FRASER, B.J. (eds) (1990) *Windows into Science Classrooms: Problems Associated with Higher-level Cognitive Learning*, London, Bristol, PA: Falmer Press.

TOBIN, K. and TIPPINS, D. (1993) 'Constructivism as a referent for teaching and learning', in TOBIN, K. (ed.) *The Practice of Constructivism in Science Education*, Washington, DC: AAAS Press, pp. 3–21.

Chapter 15

Exploring Critical Distance in Science Education: Students Researching the Implications of Technological Embeddedness

J. Damian Kellogg

When asked to write a chapter regarding students as researchers from the perspective of science education I was struck again by the ironic contrast between the possibility for engaging student research within the study of science and the reality of my own past experiences in science classrooms. I found this to be particularly unsettling within the field of biology, which I studied first in high school and then later as my major as an undergraduate. With few exceptions, my experiences within biology classrooms served primarily to stifle my inherent interest in what was to me a fascinating subject. Talking with students in the biology lab classes I teach, I have found that my experience is far from unique. I count myself fortunate, however, in that it was my discouragement with the science instruction that I was receiving that kindled my interest in teaching. Thus, rather than abandoning science altogether, I became involved in education and the teaching of biology to explore why four years of biology coursework had left me with little enthusiasm for a subject I loved. Fortunately, my initiation into science education introduced me to alternative perspectives of both science and pedagogy, first through the constructivist approach to teaching (Fensham et al., 1994), then through the post-modern ecological critique of education articulated by David Orr, and later through the language of critical pedagogy.

The autobiographical perspective with which I approach this piece is an attempt to distance myself from the traditional language or discourse adopted within modernist science classrooms and their claims to objectivity. Undoubtably, my research has been and is influenced by my own education, interests, and motivations. In particular, my criticism of science education has been recently influenced by particular researchers and critics within the field of education (Carr et al., 1994; Orr, 1992 and 1994; Kincheloe, 1993 and 1995; Frankenstein, 1997). However, my discussion here of students as researchers is largely a critical reflection upon a project in which students, myself included, explored the extent to which technology shapes our moral and ethical decisions. Specifically, I have attempted a meta-analysis of the processes at play during this particular project, paying particular attention to the pedagogical implications of this research experience for my own teaching within a college biology laboratory. In using these examples, I hope not only to share one example in which students became active, engaged researchers, but also to demonstrate the value of including considerations of the ethical, social and cultural forces at work within students' lives as part of any science curriculum.

Epistemologically speaking, science is a field dominated by empirical *research*. Yet within science classrooms students are not often encouraged to participate in the process of making knowledge through the application of scientific principles (i.e. through their own research). Rather, science is often taught by the transmission model of teaching, in which students are bombarded with vast quantities of information produced by experts. Instead of engaging students in meaningful investigation, reflection, and interpretation, many classrooms and even those courses described as science laboratories are taught in a manner that focuses on content and techniques (Carr et al., 1994). Student success is then determined not based on their ability to ask and carefully investigate questions by applying the methods of science to problems within society or in their own lives, but by regurgitating predigested and decontextualized facts and by reproducing predetermined results in contrived laboratory settings. Consequently, this style of teaching discourages critical student research and instead encourages the memorization of 'the facts' and the replication of procedures previously developed by others.

In addition rather than addressing important issues of our time, such as exploring critically the role of science and technology in shaping our world and our lives, science education has traditionally avoided addressing questions of knowledge production, ethics, and applicability through an adherence to and reification of the ideals of 'objectivity' and science for science's sake. Thus, science is often presented as a value-neutral, universal epistemology, which enables its user to transcend cultural influences and discern an 'objective', reality (Alvarez, 1992). Therefore, the ways in which scientific knowledge and technological advances transform power relationships among groups and individuals within society are rarely explored. Furthermore, discussion of these topics is not considered a legitimate realm of inquiry within science and science education. And yet, most science educators and researchers uncritically accept the assumption that technology and the advances in our 'knowledge' achieved through the increasing application of new techniques are both beneficial and necessary. Technological and economic growth and development are thus implicitly portrayed as being 'natural' and part of evolutionary processes working within society and the world. This view can be observed in a perpetual concern with bringing new technologies and equipment into the science classroom in the name of enhancing student interest and learning. The job of science educators is merely to prepare students to understand and function facilely within the technologically dominated world in which we live. However, the role of science in perpetuating detrimental and life-destroying processes within of our economy goes unexamined. I would argue that another useful analogy within biology and with which we might also explore and explain the uncontrollable growth of our consumerist economy is that of a cancer. However, the teaching of such an analogy, while instructive and perhaps equally valid, is not politically expedient and therefore seldom taught.

I recently reminded of the prevalence of this unquestioned myth of technological progress while visiting an introductory biology class at a large research institution. On this particular day, the lecturer, a geneticist, informed the nearly 900 students gathered in the auditorium/lecture hall that we are now in the golden age of biology. Somehow, this struck me as odd, and I waited for an explanation. Based on his ensuing monologue, his optimism was apparently buoyed by the advances in cellular and molecular biology in the latter half of this century. Many discoveries within these particular fields have occurred through the development of new research techniques unimaginable just decades ago. What struck me, however, was that his grand pronouncement seemed uninhibited by, and unaware of, the continued destruction of huge reservoirs of genetic information (not to mention life) as we destroy tropical rain forests and other fragile ecosystems every day. I for one, paused to wonder how many species had come to an untimely exit from the world between the discovery of the first archebacteria and the decoding of its complete genome, two pieces of information that he found worthy of note simply for their contribution to the ever-expanding stockpile of scientific knowledge.

However, he also seemed unable to connect the vacuous stare of the students upon which he gazed daily with the repressive modernist pedagogy of control employed in his course. I cannot say whether it had occurred to him that his teaching was helping to create passive students and reify the perception of scientists as the official and legitimate providers of information about the world. However, regardless of his intentions, a uniform and constricting form of instruction such as lecture, when used on a large and heterogeneous audience, ignores the diversity of learning styles among students and is destined to produce passive, detached, and bored students who find little chance to connect academic biology to their lives. Certainly, as a technique, it is not likely to foster creative and engaged young scientists.

This to me is the irony: while the rate of species extinction approaches levels unprecedented in hundreds of thousands of years as a result of human actions, many biologists stand transfixed by the wonders of our technological advances praising them as the road to a new and brighter future. They seem unable to make the connection between the disjointed and clinical view of life taught through our classrooms and the rapid extinguishing of the diversity and beauty of this wondrous living planet. Somewhere along the line 'the study of life' has lost its ability to recognize the destruction of its subject. This failing has carried over into the classroom as students have been subjected to moribund pedagogy based on reductionistic and normalized models of student learning which strive for control and uniformity rather than celebrating diversity and encouraging creative critical thought.

While writing this piece I have attempted to explore the ways in which I have been encouraged to become critically reflective in my learning, both in my own research as a student and within my own teaching where I attempt to encourage my students to address their own issues. Throughout this piece I have approached this exploration from two voices, namely that of myself as a researching student and secondly as a reflection and commentary on the role of teachers (myself included) in encouraging and engaging students in conscientiously critical research. Thus, to simplify the transition between these voices and hopefully provide for ease of reading, I felt that an explanation of the structure of this essay might be helpful.

This exploration is organized around a series of excerpts from the final paper I produced as part of an ethnographic and autobiographical research project in a graduate class within the Science, Technology, and Society (STS) department at Penn State University. My account of the project as given in this summary portrays fairly accurately, I believe, the methods and purpose of the instructor in engaging the students in this activity. While many of the selections are obviously highly contextual and limited to my own particular perspective at a given point in time, it is my hope that this contextually grounded example will speak to the potential of this method for encouraging students in critical reflection on their world.

The remainder of this section consists mainly of excerpts from my own research as a student. To explain further the pedagogical and practical dynamics at play both within my own thinking and that of the instructor under whose auspices I was working and to reflect on my original work I have displayed all commentary not occurring in the original text throughout the remainder of this piece as quoted material.

> It may also be helpful to note that the structure of my initial summary was couched within the modified framework of a traditional scientific lab write-up (i.e. the Introduction, Methods, and Results sections). When I initially chose to present the material in this format, it was an intuitive response to my feeling that in many ways, although this was the summary of a self-reflective journal with a loosely defined research methodology, the project in which I had just partaken was an example of personally relevant research, facilitated by a pedagogically informed instructor. By presenting my results in a format which I had learned through my years of scientific research training, I felt that I could benefit from the clarity of the techniques of scientific writing for presenting research in a logical and accessible medium and at the same time demonstrate how reflective qualitative methodology and an acknowledgment of the positionality of the researcher within both the investigation and the resulting text allows for more accurate and truthful knowledge production within the context of the presentation of one's findings.
>
> From a pedagogical perspective, I find that combining methods from disparate research traditions allows room for us as educators to introduce and acknowledge some of the practical, technical aspects of producing research within the scientific community, while simultaneously providing a rhetorically defensible platform and modicum through which we can initiate a critique of the weaknesses of the scientific 'objective' approach to knowledge production. In short, this postmodern approach to research allows us to creatively and explicitly examine the processes by which knowledge is produced, validated, and transmitted from a critical perspective. At the same time, this is achieved in manner such that we, both as students and teachers are able to engage in rigorous reflective research that observes, yet transcends, narrow disciplinary boundaries to address broader questions and issues relevant to our lives.

Introduction

This project and the resulting journal began as an attempt to examine the extent to which technology bounds the (or my) moral identity and affects (my) moral decision-making. To appreciate the extent to which our lives are permeated by technology, the use of specific technologies was disallowed by week during a five-week period. Non-use was intended to provide a necessary 'critical distance' from the technology and to provide the opportunity for temporary disengagement, thereby allowing for deeper consideration of the value and embeddedness of each technology. Additionally, it was intended that through this exercise, a clearer perception would be obtained of the extent to which technology is autonomous.

Methods

As agreed upon in an initial class meeting, for each of five weeks we (the students in STS/PHIL 489/589) refrained from using a specific technology. During the course of this project, we were to keep a journal reflecting on our experience with 'giving up' each technology. When appropriate students made substitutions by week for technologies which an individual either could not disengage or with which they previously had minimal engagement. For example, a student employed as a receptionist might be unable to forgo use of the phone or a student who does not own or watch television would not truly be gaining 'critical distance' from a technology which was not previously used. The technologies that I sequentially gave up were: the wrist-watch, dishwasher, private transportation, telephone, and the personal computer.

> In the above report from my previous research, as I continue to do in this paper, I intentionally write in the first-person. This is done to remind myself and my students, that we cannot truly remove ourselves from our experiments/research; the detached objective observer is a myth. Our biases are built into the experimental design and our instruments and influence the observations we make.
>
> Speaking to my own biases, I feel it necessary to mention specifically the teaching methods of my instructor for the above-mentioned course, Dr Shannon Duval, which I had not included in the description of my own research. Mostly, because, I felt that the reflective nature of the class's research testifies to the strength of her teaching methods and impressed upon me the value of an inclusive classroom pedagogy. Notably, rather than simply imposing this research project on us, she engaged us in a discussion of the aims and methods of the project. Thus, we were able to discuss and negotiate the terms of the project. In addition, we were able to address practical concerns regarding how this research might impact us, any difficulties that we thought might arise, and how they should handled. For example, by not requiring that students all abstain from the same technologies, we were encouraged to consider among our options and to make choices that were most relevant to our lives and the project at hand. In short, Dr Duval's use of a democratic pedagogy was consistent with her purported beliefs and reflected the confluence of her own research and her teaching.

Before beginning this period of sequential disengagements, one week was spent monitoring or reflecting on our personal use of technology, including appliances and entire systems. This initial week was intended to heighten personal awareness of the extent to which we depend upon and are enmeshed in technology. Also during this week, we were asked to reflect upon our ability to 'build, maintain, or repair' the technologies with which we engage.

On the seventh and final week of this project we were asked to provide a comprehensive evaluation of our journals, focusing on 'the extent to which [our] moral identity and values are shaped by the use of technologies'. Additionally, we were asked to reflect on and address the following questions: 'What did [I] learn about [my] relationship to technologies and the moral choices [I made] during this period?', 'What changes, if any, will [I] make in [my] use of technologies?', and 'Why?'

> Before continuing to my reflection on these questions, let me begin by addressing a number of technical aspects regarding this research methodology that may not apparent from the above description. As a data collecting strategy, this project entailed students' consistent use of a project journal which was turned in with a summary paper at the end of the project. However, in addition, during the course of our research some in-class time was provided each week for small group discussions, which included sharing thoughts and insights into the ongoing project. Further, class readings and discussions also focused on issues related to technology and ethics including the implications of different beliefs regarding 'human nature' and the autonomy of technology. The decision to use a journal format and to write the summary essay as a means of assessment upon completion of the project were initially made by the instructor, but appeared to work well for most students. However, the extended period between the initiation of the project and the collection of the written work left room for procrastination on the part of some students, who may have benefited from more frequent interaction with the instructor and an ongoing assessment of their progress.
>
> Beyond the technical, I find it necessary to address the thoughts and values motivating this piece. For example, this project is autobiographical in nature, or perhaps, interbiographical in that in this work the students are asked to explore the ways in which they and their subject affect each other. It is arguable that it is not necessary or useful for students to examine their lives and/or personal histories to learn about science, get good grades, or get a high-paying job. Some would even argue that such introspection merely takes time away from students' studies of science content. However, it can also be argued that the science students learn is of little use if they are unable to connect it to their own understandings of the world. From a critical perspective, whether students succeed or fail to 'learn' science content is less of a concern than the effects that the scientific worldview has on students' ability to act in a just and humane manner within a democratic society. This is not to say that a basic understanding of scientific dogma from atoms to evolution is not helpful in understanding our modern world. In fact, the contrary is true. If we can understand the complexity of these concepts and the circumstances under which they came into use, we can gain critical insight into the myriad ways in which science has successfully managed to transform our modern consciousness. However, what critical pedagogy insists is that there are structures and assumptions

embedded in the discourse of any field, whether it be biology, physics, sociology or art, which have ethical implications that are manifest in the physical world and our social interactions. Often, these assumptions remain hidden and maintain current inequities within our society and the world. Thus, by exposing the previously invisible, we are able to see and address inequality and oppression and promote decision-making based on ideals of social justice and democracy. Rather than perpetuating the creation or development of knowledge as morally neutral, teaching informed by critical pedagogy can instead ask students to recognize the ethical aspects of their perspectives and choices, to consider the ways in which all of our decisions have political and ethical consequences.

While such pedagogically pro-active teaching may be easily promoted, the average student and many teachers may not readily embrace this perception or share in this perceived need to motivate students to action. In fact many teachers feel that it is their responsibility to remain politically and ideologically neutral within the classroom. However, from the perspective which I share, neutrality is greatly overrated. From a critical position, power relations are nearly always unequal; thus, claiming a position of neutrality is to accept the status quo with all the inequities that this entails and to surrender one's own ability to act. Students in particular, may be readily aware of this inconsistency, particularly with respect to a teacher who talks about empowerment and liberatory pedagogy yet fails to relinquish many of the trappings of authority. Research which engages students to ask questions about their own lives and in which they decide which concerns are most pertinant is destined to encourage exploration and reflection. Further, such reflection can lead to positive change when students come to accept and understand that any choice they make involves the privileging of certain values. In the following section I explore taken-for-granted practices and structures in my own life that became more apparent through my research as a student in Dr Duval's class.

Results and Discussion

Connections and Implication

In the initial week of this project, if was readily apparent that my life is currently heavily dependent on technology in a multiplicity of forms. The design of my apartment and the composition of many of the tools and materials I interact with daily reflect technological 'innovations'. The temperature in my apartment is maintained within certain boundaries that I choose by the technological wonder of my air conditioner/heat pump. My climate control system, as well as my refrigerator, stove, hot water heater, lights, stereo and other appliances are all powered by electricity that is provided to me via a large technological system that I know very little about. I do know that it is quite likely that my electricity was the product of a long and environmentally damaging energy extraction process that included strip mining and the burning of coal. I also know that alternative methods for providing the power upon which I so readily depend are exceedingly limited in my current circumstances.

My limited choice among the technologies I use extends beyond the realm of my immediate environment. Included also are the means by which I obtain my food and to some extent the way I transport myself from place to place. Whether obtaining food means going to the grocery store or eating at a restaurant, I inevitably participate in a system that involves the transportation of food for hundreds or even thousands of miles investing huge amounts of energy to supply my dietary needs. When I ride my bike or drive a car, I am carried by a vehicle that was constructed from alloys, plastics, rubber, and coated with paint. The materials used to build these vehicles were products of technologically complex processes of which I again have virtually no understanding; there is little doubt that the manufacture of each component has contributed to a more polluted environment in some part of the world. Thus, in essence, my first week of reflection served mostly to heighten my awareness that like most Americans today I was born into and live in a privileged position which is maintained largely at the expense of the environment and peoples in other places. Further, it was apparent that in many cases we are severely limited in our alternatives to technology. As an ecologist, it was apparent to me that the sources for my daily existence extend over a large part of the planet, and the amount of energy needed to maintain my lifestyle are exceedingly large when compared to the flows in a biological system.

Adding Depth of Perception

Abstinence from the wristwatch was a fitting initiation to the power or non-use or critical distance as a technique. For me, not using a watch revealed the extent to which my world is shaped by technology. In releasing my wrist watch for a week, I found that my understanding of the passing of time and in essence my present life is mediated and dictated by the regime of the clock. The idea that time has broken down into discreet segments, each of equal duration and that this concept is a fairly recent technological 'innovation' had previously not occurred to me. Attempting to distance myself from this mechanized reality was perhaps my most instructive and disturbing experience since entering Penn State.

The idea that our modern conception of time should be so strictly dictated by clocks and to a larger extent the calender was not in itself that earth-shaking. Bedtime, story hours, recess, and birthdays were all part of my growing up. However, a realization of the extent to which my entire life has been surrounded and shaped by this modern reality was profoundly unsettling. The inability of our modern culture to recognize or examine the strictures of our culturally created, clock-dominated reality and the rigidity built into this system is indicative of the short-sightedness of our current norms. By giving up my watch for a week, I felt as though I had undergone a transformation.

In nearly every segment of my daily life, the clock rules. I wake either at a time set on my alarm clock, or on some days, on my own in anticipation of an appointment demarcated, again, by the clock. From the moment I rise, until I go back to sleep, and every moment in between, my watch is running. It tells me what time it is and the day of the week and of the month. In a sense, it defines my sense of place and gives me grounding. By consulting this instrument, I make decisions on what I should do and where I should be. Whether it's dark or light, whether I'm wide awake or exhausted, regardless of the seasons or the weather, the clock does not differentiate in its measurement. Our concept of time has become separated from the biological or ecological cycles of the natural world.

This distance from the natural world is in fact seen as one of technological society's crowning achievements; we can now function in nearly any habitat, no matter how inhospitable to human life, with the requisite technologies surrounding us. The progressively widening schism we have created between the human and natural environments has allowed us for a time to expunge the environment from our collective consciousness, and particularly from our moral and ethical frames of reference.

Additionally, time has become a unit of value, of worth. I found the permeation of this way of thinking deep within my own actions and aspirations. Being a competitive runner, my goals and training are centered on times. Using my watch's precise reality, I measure my performance. Four minutes and 29 seconds to run a mile is good, but wouldn't it be nice of if I could run one or two or 10 seconds faster? I also extend this logic to my academic work. I may have just read two articles, which took me nearly four hours. Maybe I just don't get it. The oppression of the clock leads me to doubt; perhaps I wasn't meant to lead a life of scholarly inquiry. Daily life races on. Efficiency and meeting deadlines become the criteria by which our lives are given value and for which we receive rewards. But, why not? Isn't running a four-minute mile inherently better than running one in 10 minutes? Taking only two hours to complete an assigned reading is certainly preferable to four hours. Perhaps it is the case that faster is better. However, when time becomes the only measurement used to determine the value of any part of our lives, something is terribly amiss. And yet, time is the one aspect by which our modern lives are unquestionably ruled.

Moving on: Is There Life Without Personal Transportation?

Private transportation has been an ethical consideration of mine for the last few years. Thanks to the serendipitous destruction of my personal automobile, my great fortune to be living within a few blocks of the university, and my interest in environmental education I have been able to reflect on and weigh my transportation options carefully without having to commit myself to the expense of an automobile. However, were it not for the loss of my own car in a crash three years ago, and my decision for financial reasons not to replace it, I would in all likelihood still be zipping around in my little sports car consuming huge amounts of energy and adding steadily and heartily to the greenhouse gases accumulating in the atmosphere. Having owned a vehicle since I was 16, this loss provided me the critical distance I needed to re-evaluate my relationship to this technology that had become an unquestioned part of my life. I count myself fortunate to have been living in a location where I was able to discover the freedom from owning an automobile.

This week of non-use, I reflected on the value that I have found in not owning a car, the conditions that perpetuate the use of this particular technology, and the costs of our system of personal transportation. In terms of immediate and direct benefits to me, not owning a vehicle returns some amount of economic freedom. Without a car, I no longer have the expense of maintenance, insurance, or parking. Additionally, I am no longer burdened with the responsibility or driving safely, of driving a potentially deadly weapon, or for personally contributing to the emissions of greenhouse gases through my vehicle use.

This line of thinking, however invariably brings me back to the question of freedom, privilege, and the extent to which we shape and control our own lives. Undoubtably, being without a car has disadvantages. I am less able to leave the immediate vicinity in which I live. I have forfeited the social status of owning a particular type of car and the privileges that car ownership provides. Current land use and development practices frequently assume the availability of private automobile. Jobs, businesses and civic establishments are frequently located at considerable distance from our homes and require some form of mechanized transportation for ready access. Further, because public transportation is often not available, insufficiently flexible, or culturally devalued, it often fails to provide a viable alternative to private transportation. Thus, although I may choose not to have a car, I may simultaneously be severely limiting my access to recreation in remote areas and to my parents in north-western Pennsylvania who are a couple of hours away by car, but an entire day distant by public transportation.

As further development occurs based on the premise that everyone has an automobile and the distance over which we travel in our daily lives increases, options that would not require car use become less feasible or further outside the norm. Thus we become trapped into a specific technologically dependent mode of living. It is this normative technologically based thinking that fails to recognize the political and ethical choices inherent in the technologies we embrace. If we hope to engender socially and environmentally responsible decision-making among 'middle America', a hiatus from automobile use might work wonders.

Communities Without Boundaries

The technological infusion extends even beyond my environment, world view, and space; it reaches into my social world as well. In giving up the telephone for a week, I realized that without the use of the telephone, many of my relationships as I currently experience them, would simply cease to exist. Telephones and to a lesser extent answering machines are an integral part of my social life. Bell Atlantic and AT and T provide me the means of communicating with my brother in Maryland, my aunt and uncle in North Carolina, and my parents and grandparent in Warren, Pennsylvania. Since, I have no car and seldom make visits, the phone has become the primary means through which we maintain our family ties.

Among four friends with whom I regularly run, two live on either end of the university campus, one lives a couple miles north, and the fourth lives around four miles south of my apartment. Our work is largely in unrelated areas and thus we typically would not see each other during the course of a day. However, each night

I talk with at least one of these persons to arrange or confirm a run for the following day. Thus, our rather informal running 'community' is currently contingent on the use of phone, which allows us flexibility without which we would not meet. Another friend with whom I meet only sporadically, whose lab is located on the opposite end of campus from my department and class meetings, would become more distant were I not able to call her at home on any evening. In addition, my closest friends are scattered around the country and the world in Miami, Boulder, San Francisco, Boston, and Japan. Without the phone we would be in touch much less frequently. Thus, the phone keeps me connected to the 'closest' people in my life, and even allows for the formation and maintenance of 'community'.

As is obvious by these statements, to me the phone has the positive value of creating and maintaining a sense of community in a world in which the persons we love and care for are located beyond easy or convenient reach. This feeling is amplified by my chosen means of transportation, my feet, which limit my range of interaction. My poor attempt at restraint from phone use during this week served to confirm my current addiction to this technology and to emphasize the role it plays in my life. This technology, too is maintained via the use our electrical system and probably includes hundred of thousands or even millions of miles of wires strewn across the globe, and perhaps even some satellites orbiting the earth. Previously, my decision as to whether or not to use this technology was never a question. The phone is rather firmly entrenched in my life. While this may not change, I now better understand the values that I am promoting, both positive and negative from my perspective, when I use the phone. In addition I can now see that I do have options and I can begin to assess the costs associated with any decision I make.

Applying an ethical framework to my phone use, quite honestly can be highly frustrating, largely because of the contradictory values which are promoted by the choices I make. However, it becomes obvious that at some point all of our decisions entail judgment calls, or choosing which values we believe are most important. In this case, the values on which I am more inclined to focus and feel capable of monitoring are social-responsibility aspects of this technology, such as using the phone only in a manner which enhances community. Thus, as an example of an alternative, where possible I might attempt to meet in person rather than to talk at a distance. Through this decision I privilege and assert my belief in the value of face-to-face personal interaction as a way of promoting honesty and fostering understanding over the flexibility, expediency, and physical separation allowed by telephone use. Ironically, my difficulty in giving up the phone was that it would have stranded me from my 'community'; yet, if the phone were non-existent, I would be more inclined to converse with those nearest me, a situation that could work wonders for enhancing my local community and which wouldn't be mediated by technology.

Conclusions

In participating in this period of non-use of technologies, I was particularly aware of the extent to which my world and all of my actions are embedded in a technological matrix in deep and often unexplored ways. Since coming to Penn State I have been particularly critical of the value of technology and the role that technological development has played in the degradation of the environment (in a holistic sense). I feel that I may have begun to identify the source of my distrust of technology and persons who seek to further its advance. It seems quite likely that my ill ease has been a reaction to the lack of moral and ethical consideration that is often given to the work we do and the actions we take daily. As part of generation born after WWII and the industrial revolution, I have been brought up to accept and value each new technological innovation and to expect that science will provide that answers to all of our troubles. However, exposure to the readings of persons such as David Orr, Wendell Berry, Aldo Leopold, and others lead me to question the success or likelihood of technological solutions to increasing environmental destruction. In addition to these latter authors, my own exploration of literature by critics of modernism, growth economics, and capitalism strengthen my distaste for technological development and increasing individual consumption. Arguments that technology is autonomous seem to strip responsibility and agency from individual humans, and further a sense of helplessness.

In contrast, stepping away from technologies even for a week, has provided me with a means of assessing the extent to which I find myself entrenched and trapped in a technological world. Abstinence even for a short time assures me that I still retain some agency. Where I fail, I realize I have much work to do. I personally find reliance on huge technological systems to be rather deplorable. Immense systems allow for little control of the participants, make comprehending the results of individual actions and their effects difficult or even impossible, and thus hide the ethical nature of our daily decisions. And yet, if I pass a judgment using the avoidance of large-scale technologies as a yardstick, my own actions become unconscionable. This exercise has been instrumental in helping me acknowledge my own complicity in supporting many hyperextended systems, and allowed me to consider the possibility of implementing alternatives.

While I can't change the way we perceive time and I may not want to give up my telephone or dishwasher, I can and have made changes in my own actions. In the last few weeks, I have been steadily decreasing the extent to which I rely on gasoline-powered personal transportation. I have been writing more of my assignments by hand with a pencil, rather than with a disposable pen or on a computer. I have been waking up with the sun and going to bed earlier while minimizing my use of electric lighting. I now walk or ride my bike to get my groceries from locally owned stores rather than frequenting a supermarket via my friend's Jeep. I turn my computer on less, and read more. I am also conscious of my telephone (ab)use, and see this as an area for definite improvement. I haven't changed the world or escaped from technology, but I have found myself more aware of the ethical implication of my actions, and learned a new technique for assessing my own dependence and attachment to particular technologies.

When looking back at this autobiographical research, I see in vivid detail the effects that this class undoubtably had on my thinking, and more notably my action. Certainly, I was moved to make changes in my behaviors based on my new understanding of my complicity in supporting particular oppressive economically, socially and politically motivated ways of understanding and interacting with the world. And there is little doubt that this movement was a result of examining the ethics of my relationship with technology. While a direct desire to change students' behavior through a heightened awareness of the ethical implication our actions was never stated as a goal of this research, change undoubtably occurred. The effectiveness of this method in eliciting change was, I believe, the result of its ability to help students acquire a critical distance from their typical manner of interacting with technology. In this instance, a method as simple as not using a given technology for seven days and reflecting on this experience in reference to several carefully considered questions was enough to facilitate the development of insight into my own behavior. I believe that the motivation I found to make change resulted from the enhanced awareness of the pervasive technological matrix within which I find myself located and the extent to which I unquestioningly rely on it daily. The research we produced as students in this class allowed us to explore ways in which we might extract ourselves at least temporaily within a limited context. It may be unrealistic to believe that we could ever truly step outside of technology, particularly as a person growing up in the US in the late twentieth century. However, the use of temporary disengagement in this case created the space for critical consciousness to take root. The critical aspect of this project I see as *as* should be obvious throughout this paper, however, I had not previously been able to explicate my own position as clearly.

Thus, for students and teachers seeking to develop a critical perspective, the concept of critical distance as employed here may particularly useful. For myself, when simply introducing students to these ideas for the first time, I find that a number of questions can be used to facilitate the recognition of the non-neutrality of a given position. The following are a few that I have learned at some point and now commonly employ in my own thinking: Who gains? Who loses? How does this affect the poor, women, persons of color, or the earth? Could it be any other way? If so, is there resistance to alternatives, and again if so, where and why? Obviously, many more exist and the questions that help to stimulate critical thinking will differ by person. When approached from a position that acknowledges the social, historical, and environmental context within which our understandings are shaped, one gains an entirely different perspective when applying these questions to specific inquiries such as: 'Why is biology taught almost exclusively indoors at a university?', 'Why is half of an introductory course in biology now spent on genetics, cellular and molecular biology?', or 'What are the purposes of classification and taxonomy within the study of life?'

In addition, I believe that the distance I was able to gain from technology was further enhanced by the use of autobiography and my move to action cannot be separated from the use of autobiography as a research methodology. By being able to pick up and analyze my journal entries, which are in a sense snapshots of my autobiography through time, I was able to examine my perspective from more than one position within the autobiographical present. Within the framework used by this class, the past was explored mostly to the extent that the students recognized that their present actions have been and are shaped by past experiences and practices, which in turn were likely influenced by the evolving social and cultural system in which they are embedded. By examining these sources in the present we gain insight into where we have been in recent time. In addition, because we do not merely observe where we were in the yesterday, but in essence re-conceptualize both our perception of our position in the past and our location in present based on this reflection, our reflection leads to change. A similar and excellent description of the way in which autobiographical has been taken up in education theory, including the need for 'detachment from experience' within such research is described in the 'analytical' step of curriculum theorist William Pinar's method of currere (Pinar, 1994, p. 26). Pinar's more fully developed theoretical work helps explain the way in which autobiographical research can be used to explore the relationship between one's Self and the educational (or other pedagogical) experience in which one is immersed. Pinar's method is 'regressive', 'progressive', 'analytical' and 'synthetical' and provides a model with which the method used here could be deepened. By extending the researcher's reflection further into the past (regressive) and explicitly examining hopes and possible directions for future direction (progressive), including these additional steps of currere within this useful research method would help ensure that students extend even further their critical understandings.

References

ALVAREZ, C. (1992) 'Science' in SACHS, W. (ed.) *The Development Dictionary: A Guide to Knowledge As Power*, Atlantic Highlands, NJ: Zed Books.

CARR, M., BARKER, M., BELL, B., BIDDULPH, F., JONES, A., KIRKWOOD, V., PEARSON, J. and SYMINGTON, D. (1994) 'The constructivist paradigm and some implications for science content and pedagogy', in FENSHAM, P.J. et al., (eds) *The Content of Science: A Constructivist Approach to Its Teaching and Learning*, London, Bristol, PA: Falmer Press.

FENSHAM, P.J., GUNSTONE, R.F. and WHITE, R.T. (1994) *The Content of Science: A Constructivist Approach to Its Teaching and Learning*, London, Bristol, PA: Falmer Press.

FRANKENSTEIN, M. (1997) 'Breaking down the dichotomy between learning and teaching mathematics', in FREIRE, P. *Mentoring the Mentor: A Critical Dialogue with Paulo Freire*, New York, NY: Peter Lang.

KINCHELOE, J.L. (1993) *Toward a Critical Politics of Teacher Thinking: Mapping the Postmodern*, Westport, CT: Bergin and Garvey.

KINCHELOE, J.L. (1995) *Toil and Trouble: Good Work, Smart Workers, and the Integration of Academic and Vocational Education*, New York, NY: Peter Lang.

ORR, D. (1992) *Ecological Literacy: Education and the Transition to a Postmodern World*, Albany, NY: SUNY Press.

ORR, D. (1994) *Earth in Mind: On Education, Environment, and the Human Prospect*, Washington, DC: Island Press.

PINAR, W.F. (1994) *Autobiography, Politics, and Sexuality: Esays in Curriculum Theory 1972–92*, New York: NY: Peter Lang.

Part Three

Conclusion

Chapter 16

Making Meaning and Analyzing Experience — Student Researchers as Transformative Agents

Joe L. Kincheloe and Shirley R. Steinberg

The authors and editors of *Students as Researchers* passionately believe in the pedagogical, cognitive, and political empowerment of teachers and students. Too often the concept of empowerment in the 1990s has been used as a 'buzz word' meaning little. In the context of this book, however, we have specifically connected the process of student research with the concept of empowerment. With empowerment in mind Nancy Dana writes in her chapter about the sense of power her student researchers gained as they developed a personal perspective — a point of view. Dana like the authors of other chapters helped empower student researchers by awakening their ability to make meaning, to understand that they can know more and that they are capable of more than they had previously imagined. Julia Ellis' chapter is especially helpful in this hermeneutic context. Such revelations engender passion in student researchers and their teachers. Little life-changing or life-affirming learning takes place until our affect is mobilized, until our passions are engaged. This usually occurs when student intellect, academic knowledge, and personal experience are brought together. At this point of intersection pedagogical magic takes place — the kind of magic that produces genius, that keeps the romance of teaching alive for great teachers. If this book doesn't engage your passion, we will feel that we have failed. The authors and editors want you to feel passionate about teaching, student research, empowerment and social justice.

Student Researchers as Autobiographical Inquirers: Exploring Student Identities

Both Kathy Berry and Pat Hinchey frame the concept adeptly in their chapters: one of the central concerns of student research involves students investigating the formation of their consciousness, their subjectivity. Engaging their passion and moving them in an empowered direction, Berry and Hinchey want their students to understand how their consciousness is constructed and how such an understanding is a prerequisite to critical civic action. These goals are central in student autobiography; indeed, outside of such concerns students' research of themselves is trivialized and too often becomes little more than a self-indulgent dabbling. Many social psychological analysts believe that one of the most important features of the human mental process involves its capacity for self-awareness. Our critical conception of student research is designed to extend this capacity by consciously focusing on these forces that work to interfere with such a process. As teachers focus on these power-generated impediments to self-awareness, they also explore ways of connecting to student ideas. A key dynamic in the effort to promote student research into their subjectivities involves making use of these connections. In this context teachers affirm the importance of student ideas and the value of finding out where they originated. There is much to gain from such knowledge, new realms of consciousness to experience from such genealogical investigations.

In her unique chapter on girls' notewriting in school Sandra Spickard Prettyman illustrates this concern with the construction of consciousness/subjectivity. In Prettyman's case notewriting becomes a form of action research by girls that can be read as acts of resistance to the traditional passivity curriculum for female students. Upon exploration Prettyman found that girls used notewriting as a form of indigenous therapy, a chance to express what was hurting them. This self-generated practice of notewriting is fascinating when viewed in the context of student autobiographical research. Though traditionally dismissed as 'merely' a feminine practice, notewriting is undoubtedly one of the most honest forms of self-analysis in school classrooms. Indeed, such notewriting might be used by a creative teacher as a first step in a reflective analysis of one's lived situation. Careful interpersonal negotiations by a *female* (not a man) teacher with the permission of the girls involved could initiate a set of activities connected to the notewriting designed to help these students become more aware of their lives and the gender forces that shape them.

Ellen Swartz's insights in her chapter on dramaturgy in educational research extend Prettyman's work, as she suggests that students build upon what they know. In the case of Prettyman's students such a pedagogical process might involve Swartz's questions about narrative vantage points, the construction of subjectivity and inter-subjectivities (the construction of identity and the meanings made in personal interaction), power relations and the interests they serve, and the connections between what teachers and students teach and learn, especially in relation to their individual and collective lived realities. Such teacher questions could generate some of the most profound school experiences a young woman might have. What is especially interesting in these contexts for students of pedagogy involves the origin of profound student research in what traditional educators typically view as a trivial (and improper) student behavior. In this example a savvy teacher researcher instead of punishing her students could help them understand the personal and social/gender significance of their notewriting — why they feel so drawn to the activity and the meaning of that attraction.

Since our understanding of pedagogy involves the production of knowledge both inside and outside the classroom, a critical pedagogy of student research directs us to the analysis of so-called 'trivial' activities such as girls' notewriting. The profound like a hologram rests in the trivial (the whole in the part) and in this context critical teachers and students as researchers adjust their attentions accordingly. As critical observers, we explore those places where students construct meanings — especially those meanings that situate them in relation to academic assumptions and knowledge. Indeed, a student's identity is closely tied to such a relationship in a manner that shapes the way the school categorizes, tracks and admits/not-admits them to the community of the capable, those with the acceptable test scores and bright futures. How does a teacher who understands these concepts structure a research project on, say, the Battle of Wounded Knee and the cultural implications it holds for the racial politics of the US? In what ways does the teacher ask racially privileged and racially marginalized students to autobiographically engage with the horrors they uncover? As the present is linked to this knowledge of the past, how do these different students connect their research to their lived worlds? Teacher researchers such as Swartz help them sort out the social and personal meanings engendered in their inquiry (Mullin, 1994; Allison, 1995; Giroux, 1992, 1994; Capra, Steindl-Rast, and Matus, 1992; Long, 1995; Lave and Wenger, 1991; Marker, 1993).

Students as Researchers of the Nature of Experience, the Nature of Their Own Experiences

Critical research regardless of where it is performed refuses to accept human experience as unproblematic and beyond questioning. Thus, experience never speaks for itself — it is always an understanding derived from a specific interpretation of a personal engagement with a constellation of symbols, socio-cultural practices, and political encodings. Particular experiences, critical researchers maintain, must be respected but always made problematic in terms of their interpretation. William Pinar and Joe Kincheloe (1991) address this concept in our theory of place which brings particular experience into focus but in a way that grounds it contextually through a consideration of the larger political, economic, social, and linguistic forces that shape it. Here, interpretations of experience are contextualized by the particularity of visceral experience. Such experience grounded in lust, fear, joy, love, and hate creates a synergistic interaction between interpretive understanding and the intimacy of the researchers' own autobiography. Students acting on these insights gain the ability to place themselves hermeneutically within the often messy web of power relations without losing touch with the emotion of their everyday lives.

Students as researchers come to understand that there is more to experience than initially meets the eye. As student researchers learn to interpret their experience, their imagination is released in a way that allows them to imagine new possibilities for themselves. In a critical context wise teachers help student researchers understand the unseen ways cultural forces shape their interpretations of their own personal experiences in modes that resonate with dominant forms of race, class, and gender power. Student experiences *and their interpretations of them* are the building materials used to construct versions of who they are. Teachers who want to cultivate student research on the nature of experience in general and their own personal experiences need to learn how to help students understand, validate, and challenge such activities. When teachers dismiss student experience, they blind themselves to the ways students learn, construct identity, and negotiate their place in the world. Students inquiring in this manner move into the meta-cognitive, meta-analytical terrain of epistemological analysis. In this domain, so uncharted in most classroom settings but so essential to the development of critical thinking, teachers and students deconstruct and reconstruct experience and its meaning.

Such analysis focuses attention on the relationship that connects and disconnects experience, action, reflection, and language. Making these connections might involve teachers and students researching and questioning particular experiences. The tentative answers they provide to such inquiries might be formulated by viewing experiences through new lenses provided by the meta-analytical frameworks of critical epistemology, post-formal thinking, and democratic ethics. Using the post-formal framework as an example, student researchers might re-visit experience by asking about the conditions in which it took place (contextualization), what led up to the actions in question (etymology), what connections might we find among the conditions, historical background, and the experience itself that would provide insight into the meaning of the situation (pattern detection), and what new forms of analysis might grant previously neglected perspectives on the experiences (process considerations). Being able to take student researchers through such a post-formal inquiry method will establish a thicker, more mature understanding of experience as a complex, less-than-transparent entity that must be carefully researched by those pursuing profound personal, social, political, and ethical understandings and meaningful cultural action. Simply stated, such research moves us from merely undergoing an event to an understanding of the consequences of an experience in our own and the lives of others (McLaren, 1992; Greene, 1993; Giroux, 1997; Freire and Faundez, 1989; King, 1990).

Using post-formal thinking as a conceptual framework for student and teacher research opens up a previously impoverished conversation on the nature and purpose of inquiry into experience in a pedagogical context. Understanding the elastic nature of post-formal thinking and post-formal research, we attempt not to 'define' these dynamics as much as 'perform' or 'do' them. The way these post-formal processes are 'done' always involves the interaction between our general conceptions of them and their interactions with the specificity of ever-changing experiences, the new contexts in which post-formal researchers find themselves. Post-formal inquiry and analysis facilitates our attempt to understand who we are and where we conceptually, politically, and pedagogically belong. Such understandings are always inseparable from the ability to make critical choices. Post-formal researchers gain the ability through the subtle process of learning via experience to make informed choices concerning interpretations and methods of inquiry best designed for particular circumstances. Outside the boundaries of such critical appreciations, student research operates superficially at best. Aware of how radical such a pronouncement sounds, we nevertheless believe that classrooms where the previous issues are missing often work to cognitively and ethically de-skill students. In such a context students consider it normal that schooling immerses them in busy work and mindless rote-based, text-driven, unreflective exercises. Who in the hell could find this interesting?

In our consideration of the post-formal 'take' on experience we reflect back many of the essays in this book that consider these issues in relation to student research. Again Sandra Spickard Prettyman's chapter on student notewriting is valuable to a broader pedagogical and cultural understanding of students as researchers in its concern with connecting everyday life's multiple levels of experience with larger socio-political structures. In a post-Vygotskian manner that connects Vygotsky's insights to advances in critical theory over the last several decades, critical teachers struggle to engage themselves and their students in a mode of research that uncovers the imprints of the structural aspects of reality at the experiential level — the domain where life is lived (Lave and Wenger, 1991). This intersection of the structural (macro) and the experiential (micro) creates a wormhole in the space of knowledge production through which critical teachers can help lead their student researchers. Crawling through this conceptual tunnel, teachers and students emerge in a new dimension of analytical insight where they find themselves capable of a sort of stereoscopic vision: a cognitive ability that allows them to concurrently see macro-structural inscriptions on the individuals and their lived experiences and the micro-level impact of individual actions that either support or challenge macro-structural forces covertly operating throughout the society.

On one level we might describe this form of experiential research as students conducting sophisticated sociological research on their lives, the construction of their consciousness (Long, 1995). Melissa Butler describes in her chapter such a process in the critical experiential inquiry of her second graders, as they struggled to understand the forces that shaped their lives. As Butler highlighted (or bracketed in the phenomenological sense) her children's lived experience, she engaged 7-year-olds in an amazingly sophisticated version of this macro/micro form of inquiry. Even at this young age Butler's second graders were coming to understand their own subjectivities in relation to the world and other people. John Fiske (1994) is insightful in this context with his description of ideology in cultural studies. Students as researchers using Fiske's analyses study the ways that ideology shapes identity, the ways they become 'subjects-in-ideology'. As such ideology-driven subjects, they make sense of social relations and experiences through the filter of dominant ideologies.

As students understand these dynamics in a more and more sophisticated way, their ability to analyze experience deepens. Using Butler's second graders as an example, we maintain that students from all ages and backgrounds can become critical students as researchers who on some level deal with these macro–micro aspects of human experience. For example, elementary, secondary, and university students can explore their socio-economic class backgrounds, focusing on the kind of work in which their parents and grandparents were involved. In this context the lives of these relatives could be compared to their own lives in terms of macro-power issues such as socio-economic class, race, gender, and religion (Mayo, 1996). Thus, teachers cultivating students as researchers become scholars of power, working to help their students whatever their academic level understand both how power operates and how it shapes their own and other people's lives. Marc Pruyn (1994) argues that these types of understandings lead directly to more sensitive, emancipatory views of the world. While this emancipatory form of student research can be employed by all students regardless of their social position, it can be used especially effectively with marginalized students such as Melissa Butler's inner-city second graders to make sense of the nature of their subordination. Armed with this knowledge such students can begin with the help of critical teachers to figure out ways of overcoming the obstacles that block their success and empowerment. First, critical student researchers gain the confidence to change their lives and then the skills needed to negotiate the specifics of the process.

Teachers Nurturing Student Research: Analyzing Experience in the Classroom

The cultivation of students as researchers requires teachers who understand the experiences of their students, the subject matter of the disciplines, excluded critical modes of analysis, and various other forms of subjugated knowledges. Such teacher requirements demand reconceptualized colleges of education with far more rigorous curriculums and an energized democratic sense of purpose. Teachers emerging from this rigorous background, focus their scholarly attention (a critical action research) on how school knowledge intersects with student experience in everyday classrooms. The insights teachers gain in this context helps them shape lessons, interpersonal relations, and possible research projects. Such teachers must work hard to both affirm their students' right to speak of their experiences and to develop a point of view about them. This does not mean, however, that teachers cultivating student research on their experience simply affirm their experiences uncritically. Such teachers must develop the subtle pedagogical ability to create a sense of trust in their classrooms that allows them to point out the moral, ethical, and political contradictions within their stories and histories. Without this critical facility critical teachers often lapse into a romanticization of student experience that shuts down the possibility of conceptual growth.

A central feature of the classroom role of the teacher as cultivator of student research involves understanding the types of visceral, common sense knowledges students bring to a classroom, engaging them in an analysis of these knowledges, and motivating them to develop new forms of perceiving in relation to this original storehouse of information. Paulo Freire (Horton and Freire, 1990) maintained that students have 'the right to know better what they already know' (p. 157). Knowing better, he maintained, means moving to a new cognitive and epistemological level that interrogates common sense in a way that exposes the reasons some information is viewed as factual while other information is not. Ellen Swartz in this book understands this Freirean dynamic, when she advises teachers facilitating student research to view student knowledge as a foundation for subsequent student inquiry. Such critical teachers' respect for students and their knowledge is displayed by their refusal to let it lay fallow, unquestioned, unutilized in the effort to empower students cognitively, politically, and vocationally. Lana Krievis understands these pedagogical dynamics in her chapter on deaf students as knowledge producers, as she admonishes educators who don't listen to deaf and other students with handi-caps. The sophisticated knowledge that students who see human experience from a different angle due to some form of exclusion from the mainstream can become some of the most important knowledge we ever encounter. Indeed, as Krievis well understands, it can lay the foundation for emancipatory breakthroughs for teachers and students from a wide variety of social locations.

It would be remiss not to point out in this conceptual context that teachers working with student researchers not only focus on what students know but what they don't know as well. On one level this seems to go without saying because that data unknown by students is what schools normally address. Thus, it is import-ant for humble teachers to talk with student researchers about what none of them know. Not only does this create a safe classroom climate, but it allows teachers the opportunity to model ways of researching what we don't know. Always alert to methods of illustrating the complexity of knowledge, teacher facilitators of research illustrate the possible layers of ignorance that underlie not knowing something. As researchers of the unknown, we may find that understanding demands an appreci-ation of context, prerequisite conceptual insights, or the ability to sift through super-fluous data. In addition we will undoubtedly be faced with problems concerning what resources to use, where to get them, and which ones to believe when we find conflicting answers. Such daunting difficulties are the bread and butter questions good researchers must address (Marker, 1993). A teacher who can highlight them for student consideration and provide specific examples — as Leila Villaverde and I attempt in our chapter on the exploration of Thanksgiving — is performing the necessary trenchwork of engaging students in rigorous research.

Students As Cultural Studies Researchers: Examining the Power of Contemporary Popular Culture

One of the most inspirational aspects of student research for teacher facilitators emerges when students recognize that they can know more, that they have the tools to learn what they don't know and to know better what they already knew (Freire and Faundez, 1989). At this point it is important to focus on student knowledge of and experience with popular culture. One of the most important ways of promoting the analysis of student experience and thus students as researchers involves using popular culture as a site of knowledge production, meaning making, and social conflict. Bluntly put, student voices are muted when their popular culture is either vilified or ignored. Students resent and often take personally teacher degradation of cultural forms that hold so much meaning in their lives.

I still feel the sting of one of my eighth grade teachers' 'dark sarcasm' and ridicule of my enthusiastic analysis of the social significance of the music of the Rolling Stones in 1964. It is significant to the topic at hand that 34 years later (gasp!) I can still feel the embarrassment and anger of that moment and its effect on my relationship with not only that teacher but with school in general. The incident had a profound effect on my life, as it contributed to a growing disdain for traditional schooling. How lucky I was compared to other students with the same feelings and from a similar social background as myself. For whatever reason I had the confidence to first flaunt my oppositionality and then draw upon it for academic analysis. The vast majority of my disaffected compadres were unable to use their hurt for such a positive outcome. They and the generations that followed them, as I have found out from countless interviews, located fault for their disaffection within themselves — not in a system uninterested in who they were or what they knew and felt.

Again, utilizing cultural studies in education critical teachers take popular culture seriously; this attribution of significance is manifested by the teachers' attention to the process by which students use it to make meaning in their lives. Teachers facilitating student research induce students to examine how their identities, their relation to schooling, and their world views are often produced in the context of pleasure. Thus, TV, popular music, movies, video games, comic books, and other commercially produced youth culture or kinderculture (see Steinberg and Kincheloe, 1997) become cultural artifacts to be examined around the questions of experience and identity raised in this book. In critical teachers' studies of these popular cultural entities they focus their own and their students' attention on the politics, cultural aspects, personal meanings circulating within them and between them and their audiences. The meanings such popular cultural productions make are not always rational but affective/emotional in relation to the politics of pleasure (Giroux, 1992; Sholle and Denski, 1994). In this context the notions of self and social transformation must be viewed in a new perspective. Because the process does not take place in a linear and predictable way, teachers and students researching the production of identity must account for the multidimensional forces that interact with the libido in the new cosmos of electronic, mediated reality.

When the libidinal impulses (the desire) of young people interact with these popular cultural dynamics, explosive results occur. Sandra Spickard Prettyman pushes our understanding of youth culture in her chapter in this book, contending that popular culture is not simply a product but a process developed by consumers' interaction with what the culture provides them. This is an important understanding for teachers and students exploring the role of popular culture in the formation of identity. It reinforces our notion that little is linearly predictable when popular cultural artifacts intersect with libido and cultural context. A pedagogy of popular culture takes popular cultural artifacts and the uses young people make of them as material with great curricular significance. One doesn't have to be excessively creative to imagine a series of research projects on the ways particular students make meaning, create knowledge, and produce identities via the dynamics of popular culture. In the process of students researching their own popular cultural artifacts, their use of them, and the consequences of the interaction, they begin to uncover the framework for how youth culture, its knowledges and practices are produced. The levels of self-awareness that young people can achieve are limitless when these previously invisible dynamics are made visible.

Students As Researchers of Their Own Academic Performance

In my work on post-formal thinking I have argued that the reasons many students fail in school has less to do with some innate lack of ability and more with whether or not they come from a cultural/family background that understands the structures and purposes of school (Lave and Wenger, 1991). In other words, do they enter the schoolhouse knowing how to 'do' school? Many of my schoolmates who came from especially poor Appalachian families (everyone was poor) in rural Sullivan County Tennessee were brilliant kids who could perform a variety of cognitively sophisticated tasks. The moment they hit the classroom, however, they were stymied, for all of them came from homes where no-one had stayed past the first few grades in school. There were few reading materials within my young friends' homes, thus their sense of displacement was enhanced by a lack of attention to the written word. Linguistic skills were absolutely necessary to school success and not only did most of my especially poor friends not have them (or even have a notion that they were important), they knew no-one who had such skills. I remember so clearly Larry, Jacob, Bobby, and Roy turning to me in despair in the first three or four years of elementary school, asking what the teacher wanted them to do. By the third or fourth grade the boys no longer asked — they had given up trying to make sense of it all.

Lilia Bartolome (1994) writes of the necessity of teachers introducing students such as my friends not merely into the culture of the classroom, but even more deeply, into the discourse of schooling in general and school subjects in particular. Discourse, as Bartolome uses it here, refers to the unspoken rules, assumed understandings, and implicit power relations which shape who is an 'insider' or an 'outsider' in a particular cultural context. Larry, Jacob, Bobby and Ray had no-one to provide them an apprenticeship into the school discourse's definition of school success, ways to acquire content and what content was the most important, methods to organize content, proper modes of deportment, and approved ways of using language — both orally and in writing. Without these discursive understandings my friends' pedagogical tombstones were already inscribed with the dates of their educational demise: 'Here rests Jacob K. who despite his good spirits and almost saintly disposition failed to do school well because of his almost total unacquaintance with the written word. His educational life ended in his third grade year circa March 17, 1959. He was not missed by his teachers.'

Having lived these experiences and witnessed the educational deaths of so many wonderful acquaintances, I am passionate in my desire to help teachers apprentice students unfamiliar with the discourse community of school. The central feature of such an apprenticeship should involve students as researchers of the discourse community of school, researchers of the power dynamics of their own educational experiences. Students who are not members of this discourse community often feel that teachers are withholding information from them — this feeling is intensified when teachers are using inquiry or discovery methods of teaching. Certain of my southern Appalachian classmates felt this way, as they struggled to understand what the teacher expected of them. Until students understand the discourse community of schooling, empowerment, motivation, and cognitive growth are impossible. Traditional remedial pedagogies miss this dynamic when they engage in decontextualized and fragmented drill and test methods. Such strategies not only fail their primary goal of delivering subject matter but do nothing to bring marginalized students into the discourse community. In a critical pedagogy of student research students could explore the concept of a discourse community. They could formulate questions about discourse communities to which they already belong: What do you have to know to be a part of your peer group's discourse community? What happens to those who don't have this knowledge? Who gets to speak and who has to listen in your discourse community? How is this power to speak obtained, recognized by others, and practiced? How do those with the power to speak protect their position? What benefits do they receive as a consequence of their privileged position?

What fascinating research marginalized students could conduct around these questions. As they began to put together a picture of how any discourse community works, they would gain a meta-analytical understanding of those hidden structures, assumptions, and rules that tacitly shape everyday life. The dramatic act of transferring these insights into the context of schooling opens unprecedented possibilities for democratizing education and bringing the marginalized into the community of achievers, of the talented, of those who *get it*. Understanding the concept of a discourse community in their own lives, these student researchers could begin to explore the specific characteristics of the discourse of schooling. In this context they might make many sophisticated social and cultural observations, such as the wealthy kids from Ridgefields seem to always do better in school than the poorer kids from Highland Park. They may find that the voices of those rich Ridgefields students are valued more by teachers than their own voices. And they may get angry at the realization that it is not a lack of ability that undermines their performance at school but their proximity to the discourse community.

The expertise of the teacher facilitating student research is desperately needed at this critical juncture. The goal of the teacher is neither to fan the flames of student anger or attempt to douse it. A critical teacher can validate the anger, letting the student researchers of discourse know that it is an understandable reaction to the injustice they have uncovered. The salient question becomes, however, what do we do about our unenviable situation. How do we draw upon our anger in a way that accomplishes three goals:

1 challenges the injustice;
2 allows students to learn the features of the discourse that will enable them to succeed in their academic pursuits; and
3 enables student understanding of the ways the school and other social discourses work to embrace and exclude them.

Such an understanding allows students to succeed in school, while working to preclude schools from continuing the exclusion of new generations of outsiders. Here, the enabling teacher engages students in the social responsibility that comes with this knowledge. Such a teacher also helps students appreciate the positive features of the academic discourse and how such literacy- and numeracy-related skills can be used for a variety of goals.

The teacher who facilitates student research and interpretation in this context must subtly point out the relationship connecting identity, knowing, and discourse communities. As marginalized students learn about the nature of such communities and come to understand the specific information and skills required by them, they will develop different relationships to the various discourse communities they operate in and around. They will see things that others don't see. This is to say that they will change, they will not be the same people they were before. Such changes will hold consequences both sweet and bitter, and the teacher facilitator must prepare students for the emotional roller-coaster ride that awaits them. As students gain post-formal meta-awarenesses concerning the tacit political, epistemological, and cognitive subtexts of the educational discourse, their interests change.

Teachers working with student researchers of the unstated features of the discourse of education ask about the nature of the knowledge that is generally taught in mainstream schools. In this epistemological domain student researchers may find that a 'rationalistic irrationality' shapes school's treatment of knowledge. As part of their research marginalized students might study the knowledge that teachers emphasize, high-achieving students write down and/or commit to memory, and shows up on tests. Like so much of the marginalized students' research on the relationship between their low achievement and the educational discourse, this phase of the research has dual purposes. One level of the student research is designed to help them learn the rules of the game: What type knowledge is the most important to success? How do you pick that knowledge out? How do you 'massage' that data for the test? The second level involves a higher-order post-formal understanding, a critique of the trivialization of information resulting from its irrational fragmentation and decontextualization. Here I am asserting that low-achieving students can gain a meta-understanding of ways that meaning is undermined through the bureaucratization of curriculum making, teaching, and evaluating. They can both learn to succeed in *and* conceptually transcend schooling's discourse community.

Bruce King (1990) is instructive in our effort to imagine student research in this context. He argues that students as researchers adopting a Freirean problem-posing method could ask of the fragmented curriculum very simple questions: What is worth knowing here? How do we come to know it? To King's research questions I would add: What benefits do we derive from knowing it? What can we see and do as a result of gaining a specific understanding that we were unable to see and do before? For example, when white students learn that the prototypical crack cocaine user is a 40–50-year-old white businessman and not a young black male, they are almost always shocked. The value of such a piece of data does not merely involve achieving a more accurate picture of who smokes crack, but the development of skepticism about white stereotypes concerning the behavior of African-Americans. Such a skepticism may be drawn upon as a motivation to examine other comfortable white beliefs about Blacks. Thus, marginalized student researchers as meta-analysts of school knowledge begin to understand that knowledge emerges from specific cultural locations. These venues hold certain assumptions and values that help create specific questions. All knowledge, school knowledge in particular, emerges from these cultural spaces. Students who analyze and understand these dynamics understand what's happening in school at a level not understood by most educational leaders. Such previously excluded students — now student researchers — can help educate educational leaders and community members about the social and political implications of how schools operate.

If these excluded student researchers can contain their anger about their treatment by the schools, they can not only succeed in the traditional 'game' of education but work as critical agents to change it. As they research and learn the mainstream conversation about schooling, they empower themselves to imagine a new more cognitively sophisticated and socially just educational discourse. They gain understandings such as those delineated by Ivor Goodson (1997) on how subject-matter fields get constructed in ways having remarkably little to do with considerations of what knowledge and skills are of most worth. Such insights move us back to post-formal thinking's concern with new cognitive processes or as Ellen Swartz puts it in her chapter, expanding our ways of knowing and becoming authors of ideas and questions that empower us to operate as critical agents. Discursive analysis as a form of student research is a meta-cognitive act that moves us beyond the blindnesses of modernist cognitions. This second level — the post-formal level — of student research on the discourse of schooling can change schools as we know them, as it empowers the disempowered. In the case of traditionally high-achieving students, engagement in such discursive research can open windows on an understanding of their own privilege. In addition to granting them access to more complex ways of knowing, such students may gain a humility and empathy with those who haven't had their access to the esoteric educational discursive knowledge.

Reaping the Benefits: Student Research As a Cognitive Act

We're not sure what intelligent is, but whatever it is it probably has little to do with the ways psychometricians measure it on their IQ tests and 'normed instruments'. Operating in a post-formal context, we maintain that the ability to engage in discursive analysis makes us smarter, better able to make meaning in a complex world. In this concept we can all understand that sophisticated research is a cognitive act. When former doctoral students discuss their graduate programs, those who did more than a plug-in-the-data, procedural empirical study chosen by their dissertation director will often testify that the most valuable aspect of their program involved their dissertation. The experience taught us to write, to use the library, to gather information, to make an argument, and to think, they will say. When a student has a voice in the negotiation of the form a research project takes, the methodology of inquiry moves beyond a set of predetermined procedures and the research becomes a valuable cognitive experience. Few activities can move students (and teachers) to new cognitive vistas as effectively as rigorous research. The following is a tentative list of cognitive benefits to be accrued from student participation in research. Critical student research:

1   Moves students to the critical realm of knowledge production, as it induces them to organize information, to interpret. As active inquirers students no longer see themselves as the passive receivers of expert produced knowledge. They become responsible agents who engage in their own interpretations of the world around them. Thus, there is a power shift in this situation that democratizes the process of naming the world. Student researchers are 'uppity', as they maintain that their interpretations are worthwhile. Such a perspective changes their view of how they approach knowledge — indeed, it changes the way they approach knowing in the first place.

2   Focuses student attention on thinking about their own thinking, as they explore their own consciousness construction, their self-production. Student research induces them to take seriously the ways that they are moved to see the world. As they become more familiar with the concerns of critical action research, students become more conversant with who they are. The genesis of the images they adopt of what it means to be an educated person is interrogated for the ways it reflects representations of conventionality and manifestations of power. Such questioning grants them a higher perspective on who they are — a perspective that moves them in a post-formal direction.

3   Creates an analytical orientation toward their lives. Simply put, students develop a reflective attitude toward their lives that motivates them to contextualize events that take place. They come to see events in ways that grant them meaning not readily apparent when they are viewed in isolation. In a post-formal context students begin to uncover the deep structures, the implicate order that connects events.

4   Helps students learn to teach themselves. Few activities better prepare one for such a task than an ability to conduct research. Individuals who are able to conduct research not only have access to primary and secondary information sources, but are able to do for themselves what others rely on experts to accomplish for them.

5   Improves student ability to engage in anticipatory accommodation. Cartesian-Newtonian researchers assume that generalizations derived from one classroom are valid in all classrooms with that same population. Anticipatory accommodation involves one's ability to anticipate what one might encounter in similar situations and what strategies might work to bring about desired outcomes. In other words, when students engage in anticipatory accommodation, they learn from their knowledge of a variety of comparable contexts. Critical research enhances their ability to make such accommodations by providing them with detailed pictures, interpretive understandings of the similarities and differences of the various contexts. Students' ability to think as post-formal agents is significantly improved.

6   Cultivates empathy with 'others'. As a phenomenological act, critical research helps students explore the consciousness of those they encounter. Their ability to understand the joys and pains, the dreams and motivations of their friends and colleagues is significantly enhanced. Thus, critical

research becomes a vehicle for connected consciousness, a central form of knowing in a critical education.

7 Negates reliance on procedural thinking. Understanding the techniques and assumptions of critical research releases students from the Cartesian-Newtonian rules for conducting inquiry. Thus, they gain a methodological freedom from rigid procedure, a freedom that allows them the right to change their strategies in the face of new circumstances. Not only do they gain a freedom to conduct inquiry in ways contingent on context, but they also are released from procedural definitions of cognition. When the need is perceived, students as researchers can embrace cognitive strategies more compatible with the situation encountered.

8 Improves thinking by making it just another aspect of everyday existence. Research becomes a way of life, a way of approaching the world. In line with higher orders of cognition, those who embrace critical research view answers as tentative — findings are always in process. Thus, students' tendency to make up their minds and ignore the evidence is reduced; indeed, because there is always further evidence to be considered, they are less likely to resort to stereotyping and overgeneralization. Such cognitive orientations are essential to the democratic project, to the effort to make democracy work.

In this critical cognitive context we focus on the way research pushes students to new depths of insight. As Nancy Dana maintains in her chapter here, student research refuses to allow for mindlessness. Waking up from cognitive anesthesia is never easy. It is far more comfortable to roll over and go back to sleep. The teacher facilitator of student research works with students to develop their intuition as a basis for their more logic-based inquiry. Intuition lets researchers know that something doesn't feel right — it wakes us up. In post-formal student research participants don't stop with their intuition but use it as a starting point. As Paulo Freire put it in his dialogue with Myles Horton, 'I have to take the object of my intuition as an object of my knowing and grasp it theoretically' (Horton and Freire, 1990, pp. 124–5). In Freire's mind this intuitive ability helped frame problems in ways that facilitated researchers' attempts to make sense of complexity. Thus, in this new paradigmatic form of research individuals value and employ their intuition, as they struggle to explain the way various parts of the world are connected to other parts of the world. Student researchers search for interconnectedness of data, inanimate objects, problems, and people themselves (Munby and Russell, 1989; Capra, Stindl-Rast, and Matus, 1992).

The Critical Dimension: The Unabashedly Political Nature of Student Research

The form of student research described here is political in its effort to challenge the fate of the marginalized. As Kathy Berry writes in her chapter, everyone involved in developing students as researchers is concerned with 'nurturing the imagination of resistance' — resistance to those unacceptable fates. Learning and knowledge production in this context become an aspect of the process of social change. Student researchers as critical agents are always concerned with how cultural meanings are produced, transmitted, and challenged. They are also interested in how particular cultural meanings prohibit student self-direction — for example, the way school-generated descriptions of model students may automatically exclude individuals from particular cultural backgrounds regardless of their character and abilities. If existentially we are a species of questioners, then we need to learn to do it adeptly. Adept questions are the critical root of emancipation and, thus, of our notion of students as researchers. Such questions in the context of student research interrogate the concepts and activities that make meaning in people's lives (Giroux, 1997; King, 1990).

As students as researchers become producers of knowledge in this configuration, the more they become agents of change. Marginalized students begin to understand that they are not always at fault, incapable, or inappropriate, that many of the problems they have in school result from macro-forces of power interacting with the specificities of their everyday lives. When one has internalized the school's ascriptions of failure, it is quite liberating to discover you're not inept or incapable. As students research the construction of their consciousness, they cannot escape the adoption of a political role. Of course, the use and application of the term, political, is controversial and raises the hackles of those who claim neutrality. Indeed, such technicists will argue that our research-based pedagogy politicizes an otherwise objective school. The argument that the schools should remain politically neutral reflects the popular naivete that fails to identify dominant definitions of neutrality as problematic. The role of the teacher as a neutral transmitter of prearranged facts is not understood as a politicized role. If schools are to become places that promote teacher and student empowerment, then the notion of what constitutes politicization will have to be re-conceptualized. Battle with texts as a form of research, resist the demand of the official curriculum, Paulo Freire and Ira Shor (1987) argue in line with their critical pedagogical vision. This contention can be presented in the attempt to challenge the mainstream belief that capitulation to textual authority constitutes political neutrality.

Every historical period, contrary to prevailing pedagogical belief, produces tacit rules that dictate what non-partisanship entails. Different rules privilege different causes. Thus, what we 'see' as researchers is shaped by particular world views, values, political perspectives, conceptions of race, class, and gender relations, definitions of intelligence, and research methodologies. Student research, no matter how hard we may try, can never be non-partisan — for someone somewhere must choose the rules that guide the research. Understanding these dynamics, these ideological inscriptions, marks the end of our academic innocence. So, as our critical student researchers watch their academic childhood fade in the rearview mirror of their consciousness, they must face the adult responsibility of determining what type of social transformation their research supports. They must come to terms with a new mature vision of themselves as political beings who take informed action on the basis of their research. Such action is inseparable from student researchers' appreciation of the etymologies of problems and their social vision of better conditions (King, 1990).

In the research-related maturation process students learn that their political role necessitates the development of an ability to deal with conflict. When researchers present their findings to each other, controversy erupts. Such conflict can be interesting and quite valuable to everyone involved, if they learn how to emotionally and interpersonally deal with it. Unfortunately, most students and teachers don't learn to handle controversy and when differences arise they either retreat, seek a contrived consensus, or attack. Myles Horton, the late founder and director of Tennessee's Highlander Center, served as such a brilliant role model for both handling and learning from controversy and cultivating critical student research. As Horton engaged individuals in research projects such as civil rights, organizing tactics and explorations of land and mineral ownership by poor mountain people in Tennessee and Kentucky, he maintained an empathy and humility that enabled him to take criticism and learn from a variety of people. This humility, as argued previously, is basic to our notion of students as researchers. Student research is not designed to turn out arrogant students that have the answers but students who learn to listen as they become more sensitive to people who are often ignored (Horton and Zacharakis-Jutz, 1987; Preskill, 1991).

In the spirit of Horton and Paulo Freire students as researchers seek unity with democratic groups outside of the school, those who hold untapped subjugated knowledges in the local community. Student researchers find that their connections with such groups provide two-way benefits:

1 not only do student researchers awaken dormant curiosities and insights of individuals in some way connected to subjugated knowledges; but
2 such individuals also induce student (and teacher) researchers to ask questions of themselves previously unconsidered.

Such a dialogue initiates dramatic social, cognitive, political, and pedagogical changes. In an age where public dialogue is so truncated and terse, the development of student dialogue with valuable but neglected people opens a space for renewing civic life. The listening dimension of research is a neglected feature of the pseudo-democracy of the late 1990s. The renewal of the public sphere is grounded in part on the development of the skills we have discussed in this book. We are unembarrassed about this highly political aspect of our pedagogical task. May we be able to rise to the level of difficulty and dedication it demands.

References

ALLISON, C. (1995) *Present and past: Essays for teachers in the history of education*, New York: Peter Lang.
BARTOLOME, L. (1994) 'Beyond the methods fetish: Toward a humanizing pedagogy', *Harvard Educational Review*, **64**, 2, pp. 173–94.

CAPRA, F., STEINDL-RAST, D. and MATUS, T. (1992) *Belonging to the universe: New thinking about God and nature*, New York: Penguin.

FISKE, J. (1994) 'Audiencing: Cultural practice and cultural studies', in DENZIN, N. and LINCOLN, Y. (eds) *Handbook of qualitative research*, Thousand Oaks, CA: Sage Publications.

FREIRE, P. and FAUNDEZ, A. (1989) *Learning to question: A pedagogy of liberation*, New York: Continuum.

GIROUX, H. (1992) *Border crossings: Cultural workers and the politics of education*, New York: Routledge.

GIROUX, H. (1994) *Disturbing pleasures: Learning popular culture*, New York: Routledge.

GIROUX, H. (1997) *Pedagogy and the politics of hope: Theory, culture, and schooling*, Boulder, CO: Westview.

GOODSON, I. (1997) *The changing curriculum: Studies in social construction*, New York: Peter Lang.

GREENE, M. (1993) 'What are the language arts for?', *The NAMTA*, **18**, 2, pp. 123–32.

HORTON, A. and ZACHARAKIS-JUTZ (1987) 'Empowering the poor: Participatory research as an educational tool'. Paper presented at the American Association for Adult and Continuing Education, Washington, DC.

HORTON, M. and FREIRE, P. (1990) 'We make the road by walking: Conversations on education and social change', in BELL, B., GAVENTA, J. and PETERS, J. (eds) Philadelphia: Temple University Press.

KING, B. (1990) 'Creating curriculum together: Teachers, students, and collaborative investigation'. Paper presented at the American Educational Research Association, Boston, Massachusetts.

LAVE, J. and WENGER, E. (1991) *Situated learning: Legitimate peripheral participation*, New York: Cambridge University Press.

LONG, D. (1995) 'Sociology and pedagogy for liberation: Cultivating a dialogue of discernment in our classrooms', *Teaching Sociology*, **23**, pp. 321–30.

MARKER, P. (1993) 'Not only by our words: Connecting the pedagogy of Paulo Freire with the social studies classroom', *Social Science Record*, **30**, 1, pp. 77–89.

MAYO, P. (1996) 'Transformative adult education in an age of globalization: A Gramscian-Freirean synthesis', *The Alberta Journal of Educational Research*, **42**, 2, pp. 148–60.

McLAREN, P. (1992) 'Collisions with otherness: 'Traveling' theory, post-colonial criticism, and the politics of ethnographic practice — the mission of the wounded ethnographer', *Qualitative Studies in Education*, **5**, 1, pp. 1–15.

MULLIN, J. (1994) 'Feminist theory, feminist pedagogy: The gap between what we say and what we do', *Composition Studies/Freshman English News*, **22**, 1, pp. 14–24.

MUNBY, H. and RUSSELL, T. (1989) 'Educating the reflective teacher: An essay review of two books by Donald Schon', *Journal of Curriculum Studies*, **21**, 1, pp. 71–80.

PRESKILL, S. (1991) 'We can live freedom: The Highlander Folk School as a model for civic education', *Social Science Record*, **28**, 2, pp. 11–21.

PRUYN, M. (1994) 'Becoming subjects through critical practice: How students in an elementary classroom critically read and wrote their world', *International Journal of Educational Reform*, **3**, 1, pp. 37–50.

SHOLLE, D. and DENSKI, S. (1994) *Media education and the (re)production of culture*, Westport, CT: Bergin and Garvey.

STEINBERG, S. and KINCHELOE, J. (1997) *Kinderculture: Corporate constructions of childhood*, Boulder, CO: Westview.

References for Chapter 1 — also by Steinberg and Kincheloe

ABERCROMBIE, N. (1994) 'Authority and consumer society', in KEAT, R., WHITELEY, N. and ABERCROMBIE, N. (eds) *The authority of the consumer*, New York: Routledge.

AYERS, W. (1992) 'Disturbances from the field: Recovering the voice of the early childhood teacher', in KESSLER, S. and SWADENER, B. (eds) *Reconceptualizing the early childhood curriculum*, New York: Teachers College Press.

BARTOLOME, L. (1994) 'Beyond the methods fetish: Toward a humanizing pedagogy', *Harvard Educational Review*, **64**, 2, pp. 173–94.

BOHM, D. and EDWARDS, M. (1991) *Changing consciousness*, San Francisco: Harper.

BOZIK, M. (1987) 'Critical thinking through creating thinking'. Paper presented to the Speech Communication Association, Boston.

CAPRA, R., STEINDL-RAST, D. and MATUS, T. (1992) *Belonging to the universe: New thinking about God and nature*, New York: Penguin.

DEWEY, J. (1933) *How we think*, Lexington, Massachusetts: Heath and Company.

FISKE, J. (1994) 'Audiencing: Cultural practice and cultural studies', in DENZIN, N. and LINCOLN, Y. (eds) *Handbook of qualitative research*, Thousand Oaks, California: Sage Publications.

FOUCAULT, M. (1980) *Power/knowledge: Selected interviews and other writings*, New York: Pantheon.

FREIRE, P. (1972) 'Research methods'. Paper presented to Studies in Adult Education seminar, Dar-es-Salaam, Tanzania.

FREIRE, P. and FAUNDEZ, A. (1989) *Learning to question: A pedagogy of liberation*, New York: Continuum.

FRIED, R. (1995) *The passionate teacher: A practical guide*, Boston: Beacon Press.

GARDNER, H. (1991) *The unschooled mind: How children think and how schools should teach*, New York: Basic Books.

GIROUX, H. (1992) *Border crossings: Cultural workers and the politics of education*, New York: Routledge.

HAUSER, J. (1991) 'Critical inquiries, uncertainties and not faking it with students'. Paper presented at the Annual conference of the Center for Critical Thinking and Moral Critique, Rohnert Park, California.

HORTON, M. and FREIRE, P. (1990) 'We make the road by walking: Conversations on education and social change', in BELL, B., GAVENTA, J. and PETERS, J. (eds) Pennsylvania: Temple University Press.

KINCHELOE, J. (1993) *Toward a critical politics of teacher thinking: Mapping the postmodern*, Westport, Connecticut: Bergin and Garvey.

KINCHELOE, J. and STEINBERG, S. (1993) 'A tentative description of post-formal thinking: The critical confrontation with cognitive theory', *Harvard Educational Review*, **63**, 3, pp. 296–320.

KINCHELOE, J., STEINBERG, S. and HINCHEY, P. (1998) *The post-formal reader: Cognition and education*, New York: Garland Press.

KING, B. (1990) 'Creating curriculum together: Teachers, students, and collaborative investigation'. Paper presented at the American Educational Research Association, Boston, Massachusetts.

LAVE, J. and WENGER, E. (1991) *Situated learning: Legitimate peripheral participation*, New York: Cambridge University Press.

LAWLER, J. (1975) 'Dialectical philosophy and developmental psychology: Hegel and Piaget on contradiction', *Human Development*, **18**, pp. 1–17.

LONG, D. (1995) 'Sociology and pedagogy for liberation: Cultivating a dialogue of discernment in our classrooms', *Teaching Sociology*, **23**, pp. 321–30.

MACEDO, D. (1994) *Literacies of power: What Americans are not allowed to know*, Boulder: Westview Press.

MAHER, F. and RATHBONE, C. (1986) 'Teacher education and feminist theory: Some implications for practice', *American Journal of Education*, **94**, 2, pp. 214–35.

MARKER, P. (1993) 'Not only by our words: Connecting the pedagogy of Paulo Freire with the social studies classroom', *Social Science Record*, **30**, 1, pp. 77–89.

PIAGET, J. (1969) *Psychology of Intelligence*, New Jersey: Littlefield Adams.

PIAGET, J. (1970) 'Piaget's theory', in Mussen, P. (ed.) *Manual of child psychology* (Volume 1), New York: Wiley.

PIAGET, J. and INHELDER, B. (1968) *The psychology of the child*, New York: Basic Books.

POSTMAN, N. (1995) *The end of education: Redefining the value of school*, New York: Knopf.

RAIZEN, S. (1989) *Reforming education for work: A cognitive science perspective*, Berkeley, California: NCRVE.

RAIZEN, S. and COLVIN, R. (1991) 'Apprenticeships: A cognitive-science view', *Educational Week*, **26**, December 11.

SENGE, P. (1990) *The fifth discipline: The art and practice of the learning organization*, New York: Doubleday.

SHOLLE, D. and DENSKI, S. (1994) *Media education and the (re)production of culture*, Westport, Connecticut: Bergin and Garvey.

SLATON, C. (1993) 'Mission and methods of democratizing the classroom', *Thresholds in Education*, **12**, 1–2, pp. 27–31.

List of Contributors

Editors

Joe L. Kincheloe teachers Cultural Studies and Pedagogy at Penn State University. He is the author of numerous books including: *Teachers as Researchers: Qualitative Paths to Empowerment; Toil and Trouble: Good Work, Smart Workers* and *The Integration of Academic and Vocational Education* and (with Shirley Steinberg) *Thirteen Questions: Reframing Education's Conversation.*

Shirley R. Steinberg teaches Educational Foundations at Adelphi University. She is the co-author of *The Stigma of Genius: Einstein* and *Beyond Modern Education* (with Joe Kincheloe and Deborah Tippins) and with Joe Kincheloe, *Changing Multiculturalism.* She is the founding editor of *Taboo: The Journal of Culture and Education.* Both Steinberg and Kincheloe travel and lecture extensively on issues of cultural studies, social justice and pedagogy.

Contributors

Paulette Alli teaches in the Dade County Public Schools, Miami, Florida.

Kathleen S. Berry is a professor at the University of New Brunswick.

Melissa A. Butler teaches in the Chicago city schools and is a graduate student at Penn State University.

Nancy Fichtman Dana teaches at Penn State University.

Julia Ellis teaches at the University of Alberta, Edmonton.

Penny J. Gilmer teaches at Florida State University.

Patricia H. Hinchey teaches at Penn State University.

J. Damien Kellogg is a lecturer in biology at Penn State University and is completing his doctorate.

Lana Krevis teaches in the Covina Valley School District, Covina, California.

Sandra Spickard Prettyman teaches at Eastern Michigan University.

Ellen Swartz is an educational/curriculum consultant in Rochester, New York.

Leila Villaverde is a lecturer in education at Penn State University and is completing her doctorate.

Nina Zaragoza teaches at Florida International University and in the Miami Public Schools.

Index